Quareia—The Apprentice
Book Two

Josephine McCarthy

For more information and all course modules please visit www.quareia.com

Copyright 2014 ©Josephine McCarthy
ISBN 978-0-9933480-1-3

All rights reserved

Without limiting the rights under copyright reserved above, no part of this publication may be reproduced, stored in, or introduced into a retrieval system, or transmitted, in any form or by any means (electronic, mechanical, photocopying, recording or otherwise) without prior permission of the copyright owner and the publisher of this book.

Published by Quareia Publishing UK

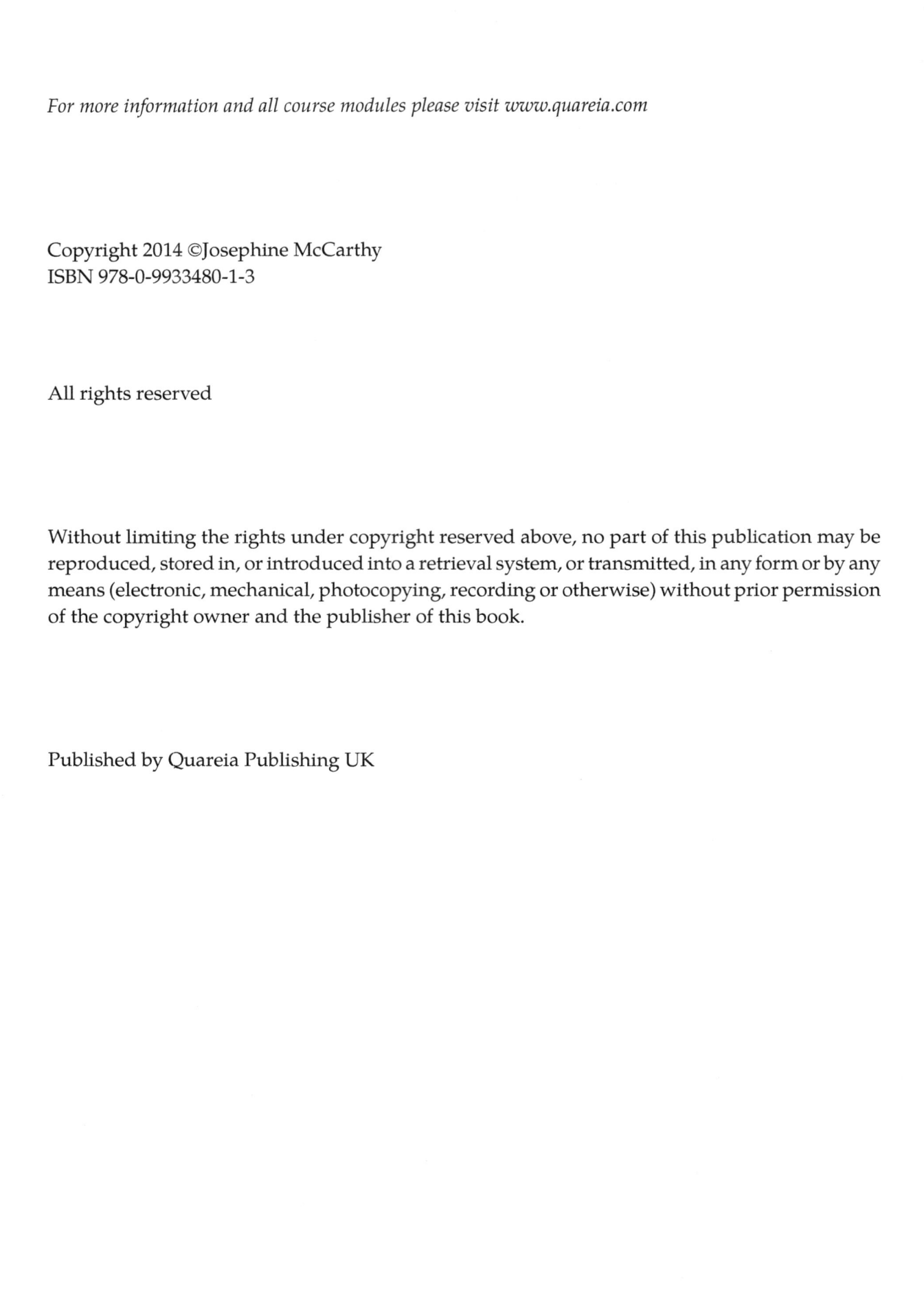

Cover illustration by Stuart Littlejohn

Acknowledgements

Thanks to the Quareia team that made this course possible:
Frater Acher, Alex A, Stuart Littlejohn, Aaron Moshe, and Michael Sheppard.

And thank you to all the donors who made this course a reality.

Course Advisory

The Quareia takes a magical apprentice from the beginning of magic to the level of adeptship and beyond. In order for this course to work, it is wise to work with the lessons in sequence. If you don't, it will not work properly.

1. *Pace yourself.* Some modules can be done together, some cannot. You will quickly realise which ones are weekly exercises that are ongoing, and which ones you need to focus on exclusively. Work out a rota of study/experimentation that works for you. There is no clock ticking, and it is not a race.

2. *Keep paper and online notes.* This is very important. Get an exercise book for each module. Clearly mark which lesson the notes refer to and when you finish that module, put the notebook away. It is important that you work on paper as well as computer. Do your essays and written tasks on computer and store them on a USB stick so they are safe. If you wish to be mentored through the Initiate and Adept training, these online and paper written notes will be a part of your application. Without them, you cannot be mentored.

3. *Learn to be flexible and adaptable.* If you come across something in the course you are not sure how to do or do not fully understand, take a step back and think about it. It is important to learn how to adapt, experiment and move forward without having every step re explained many times over – if you get stuck, work it out for yourself!

4. *Do not skim through the lessons.* You simply will not learn and you will not properly develop. Slow down, take your time.

Contents

III	**The Power Dynamics of Creation**	**9**
1	**Introduction**	**10**
1.1	Creation and magic	10
1.2	The use of visionary technique	11
1.3	The garden	14
1.4	The inner threshold	14
1.5	The polarities of creative power	15
1.6	The Inner Beings	18
1.7	*Task:* Researching *Ma'at*	18
1.8	*Task:* Researching the Scales	18
1.9	Summary	19
2	**The Inner Garden and Outer Vessels**	**20**
2.1	Talking to vessels	21
2.2	Random inhabitation	22
2.3	Magical inhabitation	23
2.4	The Inner Landscape	24
2.5	*Task:* Connecting with the inner landscape	24
2.6	*Task:* Visionary ritual of mediation	27
2.7	What just happened?	29
2.8	Readings	30
2.9	The tools and symbols	31
3	**The Grindstone**	**32**
3.1	The angelic power	32
3.2	The Role of the Grindstone in creation	33
3.3	The Grindstone in life	34
3.4	Examples of the Grindstone in action	35
3.5	*Task:* Grindstone tarot readings	38
3.6	*Task:* The Grindstone in your chart	39
3.7	*Task:* Grindstone ritual	39
4	**The Unraveller**	**40**
4.1	The Unraveller in creation	41
4.2	The Unraveller and magic	42
4.3	Unravelling magic: effects	42

4.4	The Unraveller in action	43
4.5	The personal Unraveller	44
4.6	*Task:* Looking in the mirror	44
4.7	*Task:* Readings	45
4.8	*Task:* The Unraveller and your astrology chart	45
4.9	*Task:* Unraveller ritual	46
4.10	Study	46

5 The Inner Guardians — 47
5.1	The realm of the Desert	47
5.2	The Weaver	48
5.3	The Three Fates	49
5.4	The Keeper of Justice	50
5.5	The Keeper of the Threshold	52
5.6	The Utterer and the Wheel	52
5.7	The Noble Companions/the Noble Ones	53
5.8	*Task:* The Vision of the Sandalphon	54
5.9	*Task:* Visiting with the Sandalphon	55
5.10	*Task:* Stravinsky's *Rites of Spring*	56
5.11	*Task:* Research	56
5.12	*Task:* Working with an image	56

6 The Laws of Fate — 58
6.1	Self	59
6.2	Fate web of the family	64
6.3	Fate and the wider world	65
6.4	*Task:* Fate recognition	66
6.5	*Task:* Looking at historical fate patterns using tarot	66
6.6	*Task:* Looking at your personal fate pattern with tarot	67

7 Working with your Past — 69
7.1	Crafting notes	69
7.2	On the rest of the module	69
7.3	Passing into the past	70
7.4	Practical Work	71
7.5	*Task:* The Egyptian Book of the Dead	74
7.6	Search terms and link:	75

8 Working with your future fate pattern — 76
8.1	Hitting the blocks in the road	77
8.2	*Task:* Viewing the web ritual	80
8.3	*Task:* Painting the spider	82
8.4	*Task:* Research	83

IV Death, Birth, and the Underworld — 85

1 Overview — 87
1.1	Death in general	88
1.2	Death and the Mysteries	89
1.3	Working magically in death while alive	92

1.4	The dead in the living world	92
1.5	The Underworld and the Abyss	92
1.6	Inner contacts and inner adepts	93
1.7	The Bound Ones	93
1.8	Summary	93

2 Regular Death 95

2.1	Slow Death	95
2.2	Upon the threshold of death	99
2.3	Religious aspects of death	100
2.4	Energetic clinging	101
2.5	Death Parasites	102
2.6	Quick deaths	102
2.7	Comas	103
2.8	*Task:* Astrology	104
2.9	*Task:* Death chart practice	105
2.10	*Task:* Tarot and death	105

3 The Magical Mysteries of Death 108

3.1	Religion versus the Mysteries	109
3.2	The Death Mysteries	109
3.3	The steps of the process: a brief overview	109
3.4	The Descent into the Underworld	111
3.5	The River and Judgement	111
3.6	The Key of the Scales	113
3.7	The Second Death	114
3.8	Fooling the Scales	115
3.9	The walk of the knives	116
3.10	The face of the angel	117
3.11	The Vista	117
3.12	Reincarnation	118
3.13	Summary	119
3.14	*Task:* Observing	119
3.15	*Task:* Finding	119
3.16	*Task:* Reading	120

4 The Underworld and the Abyss 122

4.1	Threshold of the Underworld	123
4.2	The first layer of the Underworld	125
4.3	The Goddess in the Cave	126
4.4	The Deeper Underworld	127
4.5	The Abyss	127
4.6	The Highway of the Abyss	128
4.7	About the practical work	129
4.8	*Task:* First Vision—The access to death through the Underworld	130
4.9	*Task:* Second Vision—Accessing the root ancient temples	133
4.10	The vision	133
4.11	*Task:* Working with the symbols	135
4.12	*Task:* Readings on the symbols	136
4.13	Summary	136

	4.14	*Task:* Practice	136
	4.15	Goddess	137

5 The Living Dead — 138
	5.1	Ghosts	138
	5.2	Recordings	140
	5.3	Faery or land spirit haunting	140
	5.4	Parasites and demonic beings	142
	5.5	Real long-term hauntings: dead people and composites	143
	5.6	Composites	145
	5.7	Warning—Please take note	146
	5.8	The dead that cling	147
	5.9	Staying in the land	148
	5.10	About the practical Work	149
	5.11	*Task:* Investigating sleeping warriors	149
	5.12	*Task:* Investigating the Treasurer's House in York	152
	5.13	*Optional task:* Your own investigation	153
	5.14	*Task:* Clean up	153

6 The Thinning of the Veils — 154
	6.1	Working the death cycle	156
	6.2	Summary	158
	6.3	The Lyke Wake Dirge	158

7 Inner Contacts and Inner Adepts — 159
	7.1	The process of becoming an inner adept	159
	7.2	The Inner Library	160
	7.3	Making contact with the Inner Adepts	163
	7.4	*Task:* Meeting the Inner Adept—the vision	164
	7.5	*Task:* Routine	166
	7.6	*Task:* Pondering	167

8 The Bound Ones — 168
	8.1	A hell of your own making	168
	8.2	Trapped in the sands	169
	8.3	Sinking into the Abyss	171
	8.4	Ritually Bound Ones	172
	8.5	Practical Work	174
	8.6	*Reading tasks:* clips from classical and older religious texts	174
	8.7	Task	177
	8.8	Task	177
	8.9	Module Summary	177

Apprentice Module III

The Power Dynamics of Creation

Lesson 1

Introduction

This is a reading lesson with no practical magical work, but it does have an essay task at the end of it. So after finishing this lesson, you can go straight on to the next lesson as soon as you are ready. Take your time with reading this lesson, and take notes if you get stuck and do not understand something. At the end of the module, come back to your notes from this lesson and see if you have a better understanding as a result of the practical work.

In the previous modules, you have learned the final exteriorisation of magic, which we call *patterning* or *rituals*: exteriorised physical actions that essentially hold the energy of magic in a particular form and then send that magic out into the world.

It follows the same pattern as human existence: the completion of creation is the birth of a human child. The completion of creation is also a tree, a stone, an animal, etc.: it is the final outcome of something that started as a first impulse which went through a series of energetic processes to arrive at a physical substance or an outer expression.

To be able to operate in magic to any real degree of power, you need to know all the different layers of power, energy, substance, how they operate, where they came from, and where they are going. The first step in that process is to learn the complete exteriorisation of energy (substance or form); the next step is to look at the how that energy was turned into form from a magical perspective.

Then the apprentice magician will have far more understanding of the processes in between, which is where magic happens, and will be far better equipped to engage intelligently with magical power safely and effectively.

It would be too much to expect an apprentice magician to fully grasp the true depth of creation powers from the view of a magician, as the real understanding of those depths comes from direct inner experiences of these energetic forces in action. That is a process that begins during the Initiate phase of the training.

But to be able, as an initiate, to step into those inner powers and inner worlds to observe the creative act in action, they need a basic background understanding in what it is they are looking at, what they do, and how to interact with them—which in turn gives the magician a mental vocabulary that they can draw upon.

1.1 Creation and magic

A lot of magical systems give the creation process a cursory nod in the training process. In Western magic that often takes the form of learning the Kabbalistic tree of life system, whereas some other systems look at the creation process through mythology and the acts of the deities. Some forms of magic ignore it altogether.

For many years I taught this aspect of magical learning from a Kabbalistic perspective, but slowly I came to realise that because Western magic has in general so bastardised the Kabbalistic system (in an effort to make it fit the Western worldview and its psychological theories), it is to all intents and purposes pointless to teach it that way: the student invariably wanders off into various offshoots of Western Kabbalah and finds themselves stuck in mindless loops of magical babble.

So I had to sit back and think very carefully about how to approach this, as it is a critical section of learning if a magician is to truly reach magical adeptship in a real, practical sense.

I realised that I was simply being lazy: working with inner forms of magic exposes you to key *markers*, or experiences of the powers of creation that are common throughout the human experience. Through those generic experiences, the magician learns the depths of the creation dynamic, and learns how that process affects their magic, themselves, and everything around them in very practical ways.

Kabbalah is one method (though not the only one) that systematises those key experiences. I had become lazy in that I had fallen back on already produced and packaged systems as a way to convey magical information in writing. But those ready-produced and packaged systems have baggage; they have fragmentations and also tons of modern-day misconceptions. While it is still possible to operate through that system, I decided it would be better to step away and look at things in a fresh light.

Writing Quareia has kicked me up the ass and has forced me to stop being such a *lazy* magician. Instead I am making an effort to outline these deep, powerful mystical and magical processes without their cultural/religious structures: I am approaching them by teaching about the key elements that are found in the creation process as they present to a magician, and introducing the student to the beings, powers, and realms relevant to this process.

Once you have worked with the creation process in different ways and on different levels, you will immediately be able to spot one of these *keys* embedded within a mythology or a religion. And you will be able to recognise it *because you will have seen it and experienced it in action for yourself.* That experience is one of the hallmarks of the Greater Mysteries.

To get to that stage, you first need a background understanding. This module is the start of gaining that background understanding, and more modules around this subject matter will appear in the Initiate and Adept section of the training as you slowly inch your way deeper and deeper into the realm of creation.

You will also learn the polar opposite of the creation process, and that is the process of destruction and of death (the next module). Together, those three key energetic dynamics tell us everything about how real and powerful magic hangs together.

1.2 The use of visionary technique

Unlike the more externalised forms of magic, i.e. rituals, sigils, utterances, forming of objects, talismans etc., the energetic powers of creation are best understood, interacted with and observed through visionary magic. Only once the magician has worked in vision will such powers be accessible to be worked with through more externalised methods.

This is because the magician must first have direct and unique energetic experience of these powers in order for the understanding and power resonance to settle within the mind, spirit, and also the body of the magician.

The magician works with the inner and outer worlds together when they engage with power magically, so the understanding from both sides of the fence must be active and based upon direct experience in order for such magic to be successful.

The inner worlds, where energies are formed and patterned, can only be experienced and interacted with through the use of the imagination. This expresses itself through dreams and through visions.

In some kinds of magic, those dreams and visions come spontaneously and are uncontrolled. In other forms of magic the magician uses their imagination consciously as an interface to trigger, work with, and to an extent control the visionary act.

Dreams are best left to unfold themselves naturally, so the magician uses controlled and disciplined vision, and uncontrolled, un-interfered-with dreams. That allows both sides of the human mind to express themselves in their different ways.

As we discussed in Module I's lesson on visionary exercises, the imagination is used by a magician to create windows in their consciousness that the human spirit can step through in order to interact with beings, spirits, and powers in the inner worlds (worlds that have no physical manifestation). You have worked with your mind/imagination in various lessons so far, learning slowly how to build up images using your mind's eye in order to 'see.'

In future, in all lessons, I will no longer use the term 'mind's eye,' as you should all now know what it is I am referring to. From now on we will call it by its correct name, *inner vision*. You will be using inner vision a great deal more in your magical training from now on, and using it in balance with exteriorised magic so that your mind and body become used to the balance of working in both inner and outer forms, often at the same time.

The inner dynamics of creation are observed using inner vision. The magician interacts with various beings by using inner vision, and once they have acquired a good grasp of the inner dynamics of creation, then they can slowly start to connect the inner and outer dynamics together in magical acts. The combination of the two properly plugs the magic into a power source, and gives the magic an energetic focus, a pattern of behaviour, and a stable way to complete that magic successfully.

A magician would not plug into these deep dynamics to do simple or 'surface,' everyday magic like protection, etc., but they would most certainly plug into these powers to varying degrees when undertaking long-term powerful magical work that will have a lasting effect.

This method is very similar to the pathworking that is used in psychology, the only real differences being that inner vision is not about 'you,' is not venturing into your own inner self, and is not a constructed story. The realms exist outside of yourself, and the images used in vision are key steps that describe things which other magicians have also seen repeatedly over thousands of years: it tells you what is there, and you also have your own unique experiences. The images we see in those visions are a collective human interpretation of what is actually there: they are very real and exist independently of us.

In our modern world of science, the model of 'proof' is to measure the veracity of something by the ability to reproduce findings. That modus operandi has become the gold standard for everything in our lives. Magic does not work quite so neatly and cannot be measured using that paradigm.

However, there is one gold standard that does shine in magic, and that is that there are key elements that appear in inner vision to everyone who stumbles into the inner worlds, regardless of whether they were aware of those keys or not. They are not widely discussed, and are therefore unlikely to be in the subconscious mind or memory, waiting to resurface as an 'experience.'

These key images, interactions, and experiences are a hallmark of *inner contact* for magicians, and help us psychologically by telling us in quite plain language that we are on the real and right track. Often they have slightly different presentations, but the overarching power and communion is the same.

And some major keys are not written into the course so that you can find them for yourself—once you have experienced them, you will then be able to research them for yourself and track them down in ancient images and texts. This is one of the hallmarks of the Mysteries, and one of the ways the Mysteries protect themselves.[1]

I could write reams on these different keys, but it would not forward you an inch as a magician, because you will not have experienced them for yourself. True, direct experience changes you at a deep level, and that direct experience and the subsequent change is the chariot that carries you deep into magic.

There will be many times you will have self-doubt about your visionary experiences, and that can be very healthy, so long as it does not limit you.

If you see something in vision that does not compute, do not automatically dismiss it: you may very well find that what you saw was a real power contact. So if you experience something that does not fit with what you think should be there, do not dismiss it, simply write it down in your computer log.

It can be sometimes be handy to research what you have seen after you have seen it: often you can come across ancient references buried deep in stories or myths that exactly (or almost exactly) describe what you saw. That tells you it is not just in your own head, but that you were connected with something that magicians saw thousands of years ago.

There can be times when the imagination 'plays out' in the visionary process and what you see is simply coming from you and not from the inner worlds. There is no easy way around that, unless it is really obvious in its presentation. Slowly you will learn, through work and practice, to differentiate between what is really an inner world experience and what is your own mind amusing itself. That only comes from lots of practice, having direct experiences, and having those direct experiences confirmed in retrospect, either by other magicians or from ancient texts.

The best of all confirmations come from situations where, for example, an inner contact tells you something is going to happen (someone is going to die, something specific is going to be given to you unexpectedly, etc.) and then it happens, and there was no way you would have been able, even subconsciously, to effect such an outcome.

I write more about this type of process in my book *Magical Knowledge One*, but in truth, the best way to work with vision is to treat everything as real until you slowly start to be able to differentiate for yourself, and that time will most certainly come with work. That stops you inadvertently shutting down a contact by ignoring or blocking it from your mind. Such an action will have a far more long-term negative effect on your magic and training than accepting everything, even if that means accepting something that is simply your own mind.

Every magician goes through this process, and as you develop it will become less and less of an issue. Just also be cautious of accepting everything you see and hear as 'gospel' while working in vision, particularly as a new magician, as that too can take you down a not-so-good road. The key is simply to take note of your experiences, be respectful of the experience, and then wait and see.

So let us have a quick look at the stages of this creation dynamic that we will be looking at in depth through this module.

Through the module we will start the journey into creation by stepping backwards through the creation process. We will look at the first layer of beings that most humans come into contact with in magical vision or work, beings that stand at or near the threshold between our manifest world and the deeper inner worlds. We will start with the

---

[1] And the Quareia adepts will be looking for those unmentioned keys in your submitted work for mentoring: it will tell us that you are on the right track.

outermost manifestation of creation, and that is the physical world.

1.3 The garden

The *garden* is a name for the physical world that pops up a lot in various ancient texts and temple structures. The physical world encompasses everything: the land/earth, the plants/trees, animals, insects, humans—and it also includes the moon, sun, and stars.

This is something that many magicians forget or do not think about: the planets and stars around us are also a part of the manifest world—they are not separate, nor are they a deeper or higher expression. This is one of the mistakes that magicians make when using the Kabbalistic Tree of Life: they place the moon, sun, and stars on different Sefirot on the Tree, not realising that most of the tree is actually inner worlds, not outer worlds.

Now you start to see why it is a good idea not have anyone working with Kabbalah in the course: it has become too confused and fragmented when used in Western magic. It is badly misunderstood when taken away from its mystical religious roots.

The *garden*, or physical world, is the peak of the creation process. The *inner garden*, that is to say the inner expression of the land, shows up as a balanced and harmonic landscape and it is this 'ideal' that crops up in ancient and religious texts. This is the pinnacle of creation and is the inner template for the outer land. The outer land is not balanced and it is far more dynamic in its processes of creation and destruction, depending on the interactions it has with the creatures/humans etc. that live upon it.

As soon as anything manifests physically, it moves beyond its peak and begins its slow march towards degeneration and destruction, as everything has its death programmed into its birth. So like everything else, it is a constantly flowing process of in/out, life/death.

This peak at the outflow of creation is also the point where magic exteriorises into a ritual and goes out into the world to 'do its thing.' In the last module, you learned the four directional ritual pattern that works magically with the world. In this module, in the next lesson, you will learn to take a step deeper into the magical mysteries of the physical world so that you gain a better understanding of your own 'ground zero' (the land upon which you live) before you start to work magically with any power in the physical world.

Throughout history we have found ways of ritually reiterating this peak of creation, this inner garden that upholds the outer manifest world. We see it in the biblical Garden of Eden, and we see it in the mystical Pagan history of Kaaba in Mecca (Paradise on Earth).

The pre-Islamic Kaaba was said to have been built by Adam to the specifications given to him by angels in order to recreate Paradise on Earth. The original cubic building housed different expressions of the deities and their combined energies mirrored the inner garden in balance.[2]

We also see this recreation ritual action in the botanical sanctuary at Karnak in Egypt and also at Göbekli Tepe in Turkey. These are just some examples of the ritual mirror of creation that were worked with.

This point in creation is where the magician stands: stepping into the inner garden, the magician steps out of time and begins to backtrack through that creation process to observe how that creation came into being.

1.4 The inner threshold

The *inner threshold* is the first step inwards from the creative process. This is the realm of the imagination, and the group consciousness of every living thing. It is the inner body of the land (the *inner garden*) and of every living thing. This is where the first magical interactions happen for the magician as the magician learns to work within their own imagination.

---
[2]Quick hint on reading the symbolism of old myths: "Adam" equals people/person in the far distant past from the time perspective of the writers of the myth.

Just before creation exteriorises out into the physical world, it first creates the inner pattern of each living thing. This is the stage where we find the inner spirit of a tree, a dog, a river, a human; and the stage where the mind, consciousness, and dream world are formed. We step over this threshold to go into physical life, and we step over this threshold again at death as we begin our journey back, deep into the inner worlds.

For a magical apprentice, this threshold is the training ground for inner magic, and at some point the magician has to overcome the challenge of the threshold guardian that stops an ordinary person from wandering beyond their dreams and imagination and into the deeper inner realms themselves.

The apprentice learns to use this part of 'creation' through visionary magic, learning to step through the imagination in a controlled way in order to pass beyond this threshold and gain access to the deeper inner worlds.

This threshold is often referred to as the realm of the moon, not because it *is* the realm of the moon, but because the moon affects our minds and dreams; the description is therefore a planetary association. The physical moon itself is a part of the physical world. So be careful that you do not tie too much of an association with this realm and the moon, as it could end up confusing you and leading you up a dead end.

Rather, we can study old myths, stories, and attributes connected to the moon to get a glimpse of the powers of this threshold and how that power expresses itself to us as humans.

The lower parts of the creation process (which is what this module is about) have planetary connections which do influence aspects of the creative process, but as you tread deeper into the inner worlds you will find the planetary associations fall away.

1.5 The polarities of creative power

Once we step beyond the threshold of the imagination and the inner spirit of the outer being, we reach a second energetic threshold beyond which is the deep cauldron of creation with all its inherent angelic powers, deities, beings, and Divinity itself. This energetic threshold is not so much an inner space or realm; rather it is a tense, polarised power filter that the patterns of creation flow through and past on their way to physical manifestation.

That is vocabulary that will leave many an apprentice staring blanking at the words, because we are getting into areas of power that there is no current vocabulary to describe.

Imagine it a little like this. We have an energy barrier between two powerful magnets that create a magnetic or energetic tension. This energetic tension acts like a filter: it slows things down and filters out anything unnecessary. It also acts as a catalyst that triggers the formation of shape, gender, bloodlines, race/species etc.

In the depths of the inner worlds, the creative process of something (tree, person, etc.) has been forming and has started its movement towards taking shape into a solid form. It goes through a series of changes as it interacts with the inner powers around it (something you will learn about in the Initiate section) and finally it reaches this energetic barrier/filter. Once it passes through this filter it will pass into spirit/mind form (the inner threshold), and then finally be birthed as a physical living thing.

When that 'something' that is destined for life passes through this barrier or filter, it is changed quite dramatically. It starts to take on both aspects of a polarisation at a very deep level and that polarisation or energetic tension allows it to physically manifest (every living thing has this polarised aspect).

This polarisation in its depth expresses through positive/negative energy opposites. But this is not the only polarisation that happens: the 'something' that is destined for life also takes on feminine/masculine polarisation (every living thing has an aspect of both within them). It is akin to the first division of the cell as it begins life. And the octaves of this polarisation are layer upon layer that are interwoven in the consciousness, substance and spirit of the living being.

When we as magicians, and as living beings, backtrack through magical visionary work and step into this filter, we are confronted by this polarity of power as a field of energy. How we react mentally, physically, and spiritually to this energy field very much depends on how the current health and balance of that polarity is within us.

Now this is where it starts to get interesting. You would think, because this *filter* or barrier is a deep inner energetic field, that it would be wise to ensure our deeper consciousness and spirit is fairly balanced so that is it not badly disrupted by stepping into such a powerful field. And so many magicians work on their 'psychological deeper self' through counselling and self-analysis in order to maintain and strengthen that balance.

But that is not how we are constructed. We work from the outside in, not the inside out. What we change on the surface triggers deep change within. When we work in the depths, it triggers surface changes: again, energy working in tension and opposition.

So what on earth does all this mean for the magician?

If the magician is happy to only ever work in non-powered outer ritual (ritual dramas) and not tap into deep, underlying inner powers, then all of this deeper work is meaningless.

However, if as a magician you wish to become adept at effecting change in the outer world using magic, then you must be able to work in the deep inner realms using your consciousness.

To do that, your consciousness must be able to pass through this energetic barrier without triggering a cascade of physical and mental reactions, which is essentially the first line of defence that protects the inner world from stupid people—and protects the stupid people from the impacts of the inner worlds.

So how do we find that balance in order to pass through this barrier?

We find that balance by first understanding and then working with the two polarised, opposite power dynamics that create and uphold that barrier. Those two polarised powers are within our cells, our deeper spirits, and express through our daily lives. They also express externally around us through fate—and how we interact with that externalised power in our life radically changes us. It brings us more into balance.

The externalised forms of these energies that are around us express themselves as catalysts for our individual and collective evolution. As magicians we learn to work harmoniously and consciously with these energies rather than being dragged through life by them. By working consciously with these dynamics, in their most exteriorised form, we begin a process of deep inner individual change. This in turn leads to the process of rebalancing within which allows us to work with deep power, energy, and to pass over thresholds safely.

Now this all sounds very deep and meaningful, and a tad complex, but in real terms it manifests in very simple ways. You have already been working with these two polarised power in ritual without realising it. In magic they manifest in their most outer form as the sword and the cup, the two tools that guard the power impulse as it passes into the magical space.

The sword is the most outer form of a limiting power that we will call the *Grindstone*.[3]

The Grindstone limits and slows something so that it can become stronger, denser, and more 'manifest.' That is its deepest power, and we see that in how particles and cells work.

---

[3] These powers also manifest through everyday life, which you will come to recognise through the lessons in this module.

In human fate, a totally different octave, it manifests as life events or conditions that limit and shape the individual, a nation or a race.

In magic this manifests as the 'engine governor' which stops power coming through too quickly, and also stops the magician from misusing power by stopping the magician reaching too deeply or accessing power when they are unbalanced.[4]

The opposing power to this is one that releases power and we will call that the *Unraveller*. As the Grindstone limits and polishes, the Unraveller frees things up and then dissolves them. As the Grindstone limits in order for something to solidify, the Unraveller allows a free flow of power and energy which in turn eventually brings degeneration and death.

When we die, our energies are released from the bondage of the body, for example. And we all know what happens to our living bodies if we allow free rein to our senses: we over-consume which in turn brings about our downfall.

The deepest energetic function of the cup is as a cup of the *Scales*: the sum total of your actions, development and evolution is "weighed upon the scales," that is to say, the way you develop as a spirit in life governs how the spirit travels back into death from life.

The *threshing floor* (remember that from your pentagram ritual?) is an octave of the power of the Unraveller or the cup. The 'harvest of your life' is placed upon the threshing floor and governs how your spirit interacts with the transition process into death and beyond.

You will discover, through the in-depth lessons on these powers, that within each opposing polarity there is also an inherent dualism: the complexity of the octaves of these powers are within everything, from a single cell to a city, to an animal, to a life event or a work of art.

When you step into the inner worlds, if your *body and spirit* has these two opposing influences in more or less a state of conversation if not balance, then you can pass into the deeper inner worlds without too much of a problem.

The way to achieve that is first through understanding, and then through direct conscious engagement in your outer and also magical life. Taking that first step of direct engagement triggers a whole cascade of change within you. And the lessons of this module will take you through this initial direct engagement.

The way the body and spirit balance these two opposing influences will be discussed in depth later in this module, and you will be able to work in a series of different ways to trigger that balancing/conversation process.

At this point you will be beginning to see just how complex magic can be once you get past the surface presentation. And yet it still works with very simple principles of power in opposition, tension, power moving in opposite directions, and the maintaining of balance in the centre.

The universe, the body, the mind and the inner worlds all work the same way: just as a muscle needs opposing actions, so too does the mind and spirit. The role of the magician is to work as a fulcrum, as someone who stands in the midst of the opposing powers and who conducts the orchestra of power from a place of stillness in the centre.

In today's world of commercial magic, many training groups have apprentices using counselling, psychological analysis, and drama rituals to make or even force themselves to be 'more balanced'—which of course does not work (though they are almost on the right track): these are all actions that still obviate responsibility from the magician for his or her own actions (and they tend to come away from self development rituals and go back to treating everything around them like shit).

Rather, magical balancing occurs through a subtle shift in how you live your daily life, how you understand your own body and mind, and how you first recognise, and then engage with the various beings and powers of creation as you learn to spot them active in your own life and the world around you.

---

[4] Remember the sword of Damocles?

1.6 The Inner Beings

At these thresholds, there are a variety of different inner beings that will work with the magician in order to first find and then maintain that inner and outer balance in opposition, and who act as threshold guardians, teachers, guides and workers. In the latter part of this module, you will meet these guardians in vision and ritual and learn how to connect and work with them.

1.7 *Task:* Researching *Ma'at*

The tasks for this lesson are easy and are simple study ones.

Look up and research everything you can find on the ancient Egyptian concept of *Ma'at*. Don't just find the deity and stop there: the deity is the face of a deeper power dynamic. Ma'at is the ancient Egyptians' version of this polarity power filter that creates balance—power in, power out, always working to keeping the Scales balanced.

The reason you are looking at it from an Egyptian perspective is that it is one of the few cultures we know of (they left behind a huge body of work) that engaged that inner threshold dynamic in their cultural and religious lives. And what they painted and wrote about is the closest I have ever come across to what is experienced when you step into the inner worlds. Essentially, they knew their shit.

Once you have researched and read up on Ma'at, write a short essay on what you understand Ma'at to be, and reflect in that essay how you feel Ma'at does or doesn't operate in your own life, and your country, culture, legal, and spiritual system. Do this as a computer essay so that it can be submitted later if you wish to be mentored. You will be coming back to this essay to reassess and compare with how your understanding has changed as a result of your magical work.

1.8 *Task:* Researching the Scales

Look at ancient Egyptian depictions of the Scales of Ma'at: you will notice in ancient pictures (not modern reproductions) that the feather is on the left hand scale (if you were the Scales) as is Djehuty, who is the deity of the transmission of knowledge (air). On the right hand side of the scale is the vessel which holds the person's heart, which is the harvest of their life and deeds.

Also look at the image of Themis, goddess of Divine Justice as depicted in Union Station, Washington D.C., USA. Whoever made that statue knew their Inner Mysteries. Note the nod to the threshing floor.

Then look at various depictions of the goddess of justice from various ancient cultures. What you will quickly see is that some hold the sword in their left hand (to the right as you are looking at the picture) and some are reversed.

This reversal has two reasons: one is that as the Mysteries within a culture begin to degenerate, often the power depictions become lost or reversed, and this happens in all different cultures. Whether it is deliberate or not I do not know: it could be to protect the Mysteries or it could be out of a loss of knowledge.

The other reason for the reversal could be to do with the two forms of justice. One is the Divine power of Justice, which is the two opposing polarity powers of the threshold that protect the deep Mysteries (sword in the left hand), and the other form of justice, which shows the reversal of the tools, is human justice, which is flawed. The Scales held in the left hand show the weighing up of the words (air) of a person rather than their deeds (which is weighed in the right hand/west).

These are keys that are symptomatic of the state of the Mysteries at any given point in a culture. If the powers are depicted correctly, you know that at least someone in that culture at that time was clued in to the Inner Mysteries. If the keys go missing or are reversed, cast to one side, etc., then you know it is a mystical sign of the slow descent into collapse of a culture or religion.

The depictions of the polarised powers of the thresholds are ones that can teach us a lot about the gnosis or lack thereof in a culture or religion. And the way that you as a magician work with these powers and tools will dictate how successful you are at penetrating the Deep Mysteries as an adept.

These two polarised powers are summed up as *power in* (to life) and *power out* (to death). The sword/grindstone limits and shapes, the cup/unraveller weighs and measures, and then releases.

Look through ancient art, statues, and wall reliefs, and take notes on any ideas or revelations that bubble up into your mind as you research this topic.

These tasks will help to cement the outer keys into your mind and also embed the understanding of Ma'at deep within you: by experiencing these powers through magic and then externalising through study and writing, you will gain a balance of understanding that you can then work with as a magician.

1.9 Summary

For those who find this whole concept and discussion a far cry from their ideas of magic, don't panic—although it is seemingly advanced or obscure, it is a vital part of the early stage of learning how to work in magical depth, and it is a cornerstone of adept magic, a stone which is laid in the foundations.

These dynamics play a major part in the formation of life and of magic, and without accessing these powers and energies the magician barely scratches the surface of their magical potential. These polarised dynamics are the power stations of magic, of mysticism, and of life itself.

Lesson 2

The Inner Garden and Outer Vessels

The physical world around you is the biggest source of stability, learning, power, and strength for a magician, and yet it is sadly overlooked by many a magician. It is also the most powerful gateway to inner realms, beings, and spirits if a magician knows how to operate a space productively.

All magic needs a vessel and a power source: first you learn to use what is already around you (the vessel of creation) before you then go on to work with magical tools (vessels) and powers.

Magic is everywhere: it is an expression of Divinity in substance and we as humans can mediate that power, raise it, and work with it. Everything around you has the creative and destructive powers flowing through it, and everything has consciousness in one form or another. Part of the work of a magician is to tap into that flow of power and also to communicate with everything around them. This opens the door for the magician to a path of cooperation, co-working, and mutual guardianship.

This is done in a variety of different ways, of which some are highly ritualised, others deeply mystical, and some very simple. The process of learning these skills starts with the apprentice magician doing a simple act: talking to everything. This has two actions from a technical point of view: it opens the door for power sources to flow, and it triggers natural 'vessel' actions. Why?

When as a magician you talk to something with magical intent, you mirror, at a very low level, a fundamental power dynamic of creation: the utterance. In its very deepest form, which you will learn about as an adept, it is a vibration, a sound that flows out of the 'nothing' that triggers a chain reaction that results in substance/consciousness. In a mystical form, we know this as the Word—"In the beginning was the Word." Everything in creation works in octaves, in patterns, and it is these octaves and patterns that a magician triggers when doing magic.

By talking to something with magical focus *and intent*, you recreate that act in a very small way and even though it is the simplest, tiniest form of the action, it triggers a magical flow of power: it is a catalyst. As an apprentice you learn to talk to everything while also learning the outer actions and tools that engage with this magical creative power, along with meeting some of the beings involved. As an initiate, you build on that experience and learn to engage with the beings that work with the process. As an adept you learn to utter into life.

If you talk to natural living things like plants, trees, creatures, insects, rivers, storms, you are talking to a consciousness that is already there. By talking to them, you are taking the first step towards the threshold of the inner garden: the physical manifestation of something is only the outer shell for something far more powerful and profound that fills that shell. This *inner garden*, or to put it more technically *the inner landscape*, gives you immediate access to the power source that is already partially formed and is therefore stable to work with.

By talking to everything living around you, you also signal that you are waking up; that you are willing to be an active part of the world around you, not just a passenger. And slowly you will find that things start to talk back to you, using your mind and also the physical world around you as interfaces. This begins a conversation that grows into a friendship based on mutual respect, and from that friendship the magician gains support, learning, fellowship, and companionship.

Often, working in that harmonic way eventually catches the attention of larger land beings, deities, and ancient ancestors in the area, so that over a period of time your working team becomes bigger. That also results in learning how to work magically as a team of beings, so that it is not always about you and your work, but is also often about the needs of everything around you.

This team acts like a power substation and allows you to plug into a power source that is already managed: it is like the fusebox of your house as opposed to the power generating station. So although at a magical technical level you are intentionally seeking a source of power to work with, it manifests as communicating and then working with the beings around you.

2.1 Talking to vessels

The same sideways view is also true of the *vessel*. In magic we often think of the vessel as a cup, or in advanced magic as a golem or an enlivened statue that holds consciousness and/or power. And yes, those are examples of magical vessels. But the building where you work magic and the inner landscape around you are also vessels: the inner landscape is the natural vessel and the building you work in can be turned into a vessel that can receive and hold power.

Before you learn to turn a vessel into a magical vessel (a skill which you will learn later in the apprentice section), first you must learn about the more expansive vessel potentials around you. The way to start that learning process is to 'switch on' the building vessel and then also learn to pass into the inner landscape as a vessel and work with it.

To switch on a building as a vessel, you talk to everything around and within it (opens the door for the consciousness and power), and then you tune the frequency of space though ritual magical action (working the directions and the gates). If you think of that switch action as like a dimmer switch, these two simple actions are akin to turning a light on, but very dimmed.

Later, you will learn to fully integrate a building with the inner landscape, create and open gates (both inner and outer) for that building and then join everything up. That turns the building into an enlivened vessel: the first stage towards turning it into a true power temple.

There are two basic types of vessels; those that mimic species and those that do not. Let's talk about the sort that do not (you will learn about species vessels in another lesson). The vessels we are going to work with are buildings, cars, jars...basically anything that does not have a face and is man-made. There are also natural versions of this type of vessel: rocks, mountains, etc, which we will learn about later. But the man made ones tend to surround us the most. Anything that has physical substance can be a container. A container for what?

They can contain extensions of your own consciousness (a thoughtform, for example) or they can become places of habitation for spirits. You can achieve this through the use of magical patterns, which is something you will learn later on, or through a more natural route, which you will learn first.

The natural route is triggered by talking to something as if it were a being. This creates an inner doorway for a spirit or consciousness to step into the vessel. Straight away you can see the good side to this, and also the bad side. The good side is having a being which is not parasitical step into the vessel (a parasitical being is only there to eat your energy) and which is willing to work with you in return for a home, interaction, companionship, and entertainment. The bad side tends to happen if the vessel is not properly tuned, and as a result becomes filled with parasites and low-level beings.

The way to avoid a parasitical or unhealthy being stepping into a vessel is the focused intent and approach of the magician. You will learn about beings later on in the apprentice section, but before you get there you need to know how beings operate around us. Focused intent is a major part of the skill set of the magician, and by focused intent I mean talking to something with the intention that the 'something' is a vessel for a being that you intend to interact with magically.

Let's have a look at some practical examples, which will demonstrate to you these dynamics far better than a theoretical exploration can.

2.2 Random inhabitation

An inexperienced magician spends a couple of years doing regular magical work in their home. He does rituals, calls, visions, experiments, alchemy, etc. but in a haphazard way, without any true, defined intent or focus other than curiosity, and he does it in isolation to everything else around him. He may cast a circle, do a banishing, and then get to work.

Over a period of time the magician starts to weaken, have bouts of depression and low energy, he gets a string of minor illnesses, and the house always feels 'uncomfortable' to those who visit. It always seems dark, no matter how many lights are on; it feels sticky, and no matter how much he cleans, it never quite feels right. This is the outer manifestation of working in such an isolated and haphazard way.

Now let's change perspective and look at the same situation from an inner point of view.

When our magician moves into a house and begins doing magic, it 'turns on a light' in the inner world and he becomes visible. Spirits are curious and draw near. But the magician does a circle and banishing, which appears in the inner world as "fuck off to everyone except the person I call." So the spirits draw away, disappointed and sometimes offended. The parasitical beings, however, see the energy being generated and draw nearer. They are not bothered by the magician's hostile approach and they watch him, looking for a way into that yummy scene.

The magician casts a circle and does a pentagram banishing. But such a system pattern is weak and ineffectual. The initial resistance that the parasites get from this banishing action is quickly overcome as they get used to it and see a way in.

Every time the magician does this action and then goes on to do magic, it generates energy that the parasites are drawn to. They all gather around and feed furiously upon the magician's own energy and the energy he is generating. They dress up and pretend to be the entity the magician is trying to summon, and a relationship is formed. Eventually they move into the house and begin to multiply. Think in terms of ticks or fleas.

Soon the word gets around that there is an easy source of food, and the word is passed along as to how to dodge the weak defence created by the magician. Soon the house, the magician's body, and his energy sphere are full of small, low-intelligence, low-life beings who feed happily on this new food source. If these beings are lucky, the magician uses sexual power, drugs, adrenaline, and god knows what else in their magic, which in turn creates a wonderful buffet of food for these beings.

All the while the more intelligent spirits, who feel insulted by the rejection (the magician's banishing ritual) and who do not wish to feed off the magician, watch in amusement from a safe distance. They were willing to make friends, do work, and live alongside someone who could potentially see, hear, and work with them. But the magician had, through his banishing, made it very clear they were not welcome.

That scenario is a very common one and is propagated by innocence and poor training. The first mistake is to assume that everything needs banishing; the second mistake is to assume that the magical casting of a circle and a banishment actually works and works powerfully. Most of the time they don't.

(And just as an aside, bear in mind that the pentagram ritual taught in the original Golden Dawn training—and virtually all subsequent ritual magical schools/groups—was never meant to be a powerful banishing technique: it was a beginner exercise, just as the ritual work in Module II is beginner level. The GD version just looks flashier.)

If a powerful being wants to get into your space, it will do so and no amount of banishment will stop it. Why? Because most methods of basic banishing draw upon the individual strength of the magician (regardless of the use of Divine names). This way of working also rejects beings that would be very helpful: it does not stop them getting in, but the unfriendly attitude turns them off. And it also does *not* stop beings that are looking for a dinner…

Think of it like bouncers at a nightclub. If you are the manager, your job is to manage everything, not handle the security. For that job you employ large, muscled dudes who are well-trained in conflict resolution, defence, and restraint techniques. They also usually throw a mean punch, and in some countries will be well-armed. The same principles apply in working magic. You are the manager, and you outsource the security to those better able than yourself. And for your own safety, you also learn hand-to-hand combat, weapon use, and keep well muscled: for magicians, that comes from working with different power patterns.

So what is the answer? Let's have a look at a different scenario.

2.3 Magical inhabitation

A magician moves into a house and begins to work magically in the space. He works with magical patterns that root him in the role of fulcrum: Divinity as the breath (no dogmatic religious form), the tools of balance, the rooting in the ancestral line (buffer and shield), and the working with the inner and outer directions (power sources).

The space begins to 'tune' to a certain energetic frequency, and an inner energetic pattern starts to build in the house. The four gates begin to appear in the inner landscape of the house, and through those gates, deeper inner beings that are tuned to specific powers and contacts begin to leave their energetic signature in the space.

This turns all the inner energetic lights on, and the spirits, beings, and parasites in the area become aware of the magician and start to draw near. They get to the house, but the parasites are stopped from entering the space by the guardians of the thresholds in the four directions. Also, the energetic frequency of the space (that has been generated by the focused magical work) shifts and tunes to a point where the space becomes uncomfortable for these low-life beings to stay in. It is like one of those high-frequency noises that humans cannot hear but which is unbearable for mice.

The more intelligent nature beings find that they can enter the space, usually through the gates, as the guardians of the thresholds see that their presence would be mutually beneficial for the magician and the beings. They pass into the space, join in energetically with the ritual work, and some decide to stay. Their inclusion gives the magician access to a group power from the beings who work in cooperation with him. They stay, live in the space, and earn their keep by guarding, assisting, and teaching/learning. They embed themselves into the substance of the building (which has now become a magical vessel) that is now compatible with that type of being, or they come and go from the land outside like friends popping in for tea.

From the magician's perspective, he builds

the magical patterns in the house, and he talks/works regularly with each of the four gatekeepers by lighting the directional candle, communing with the inner contact, bowing, and then getting to work. When the magician meditates, he acknowledges the gates and the gatekeepers/contacts, and that regular interaction keeps a door open that allows those guardians to have a constant presence in the house.

The magician also talks to the house itself. He tells the house when visitors are coming, or when there may be a threat, or if he is going to be away for any length of time: he talks to the house in the same way we would talk to our pets. By doing this act in a focused way, it creates a doorway for interaction and informs the beings in the vessel of changes to the space's energy, which in turn makes it a lot less likely that they would be triggered adversely by a visitor or shift in the routine of the magician (and talking to the house as the vessel, rather than addressing just the beings, helps to solidify the structure of the house as a vessel for power).

So slowly but steadily the right beings move into the house or visit regularly. The beings communicate through the mind of the magician, though sometimes also through physical acts (for example, moving things to get the magicians attention) and they begin to teach the magician how to do certain magical acts better or more productively. They also alert the magician to things that the spirits or the land may need help with, so it becomes a mutual relationship. This is a very old way of working, and has many layers to it.

The magician introduces certain working deities into the space, and eventually the house becomes a collective of humans, deities, spirits, and land beings, all of whom work together to a collective goal. That is a vessel filled with power and which mimics an octave of creation.

The first step of that is the healthy and tuned magical patterning in the house, and the second is talking to the vessels: talking to the house which allows the house to become a vessel for beings to inhabit.

2.4 The Inner Landscape

The second part of vessel/creation learning is the inner landscape. I don't want to go into too much depth here, as I want you to get on to practical work. Essentially, the inner landscape of the land is the inner spirit and template for the creation of the manifest world, including all beings/species. And that is where it gets interesting. When you go out onto the land in vision, you pass into the inner landscape, which is like the default template for that land. So it often looks like how the land would have appeared in that area before humans started inhabiting and changing it.

Now we get to the weird bit. Humans have a template of creation as well, but when you pass into one of these, it does not appear as an 'inner human'; rather it, too, appears as a landscape. For the longest time I assumed that this presentation was something to do with how my own mind worked. But once I got into deep discussions with other magicians who had also found out how to access their own inner templates, they too found that they had broken into an inner landscape. It appears that the inner landscape is the inner vessel that our spirit is poured into as we pass into life: our pattern and the pattern of the land are inextricably linked.

When you work magically you stand, from a spirit and energetic sense, in the inner landscape of the land. If the temple is tuned, it will also appear in the inner landscape, as will the gates. You can do that passively, or you can draw upon that inner landscape to further fuel and balance your magical work. So let's get to practicalities.

2.5 *Task:* Connecting with the inner landscape

The first exercise is to connect with the inner landscape around you. You can do this either in a passive way or in a magically defined way. You have already stepped into part of the inner landscape in a passive way when you went in vision across the land to connect with a river, a mountain, etc. As you walked, you passed from civilisation to wilder land. That is a simple, natural crossing of the threshold into the inner landscape in a very simple way. The way the land presented in that work is very similar to how the landscape reveals itself to you in dreams and through traditional shamanic vision quests.

As a magician working from a magical space, there is a more technical way to access this inner landscape that brings it into focus with your ritual work and space. This method still uses vision to start with, and then once you have established the ability to work with vision you introduce ritual and combine the two together to make a whole magical act. That enables you to begin the process of learning how to align with, and then tap into, the stream of creation as it flows into the world.

For the practical work of this lesson, you are going to do a vision, then a ritual, and finally a ritualised vision. Then you will do tarot readings to check your progress and the results of your work.

So let's work first with the inner landscape. Read the various steps and keys for this vision, and once you are familiar with them, then it is time to do the vision for yourself. The more you do this formed visionary method and practice it, the more your mind will begin to step into the inner worlds in spontaneous vision and dreams: it gives your mind a method of working that it will begin to play with in its own time.

The ritual

Work in your ritual space. Put a pen and paper on the east altar and also on the west altar. Put your tarot cards on the central altar. Get a piece of white thread that will fit and tie around your wrist. Place the thread on the south altar.

Go around the directions as you have learned, light all the candles, see the gates open, and then go sit down in front of the central altar, with your back to the north.

Still your mind with a brief meditation. When you are ready, with your inner vision, see the room around you. See the gates in the four directions and see them open with inner contacts standing on the thresholds.

In vision, stand up and walk around the directions, acknowledging the contacts in the four directions, and then stand before the west altar. Step through the west altar and pass through the gates and walk until you find yourself standing out on a landscape.

Look back and see your work space with the four gates surrounding a flame. Stand for a moment and just look.

As you watch, you will slowly start to see other beings appearing at the gates and standing on the threshold, looking at the flame. Watch how the guardians react to these beings. You will notice that the guardians allow some beings to pass into the ritual space and reject others. The ones who are allowed near the flame will be faery beings, land beings, or ancestral beings from your area.

If you can get a sense of how they look or feel, try to remember that, as it will help you to identify them later in your magical work. But don't worry if you cannot fix on how they present. Don't try and force it: you will pick up the necessary signatures in your own time.

Now turn away from the ritual space and start walking. You will find yourself walking in a natural landscape. Walk on the land in a large circle around the ritual space, but keep a reasonable distance.

As you get into an area of the landscape that aligns with a gate, have a look around. What does the landscape look like? Is it healthy? Is it rocky? Is there water? Sea? Hills? Caves? Go around and look at the land that is beyond each gate by walking the inner landscape around the outside of the ritual space.

Can you see buildings made by humans? If so, they are either tuned, consecrated, or have been there for a very long time. You may see buildings that do not appear in the outer world: those are buildings that slowly became vessels for one reason or another, and when the outer building was torn down the inner pattern of the building stayed. But bear in mind it is unusual to see a building in the inner landscape.

If you want to, at another time, you can use these visionary steps to explore the landscape in the wider areas around where you live: this will help you find local ancient temples, ritual burials or natural power vortexes. But for now you are going to work in a magical, systematic way.

Turn and go back to the west threshold, but instead of seeing yourself step back into the room, step over the threshold of the gate with the intention that you are going to reveal the inner landscape that runs through the ritual space (what is there in the inner land where your house does not show).

As you step through, let the landscape extend into your work space: see the land, the trees, water, whatever as they emerge, and see it appear in the ritual space until the four gates and the flame in the centre of the room appear to be in the wild of nature.

Walk around the ritual space and notice if any streams of water, ancient trees, or any sort of feature appears within the ritual space.

Go to the central candle and step into it. Stand within the flame in vision: you will realise that you do not burn; rather the flame energises you.

Stand facing south, with the east gate on your left and the west gate on your right. Feel a wind flow straight down from above onto you and flow through you: this is the Divine Breath.

Hold your arms out in vision, feel the rock beneath your feet and the wind flowing down over and through you.

See ahead of you, through the south gate, the road into the future with the noble guardians standing there, and feel a gathering of spirits/ancestors behind you: these are most likely not your blood ancestors, but the spirits of people still sleeping in the land.

Turn your head to the left and look. A large and strange-looking being steps through the east gate and stands beside you. The being is much larger that you, and they stand slightly behind you with one hand on your left hand and one hand on your left shoulder.

Now turn your head and look to your right. You find that your hand is on the rim of a large stone jar that is almost as big as you are. You can see in to it. As you look into it, you see lots of things that you recognise but cannot quite get a fix on: a bit like waking up from a dream where the memories quickly fade. The jar may be full or half full.

You keep looking at the jar, as it fascinates you. So many things in it feel and look familiar, but you are not sure what they are.

As you watch the jar, a being, once again large and strange-looking, steps through the west gates and picks up your jar. He looks down at the floor beneath the jar, and you notice that the floor is smooth, solid rock.

The being takes your hand from the rim of the jar and tips the contents of the jar onto the stone floor. He stands the jar back up and begins beating its contents on the floor with a thin stick. The contents break apart: some of it turns to dust and blows away, some of it stays behind.

The being then squats down and picks through what is left. The large being to your left pushes down on your shoulder to make you kneel on the stone floor so that you can touch the contents left on the floor. Both beings signal for you to touch one of the remaining contents.

You reach out and touch something. Immediately you have a memory of an experience you had in the past. It is a strong memory, maybe something you had forgotten about, but it comes back to you and you remember the situation, your emotions, and your actions.

Spend a little time thinking about your actions and think not about the effect your actions had on others, but the direct effect it had upon yourself.

Take as long as you need to if you wish to

touch the other fragments, and think how that situation affected you in the short and long term.

The being from the west blows upon all the contents on the stone, gathers them up and places them in your pocket. In your meditations you can take one out a time and explore a situation/memory to ascertain what you learned from it, how you have potentially matured from it (or not), and what insights it gives you into yourself and your own path.

The jar is now empty, or so you think, until you stand back up and look into the jar, and you see that it is filled with water: it is ready to receive new energetic memories.

The being from the west stays with the jar: he is the guardian of the vessel. You stand, looking at the south, with the large being to your left, who is the guardian of the sword, and the guardian of the vessel to your right.

Now open your eyes while still retaining a sense of the beings in the space with you. This is time for a break.

The walking through the west gates and surveying the land is something you can do a lot if you wish.

Now it is time to get back to work: have a stretch and then sit back down. This next part is a working technique of visionary ritual, so practice it and remember it (see notes below).

2.6 *Task:* **Visionary ritual of mediation**

You are going to work with a foundational visionary ritual method that in this instance is for a specific task: the mediation and birth (creation) process of the two main ritual tools. Although the way you are going to do this is specific to two different tools, the actual baseline technique can be used for any form of power mediation, something you will work with again in different forms.

Once more sit back down facing south with the central altar before you. Close your eyes. See with your inner vision the four gates around you. See the large being to your left and the being and vessel to your right.

Now you are going to trigger a faint flow of creative power. Do this by seeing a line of bright light come down from the stars into the room. As it hits the room it triggers a similar line of light that passes through the east gate into the room.

As it flows from the east into the room, the large being to your left holds out their left hand and slows the flow of light/power down until it changes colour to a bright yellow. The being emits a sound as the light hits his hand. Remember that sound.

The yellow light passes through the being's hand and flows into the central flame. From there it travels from the central flame to the south altar and passes through the south gates, vanishing into the distance.

Watch the south gate. The light returns as a red line of power, flows at an angle from south to west, and is held in the western flame.

You see the being in the west holding the vessel full of water, and the flame sits on top of the water. There it changes colour again, taking on a deep blue colour.

The blue light then travels back to the central flame, changing to black, and immediately flows north but also straight down below the central flame, passing deep into the earth.

You have worked with this pattern before, and it is the inner energetic template for creative and destructive energy in its completed flow.

Now open your eyes and stand up. Walk a full circle around the directions and then walk to the east altar.

With your eyes open, be aware through inner vision/imagination of the constant flow of energy flowing into the room from the east and from above.

The large being moves in front of you, standing within the east altar. The being places a hand upon your chest and you reach out, both physically and in vision, and place your left hand upon their shoulder.

Take in a deep breath. As you breathe in, a symbol appears upon the forehead of the large being. You may see it in your imagination, or you may 'sense' what it looks like. Take your time with this and do not try to force anything. When you have a good idea of the symbol shape, pick up the pen on the altar and draw it on the piece of paper.

Everyone works slightly differently with this technique. If no symbol appears in your inner vision, then simply pick up the pen and let the being guide your hand. Draw out whatever comes. After that, mark the paper with an L shape but where each side is equal length (half a two-dimensional square) above the symbol.

Once you have written that down, with your inner vision see the large being move to the right of the altar, so that he stands on the south side of the east altar. He places his right hand on the altar and stays there. Every time you work in this ritual space, keep an awareness of this being: he will now stay there until you complete your work with your soon-to-come magical sword.

Now bow, turn, and go to the west altar.

With your eyes open, stand before the west altar and keep an awareness of the large vessel that is upon or within the west altar, and be aware of the being there.

As you look at the vessel, the being draws your attention to shapes, patterns, or symbols on the vessel. Close your eyes. Use your inner vision to look carefully at the patterns on the vessel and one in particular, a symbol, stands out and is bright. Remember the shape of it, open your eyes, and write down the shape of the symbol on the paper that is on the altar.

Above the symbol write a reversed capital L (so the foot of the L points left instead of right) and again write it as half of a two-dimensional square (each side is equal).

These symbols are the sigils that will be unique to your magical tools and to the beings that will inhabit them (the beings you are working with).

The being stays in the west altar, holding the vessel, and will stay there until you complete your work with your magical cup in an upcoming lesson. So from now on, every time you work in this room, see both of these beings standing there, waiting.

Step back, bow, and walk a full circle around the directions.

Go and stand before the east altar. Be aware of the being. Close your eyes. See a wind flowing through the east gate and blowing over you. Take in a deep breath. Turn your head to the right (south) and breath out with the intention of passing to the south the breath you took in from the east.

A priest or priestess appears on the threshold of the east gate. See them with your inner vision. Do not ask their name, just acknowledge them with a bow of your head.

Take note of how this person is dressed. Do not try to dress them with your own imagination, just let them appear as they want you to see them. If you do not get a clear sense of how they are dressed or what they look like, don't worry: just be aware that they are there. They are there to simply witness your words.[1]

Take in another deep breath from the wind of the east and feel the large being at the side of the altar place a hand upon your right shoulder (right when standing facing east is future deeds).

Breathe out and recite:

> "I strive to honour the Divine Breath through my breath, my words, and my songs. I accept the guardian of the sword and I am willing to be taught by the guardian of the sword in whatever way is necessary, in my magical life and my daily life, so that I learn to work in a balanced way with power."

Step back, bow, and go to the south.

Stand before the south altar and with your eyes open, use your inner vision/imagination to see the south gate, and beyond the south gate a road or pathway in full midday sun. Pick up the white thread and hold it in your left hand. Now close your eyes.

Using your inner vision, see the Noble Ones on the path before you. These are men/women who shine brightly. One of

---
[1] See note two below.

them walks towards you, passes through the gates, and holds out their hand. See yourself handing them the white thread. Physically hold out the thread over the altar (be careful of the candle flame).

The Noble One pulls a white thread from within themselves and places it into your white thread: through this thread, you will be connected to them, and when you work in vision and stand at the inner threshold, they will recognise you (don't worry if the thread falls off before you get to that vision in a future lesson, once it has been on you for however long it needs to be there, it will fall off but leave an inner imprint upon you).

When the Noble One steps back, withdraw your hand and open your eyes. Tie the white thread around your left ankle, and do it slightly loosely so that the thread can stay there for a prolonged length of time without restricting your ankle when your ankle flexes.

Step back from the altar, bow, turn, and circle the directions, and finish in the east. Be aware of the being there. Leaving the gates open, blow the candle out, bow, step back, and repeat by putting out the candles in each direction, and the centre one last.

Note one

The emptying of the vessel is a one-off event in vision. It is not something you repeat (you get one chance as an apprentice when you step into magic to have the being assist you in the emptying).

However, should you wish to do a regular (once a year) look over your *Harvest* (also known as your deeds in the Book of Judgement), it can be useful and insightful (and can be profound at times) to spend a couple of weeks of each year meditating upon your actions (regardless of good and bad), pondering on the effect they had upon you and whether you have learned from your mistakes. In Judaism there is a form of this known as Yom Kippur. We will look again at this concept in lesson four in a more practical and magical way.

2.7 What just happened?

First you connected with the inner landscape which made you more visible to the inner beings around you, and you learned what inner powers are in the land upon which you live.

The work with the sword being and the vessel being taught you the flow dynamics of creation. Power *in* from east/above, power *existing* through east to south via the centre (the centre axis holds the void that everything flows in and out of), power *breaking down* from south/future to west/threshold of destruction, power *composting* from west to north via the centre and down. You have already worked before with that pattern, but now it needs to build in your understanding from an abstract flow of power into patterns of shape, beings, and tools.

From this understanding, you will start to fully understand the tool/direction/elemental families and the patterns and combinations they work through. Through that understanding, you will then be able to see such patterns used in ancient magic and mysticism. You will also start to see the constant dance of creation and destruction as it flows in a constant pattern in manifestation.

You connected with two beings of the tools: the two guardians and governors who oversee and work through and with the magical tools. These two foundational tools always have beings working within them. You will learn how to operate with them through the tools, and in turn they will guide you by putting learning in your path, and they will protect you from serious danger—but not from your own stupidity or arrogance.

The white thread upon the left ankle is a connection with the Noble Ones of the future, also known as the Sandalphon: these are angelic beings that guide and work with magicians deep in the inner worlds, and who also act as magical companions as you work (you will learn more in another lesson in this module). The white thread is your first connection to one of these beings and begins a very quiet, slow process of adjusting your body to their power, so that when you come to work with them in the inner worlds, your body will not be impacted by their communion with you (and they will recognise you).

It is placed on the leg that stands upon the grindstone, something you will learn a lot more about in the next lesson. This energetically connects the companion/Noble One to the energetic flow of the grindstone power that will flow through your outer and magical life. You will learn to work in combination with the Noble One, the inhabited sword, and the Grindstone power in order to learn, mature, and strengthen as a magician.

The vessel is the scale of Maat and is the vessel that records and weighs your deeds. You will slowly learn, by working with the vessel and the being, to weigh your own scales and keep your own balance in your life and magical work. The symbols from the east and the west will be inscribed upon your magical tools and will seal the connection between the tool and the beings connected to them.

Note two: the importance and power dynamic of the recitation

Done in visionary ritual, this is not a 'feelgood' or psychological affirmation: you are starting to tune into the power of the east as an apprentice magician and certain responsibilities come with that. These responsibilities are nothing to do with ethics or morals, but about how the power of utterance works for a magician.

The more you tap into power, the more your utterances will become conduits for power. Your written and spoken words will slowly gain power and will mediate power and energy. Because of this, you will have to learn to guard your words for yourself. That is a complex learning curve and the guardian of the sword will guide you when necessary, but it is better to do it for yourself (your own lessons are easier than those of the sword).

This does not mean "you must never speak a bad word"—that is an unbalanced misunderstanding of the power. Sometimes harsh words are necessary, sometimes destructive utterances are necessary. You will have to learn what, when, and how to mediate this utterance power through trial and error, as it is unique to you. Just know that you cannot switch it on and off: it is constant.

In your everyday life, from this point on, if you misuse your voice in some way you will know about it. You will be either physically, mentally, emotionally, or magically affected. What you have done by reciting in front of the witness, and engaging with the power of the sword, is that you have given permission/accepted the dynamic of governance from the inner worlds. This speeds up your evolution, learning and fate. Every time you do something that is badly imbalanced, you will get an almost immediate reaction, to teach you (not punish you) and limit you until you get back on track. Without this dynamic, you cannot step into deeper magic—or if you do you are far less likely to be guarded and taught, and far less likely to stay in one piece mentally or physically. You will essentially be on your own.

It can all seem a bit scary, but this process started for me at the age of sixteen and I can tell you, the backlash of power misuse is almost instant. But it was a good teacher and also an excellent guardian. My writing springs from that dynamic, as did a lot of my learning. The process is not temporary; it is with you for life, and it most certainly helps to form you into a better, stronger, and more mature vessel.

2.8 Readings

You are going to do three readings.

For the first one, use the Tree of Life layout and ask the question:

> "What is the power of the being that is the guardian of the sword for me?"

The last card tells you what type of power runs through the being, and that in turn will indicate to you what sort of power focus will flow through your magical sword when you come to enliven it and work with it.

For the second reading you will use the four-directional spread and your question will be:

"Show me the health of the inner landscape of the land where I live."

That reading will show you if there are any unbalanced, destructive, or unhealthy energies in the inner landscape (not just the outer land). If you see problems, just note them down for now.

The third reading also uses the four-directional layout. You will ask:

"Show me difficulties in the inner landscape that I should work on, but only show me ones that I am currently capable of working on."

If something appears in the reading that is a problem, do the vision work where you go through the gates and out into the inner landscape. See what you can find, and work according to your instincts and what you know. If it looks dirty, clean it up. If an aggressive being is there, ask it to leave. Don't put yourself in any great risk, but do what you can.

If you don't know what to do, think about what you would do if the images presented to you were something you encountered in your physical life, and go from there.

Write down all of your findings in your computer log and also take note of what you did. Make sure you write it down while it is still fresh in your mind, including any strange details.

2.9 The tools and symbols

Leave the symbol drawings on your altar if you leave your room permanently set out. If not, put them somewhere safe in the east and west of the room. You will get them back out when you come to enliven and work on your magical tools, something which is coming up soon in the course.

You should have already have ordered, bought, or found your sword by now (remember you were told to start the process of getting a sword). If you have not, now is the time to do it. If you have it, place it in the east and tie the paper with the symbol on it around the blade of the sword. Keep it in the east of the room, and do not use or touch it for now.

Also now is the time to get a vessel. You will need a cup or bowl that is metal, thick ceramic, or wood. When you get it, tie the paper with the symbol onto it and put it somewhere safe in the west. Now is also time to start looking for another magical tool, a lesser-known one, and that is a set of scales. And by scales I do not mean cooking electronic weight scales, but old-fashioned scales with a central pole and a cup on each side. Make sure you get ones that actually work, and where the T bar can move and the scales stand upright (not hanging ones). Scales like this:

Figure 2.1: Scales.

Start looking for them now, as it may take you a while to find them. Look in online stores, junk stores, anywhere that you may find them. When you get them, wash them and place them either on your west altar, behind the west altar, or in the middle of the west wall in the room where you work.

Lesson 3

The Grindstone

You have already begun to look, in small ways, at the polarised threshold powers that act as a barrier to the deeper inner worlds, and therefore to deeper magic. For an apprentice magician to try and engage directly with these powers would be folly: they are non-emotional angelic powers that simply fry anything that reaches too far across the threshold if that reaching is done in ignorance.

So first the apprentice is introduced to these powers through simple outer ritual and understanding that has no power behind it, and through basic magical and non-magical acts.

Then they inch in a bit more in vision, but still staying within their own realm. You have done both of these, even if you did not realise it at the time. This step-by-step approach allows you to strengthen, become aware of, and learn the rules of engagement before you stumble across the power lines.

The next step in your learning about these threshold keepers is to learn how their power expresses through the human life and mind, so that by learning consciously your subconscious also learns, adapts, and develops. The mind, emotions, actions, and energy drives in a human are the filter through which these powers express first.

By approaching these aspects of our own existence, we are then better armed in our subconscious to be able to walk in a balanced way between these two powers in order to enter the depths of the inner realms safely and productively. Once you have seen and recognised how these powers operate in your life, you will come to see how they operate magically and mystically. The key words of the Grindstone in its manifestation through life are *restraint*, *labor*, *perseverance*, and *patience*: the qualities of Saturn.

Through engaging these qualities with magical intent in our everyday lives, our deeper spirit also engages these qualities, and they subsequently flow through our magical acts. That in turn allows us to work with far greater amounts of power without serious risk of damaging our minds and bodies.

3.1 The angelic power

Although we will look in depth at angelic beings later in the apprentice section, it is useful to look at the angelic powers that flow through, and are the source of, these two polarised powers: the angelic manifestations of the Grindstone and the Unraveller.

These two powers are not the type of angelic beings that we have been exposed to through religious or magical teachings. Rather they are a step removed from the material and human world, and they do not have the dressing that we usually associate with angels. In essence, they are strong powers that each do one specific job, like two giant magnets: they create a barrier.

In the inner worlds that barrier appears as guardians who challenge you, and also as an unseen energy that bounces you out of vision. In life their power expresses through fate patterns, and they trigger events or they pour power into events. In magic, those two presentations become more immediate, more powerful, and more direct in their actions.

Each of these two polarised powers have many different expressions; hence each one has its own lesson in this module, so that we can look at them in depth. Some of you who already have some experience of magic (or who are magicians revisiting training) will already have an understanding of what I am saying. For those who are new or relatively new to magic, what follows may all seem a bit difficult to understand, but stay with me, as we will approach this from a human perspective which you will indeed recognise.

Although these are powerful, deep angelic beings, and they operate in depth throughout creation from a single cell to a species, landmass, or nation, how they directly affect you as an apprentice magician is best viewed, understood, and worked with through life experience and visionary ritual. This way, your conscious mind, subconscious mind and physical body can slowly absorb the knowledge, adjust to the power flows, and learn to be around and work with these vast beings without getting fried or going mad. It is also a much more direct way to learn than to sit and try to philosophically or intellectually understand them.

This lesson looks at the Grindstone, the left hand side of the polarity.[1] In magical ritual, this power is externalised in its weakest form as the sword and as the Grindstone that your left foot stands upon. That is the baby step. But then we need to grow up. So the next stage is to look at the dynamics and effects this power has on our lives. The Grindstone does not just flow through the lives of magicians; it flows through all life, and in humans you will instantly recognise its influence once we get to look at it.

The only difference for a magician is that the magician learns to consciously engage and work with this power, first through their life and outer ritual, and then in deeper vision and direct contact as an adept. To get to that adept stage and be able to have that direct contact without being destroyed, first the magician must recognise and understand its weakest, most outer influence in human life. That awareness opens the doors within you, and starts a deep energetic conversation with your subconscious and with your eternal spirit.

First we will look at the actual power dynamic of the Grindstone, and look at why it does what it does. Then we will look at the practicalities of how that expresses through your daily life.

3.2 The Role of the Grindstone in creation

In its deepest role, the Grindstone slows down the speed and vibration of energy so that it can be formed into matter. Through restriction the energy becomes denser, stronger, and more able to be contained in a vessel. The Grindstone's opposite is the Unraveller, which frees up over-restriction or breaks down the density of something in order either for it to become more fluid or to break it down and compost it.

At a magical level the Grindstone creates barriers that protect the inner worlds from stupid humans, and protects stupid humans from the onslaught of power that is inherent within the inner worlds. It limits your magical actions so that you become more solid in your power as a magician, and also helps to prevent you overreaching (unless that overreaching is necessary for you).

In terms of magical power, it is the dynamic which shapes power and gives it boundaries in order for it to be contained: a ritual is an extension of the Grindstone power, as is the sword, the key steps within visionary magic, the use of a sigil, etc. It is the power that constructs a magical form that is then filled with contact and energy. So you begin to see

---

[1] Which has nothing to do with the 'Left Hand Path' in magic.

why it is so vital for a magician to understand it. But it cannot be understood intellectually; it has to be experienced both magically and through everyday, conscious life—that way, you truly understand it on every level. Once you understand it, you can engage it magically.

On an individual level, for humans, this power weaves into your fate pattern, which is a dynamic pattern that is constantly shifting and evolving (it is not a fixed, rigid path), and drops the energy of restriction into that fate weave. This is to slow the person down, and to present them with barriers that they must overcome in order to strengthen and mature them physically, emotionally, and mentally.

It can present though life experiences, external influences, cultural restrictions, physical restrictions, disciplined training, or through mental or emotional issues. A developing magician learns to spot that action and engage it by applying the Grindstone power consciously and directly to their lives where it is needed.

The presentation of the Grindstone in the fate pattern is energy, not events: how that energy expresses itself in your life is very much dependant on your choices, actions, the society you live in, your body, mind, and the state of the species. It is both personal to you and also impersonal; it affects the individual and the collective.

The task of a magician is to recognise this energy when it is present and active in your life and work, and to work with it, fully engaging it rather than being swept along by it. That is one of the major differences between a magician and a non-magician. When the Grindstone is expressing through the collective, through your society, it is important as a magician to spot that and work with it so that you are neither its victim nor 'swept up' by the current as it passes through. Rather you recognise it, and then see where you can work with it or side-step it—whichever is appropriate to the situation.

At a creation level, this power also dynamically works through nature and is part of the constant change and evolution of the planet, the landscape, and the elements: it is one arm of the rebalancer. Once you learn to recognise this power in action in your own life and in your own society, then you will more easily also spot it in action in nature.

Throughout history, religion and magic, or aspects of such, Man has sought to control, limit, or deflect this power, which has always simply resulted in disaster at some level or other. You cannot control this power and you cannot stop it: it is a part of life itself. Once we look at the aspects of this power in everyday life, you will start to recognise where magicians throughout history have tried to dodge its power or have been swept along by it unconsciously, in ignorance.

And yet, to understand this power and to work with it in your life and magic is to tap into one of the greatest resources of power known to man. But to do that and not be destroyed, the magician needs to tap into this power with gnosis. So let's look at how this power expresses itself through the human life.

3.3 The Grindstone in life

In a non-magical life, the Grindstone presents through life situations which prevent you from doing what you want to do or which force you to do something you do not want to do. That is the simplest way to put it.

That power triggers the energy on the fate path, and how that presents depends on the person, their situation, and their culture. It is much stronger in some individuals than in others. If a person does not need that power in their lives to restrict them, or if they overly self-restrict, the opposing power is more dominant in their lives (the Unraveller). Essentially, one major way this dynamic expresses is to teach you the difference between what you want and what you need. That in turn highlights to you your weaknesses and vulnerabilities.

This same dynamic that appears in the life of an individual is also mirrored or appears in a society or culture. This power, like all powers in creation, works in octaves: the deepest pattern of the power repeats at different frequencies as it steps down and becomes more formed and personal. But the actual underlying dynamic stays the same.

When we look back in history and we come across powerful and dynamic shifts in a society, we can often spot the activation of the Grindstone, or the Unraveller, or both. People who have little internal strength or are 'switched off' are often swept along by these power tides, and the result is a huge shift in how a nation thinks or behaves. When a nation is involved (1930s Germany is a good example), there are often many different types of beings involved that are mediators of the powers of Grindstone and Unraveller: they work behind the scenes in various manifestations. An adept magician can often spot these manifestations and either get out of the way or work carefully to clear the road ahead for that nation.

In a magical life the same dynamic applies, but it is recognised for what it is: a necessary step that needs to be understood, learned, and worked with. As the magician gets deeper into magic, one of the two dynamics may (though not always) engage more powerfully than the other, the result of which being that fate is 'sped up,' or, that is to say, that the lessons come thick and fast.

So for example, an apprentice magician engages the Grindstone by being aware of where they need to apply self-restriction or patience in their life, and rather than fight blocks in their life, they learn to engage them and work with them. The initiate learns to use the magical sword in ritual/vision to create a restrictive pattern that contains and limits power in a magical act or project. The adept learns to mediate or *bridge* through themselves the raw power of the Grindstone into a magical pattern, a land area, a person, or an event.

In order for the initiate and the adept to do that powerful work safely, their mind and body must already be tuned to working with the Grindstone in their outer and inner lives so that they hold a better power balance within them. This is because every power you mediate or bridge passes through you first, affecting everything in your sphere before it is then externalised into its vessel, pattern, or project.

If an adept attempts to bridge this power and they have not reconciled the Grindstone within themselves, then it will get to work on them before it works on anything else. The adept will find themselves confronted by the Grindstone power in their health and in their everyday life.

The safest and most successful way to tune to the Grindstone power as an apprentice is through its actions in your everyday life. It is a lifetime process, and at first the apprentice magician struggles to first recognise and then reconcile themselves with the power. As they progress, the power re-presents in ever more powerful ways, working through the life pattern, the body, the mind, and the emotions. At some point (hopefully earlier than later) the magician learns to spot the triggering of this power, recognises what it needs to do, and then instead of waiting for the life bomb to drop, steps voluntarily into a situation or pattern that would obviate the need for the lesson: the step of letting go, self-limiting, or self-releasing.

Let's have a look at some practical examples of the Grindstone activating in life. We will look at some very different situations that nevertheless all have the same dynamic, and look at the outcomes relative to the way the person dealt with the power. Bear in mind that life is a very complex weave indeed, and although these two opposing powers are very present in all of life, there are also many other lesser and greater dynamics, powers, energies, and life patterns that flow in and out of a person or a nation's life.

3.4 Examples of the Grindstone in action

These following short examples are not here to bore you silly (they will be obvious to some and not to others), nor are they anything to do with moralising: morals have no place in magic. They are simple, externalised life expressions of the Grindstone which in turn prepare us to work more deeply with the inner aspects of this power.

Human society's conditioning

Each society and religion has its boundaries of 'good behaviour' and 'bad behaviour.' Some grew out of mystical understanding and devolved down to dogma, and some are simple societal control methods. The hardest thing for an apprentice magician who has grown up in a religious society or family is to step away from such dogma in a balanced way.

Usually as a young, budding magician, the person carries the dogma with them as a mode of thinking, and simply transplants it onto another dogma: we see this in many magical systems and alternative religions. They are simply rehashing the same issue. This stems from their as-yet-inability to spot and then disengage from the inappropriate restriction and engage a deeper, more magical one.

This dogmatic restriction, which often appears in magical systems as a 'code of ethics' or patterns of self-development rituals, continues to trap the young magician in an unproductive cycle of destructive restriction. The magician feels comfortable in the safety of the dogma, but is unable to truly progress to any power as a magician. The unbalanced restriction triggers the opposing power in the magician's life, and they slowly unravel.

Once the magician spots this and steps away, they restrict their desire for a predictable system with a set of rules. They learn to recognise that the true power of the Grindstone comes from the restriction of *not* having predictable walls and rules: you have to actively engage it and understand it for yourself, alone, and without guidance. That means falling back upon yourself as the maker and keeper of your own limits. That is an example of magical engagement, in the first simple step, with the Grindstone.

Alternatively, the young budding magician walks away from the dogma they were raised with and rejects all boundaries. They immerse themselves in self-indulgence, emotional and physical experimentation (Left Hand Path magic, for example) and they either self-destruct through that process or they learn to self-limit from direct experience. Again, this is engaging the Grindstone magically and consciously, but this way is reached through immersion in the power of the Unraveller.

A third way is where the magician steps away from the dogma they were raised within, and steps into a discipline of some sort, be it martial arts training, sports, or arts training: a discipline that is hard, long, and challenging. Through that process, the young magician learns to self-discipline, understands the necessity for boundaries, be they physical, emotional, or otherwise, and learns how to transplant that learning into their magical practice. This is why it is easier for lone magicians who have intensively trained in some form of discipline over a long period of time to progress well in magic.

Drama/emotional conditioning

The Grindstone can also engage through emotional dramas. When we are young, many of us project internal imbalance through emotional swings and dramas: it is the body and mind's way of trying to release the toxicity of imbalance. Think hormonal teenage outburst.

As we go through life and we have hard knocks (the Grindstone in action) we either degenerate down into a life of victimhood, or we get to a point in our life where we see that our reactions often come not just from outer situations, but also from our own need for emotional expression:

> "I am angry/sad and I don't know why, but it's not your fault."

The ability to get to that stage of self-awareness, to acknowledge imbalance and not project a reason onto someone or something else, is the first step of engaging the Grindstone. For an everyday person it is a step towards emotional maturity. For a magician is has the added bonus of alerting us to some imbalance, be it in our own minds, our own bodies, or because of some power imbalance somewhere.

The next step a magician would take is to find out, usually through divination, where that imbalance is coming from. Sometimes it is something within us that needs physical rebalancing (hormones or depression), or it is coming from unbalanced magical practice which needs changing (the engine limiter), or it is the result of magical interference from outside of the person.

The magician would identify the cause and act accordingly. If it shows up as a necessary process, the magician would then decide to 'suck it up,' tread water, and see what is coming out the other end of it. Often this happens if a lot of power is due to come into the magician's practice and they need either to go into a phase of withdrawing and waiting, or to adjust their life ready to accept the power in a balanced way when it arrives. This is the Grindstone being engaged with: it is limiting the magician in order to prepare them for something.

Through working with the Grindstone in these simple ways, the deeper aspect of the magician's psyche learns, through sideways application, how to self-limit for necessity when it comes to deeper magic and power: it becomes a second nature. That in turn allows the magician to work with large amounts of power and not go mad or get greedy. That then opens up a whole new aspect of magic for the magician, as they are stable and self-disciplined enough to work in depth in the inner worlds without temptation.

The Grindstone of magicians

Once the magician is working with the Initiate level of training (though this can also happen to an apprentice) and the powers are being consciously engaged, then the Grindstone presents around the magician in a constant dynamic I call the *Sword of Damocles*.

Here is a way it triggers for me, so that you can see it in practical action. I do a lot of magical writing and I write from my own magical experience, not from other books. I believe in 'hiding in plain sight' methods of writing and not holding information back. Occasionally though, I inadvertently cross a line. I will start to write something without realising that it should not be written about. When I do that, I begin to burn—literally. My skin, my organs; they will all burn furiously. My face will go red and I will feel very ill.

When that first started to happen, I would do a reading to see if I was ill. The answer was always the same:

> "No, you are not ill, but you have triggered the Sword by acting in an unbalanced way."

The sword would appear in my health reading with it hanging over my head—this type of situation is where the story of Damocles comes from. It is a deep magical dynamic that has nothing to do with systems or dogma; it is an energetic response to crossing a power line that should not be crossed.

When this happened, I would look back over what I had written and would then see how that text could be badly misused in a powerful and destructive way. Sometimes it was not that it could be destructive, but rather that I had, by writing a magical detail, taken away the student's chance to find out something deep and powerful for themselves; I had potentially short-circuited the magical development of another human being.

As soon as I deleted the text and then began writing with more care, the burning would instantly stop and peace was restored. That is the Grindstone in action in a magician's life.

A completely different magical application of the Grindstone is one where it is purposely engaged. Here is an example. A magician is being attacked by another adept (sigh, humans are such dicks sometimes) powerfully and dangerously: the curse or attack is to the death. An inexperienced magician would lash back, but the adept knows better—not because of ethics, but because they understand how power works. The adept does not retaliate. He simply cleans the attack off himself and carries on about his business. The attacker becomes enraged that the victim has not died, and so piles more and more magical power into the attack.

The adept on the receiving end still does not respond. Nor are they badly damaged by the attack (usually bruised but not battered); they simply clean it off again, patiently and without emotion.

The adept on the receiving end is intentionally engaging the Grindstone. They may also work with the Grindstone magically, not on the attacker, but upon themselves: ritual/vision work with the sword to guard their own temper, stay their hand, and draw strength from Saturn to persevere.

This approach does two things. The first thing is that it slowly grinds the attacker down: they are outputting a lot of their energy to use magic to kill someone—that takes a lot of energy, a lot of work, and a lot of focus. Soon they begin to obsess and pour all of their magical resources into the attack: they are emptying their inner and outer resources. This in turn weakens them considerably and eventually kills them (the effect is usually in relation to the magical intention).

The second thing that happens is that the Unraveller is triggered for the attacker. When you attack magically, you set up an energy relationship or line of energy contact. The attack travels down that route and the attacker and victim are connected energetically. As soon as the adept on the receiving end consciously and magically engages the Grindstone, it sets up a see-saw effect. And the Unraveller is the opposing power of the Grindstone: if the Grindstone appears at one end of the energy connection, that will automatically trigger the Unraveller on the opposing side.

So the attacker has the power of the Unraveller flowing through him in an unconscious way. That manifests as the magician finding it harder and harder to hold a magical pattern, and they mentally, physically, and emotionally begin to unravel as a result of their own imbalance. And if the attacker had intentionally used death magic, that triggers the death aspect of the Unraveller and speeds up their own death.

So the adept on the receiving end does nothing at all towards the attacker; they simply work on themselves and let the attacker blow himself up in his own time. By not engaging with the attacker, the adept has not bound themselves up in yet more energetic loops with the attacker, and has not outputted any energy that would potentially feed the attacker. It can be a long and laborious process, particularly if the attacker is a long holder of grudges, but the strength the adept on the receiving end gains through such restraint of action is considerable indeed.

The end result is a dead or seriously weakened attacker, and a stronger, wiser adept on the other end. In the next lesson I will look at a similar situation from the perspective of the Unraveller, and also look at a slightly different way of dealing with the same issue.

3.5 *Task:* **Grindstone tarot readings**

Your life

Using the four-directional reading layout, use your tarot cards to look and see if the Grindstone is in action in your life. To focus the reading on your outer life, use the centre for your health, the east for education/writing/learning or daily work, south for creativity, west for relationships, and north for family/home. Then look at your inner energies using the same layout and use the 'magical directions' attributes.

If you identify the Grindstone in action (it will show as a difficult restrictive card), sit and think about how instead of fighting it or trying to avoid it, you can first recognise where in your life it is playing out, why it is playing out, what you need to learn from it and then engage it through your actions, common sense, emotions, or mind. Remember the key words for the Grindstone and apply them.

An event

Choose a time in history where something major happened that changed a culture, religion, race, or land. Do the same readings that you have done for yourself: look at the outer manifestation and then the inner one to see if the Grindstone was in action. It may or may not have been.

If it was in action, read up about the history of the event, people's eyewitness accounts, and pay close attention to any art that came out of that time. See if you can see an unconscious or conscious expression of the Grindstone in the writing, thinking, art, or poetry of the time.

What you are looking for is major restrictions or disciplines that brought major growth, strength, or change to a nation. If the change was a restoration of balance, the Unraveller will also be seen in the events. If the change ultimately brought imbalance, look to see if the Unraveller was absent from the dynamic. Write up your findings on computer, and also log your readings.

3.6 *Task:* **The Grindstone in your chart**

Revisit your astrology chart and look at the natal position of Saturn and the current transit of Saturn. Look at where it is in action in your chart: see if there is any correlation between your chart's transits and the reading you did about your outer and inner life. Think about where that transit of Saturn sits in your personal pentagram pattern, and take note of the nearest direction and tool, and what power flows through them.

Bring all of the information together and see if there is a need to consciously engage the Grindstone in your life in some way.

3.7 *Task:* **Grindstone ritual**

If you are embarking on a new course of study (Quareia, for example) or college study, a new job, anything that is a major project, work ritually to draw the power of the Grindstone into that path in order to help you learn better, apply yourself consistently, and to strengthen you.

Design your own ritual to invite the Grindstone power into your life to work with you. In the design, draw upon what you already have learned about ritual and use the four-directional pattern to open the gates and directions. Look at aspects of the Pentagram work you have done and choose key aspects of that ritual work to construct your own personal ritual. Include in the ritual a recitation to call upon the Grindstone power of the east, the Noble Ones of the south, and the Unraveller in the west to guide you in the engagement of the Grindstone in your life: invite that power to work with you.

Write down the ritual in your computer log and keep diary entries over the coming weeks of any observations you may have about that power triggering in your life.

Lesson 4

The Unraveller

What I call the Unraveller is the polar opposite of the Grindstone. Where the Grindstone forms, limits, and strengthens, the Unraveller disassembles, loosens, and begins the process of weighing and dispatching energy back into the void via the power of the Scales (A.K.A. Justice).

At this point, I want to state that in this module and subsequent ones that tackle creation and destruction, I have purposely stayed away from the better-known magical and mystical names used in magic and religion for these powers.

This is to move away from the cultural and religious/magical dogmas that have built up around these powers, and subsequently only serve to trap the magician in a series of dogmatic, inaccurate patterns that serve as dead ends for true magical progression.

We are at a time in our human evolution where we want to get to the *dynamics* of things: the growth in science over the last hundred years is staggering, and that comes from a wish to know 'what is there' without overlaying supposition—and superstition. We are at a phase of magical evolution where we need to step back and look with new eyes. Hence the movement away from established vocabularies. This in turn allows the aspiring magician to learn, experience, and observe in an objective way without preconceived ideas.

Like the Grindstone, the Unraveller's influence permeates every aspect of creation from the smallest particle to the mind of the human and the lay of the land. For those students who think in a very 'science' way, view the Unraveller as the power that triggers the self-destruct process in a cell. For those who work in a more poetic way, the Unraveller triggers the start of the composting process, or literally, the mental/emotional unravelling process.

In a magical sense, the Unraveller is the power that is worked with for unbinding something, releasing something, or for magical work that is involved in the slow destruction of something large or long-term. Its action is slow, deliberate, and loosens power/energy to a point where it becomes vulnerable to any destructive power. So the Unraveller does not in itself destroy, but it *prepares* something for destruction.

Its positive action is to loosen something enough for it to be worked with better, to free up energy trapped in something, and to help reshape things. So you can begin to see why it is such a pivotal power in magic.

The two opposing powers of Grindstone and Unraveller are powers that form/disassemble just before or on the cusp of physical manifestation, a place where a lot of shorter-term magic is worked with.

As an apprentice, you will first approach the

Unraveller from an everyday perspective, from your own physical, mental, and emotional experience. From that base understanding, you will then be able to recognise this power in action around you in nature and in magic. From that awareness, you will learn as an initiate, and then as an adept, how to consciously work with, process, and create/destroy in harmony with these opposing powers.

When the Unraveller is properly engaged in your life it can be a very powerful and positive force, particularly in a culture that is obsessed with control. If the Unraveller is plunged into without due thought, its actions will destroy. Like everything, it has good and bad, balance and imbalance.

A good way to look at this process from a training perspective is that before you break the rules, you must first learn them. The Grindstone is the discipline and limitations that train you in a conformed way: this gives you technique, discipline, and strength. It also gives you a major reference point for power, and allows you to see the weakness in yourself that needs reigning in, and in the technique you study.

At that point, by engaging the Unraveller, you learn to step away from the conformity, the restrictions and barriers. You step into your own individual path as a magician, knowing what can be loosened, released, and played with, and what cannot or should not.

That wisdom comes from training, so that you learn how to engage the Unraveller in a way that does not unravel you, but which simply loosens whatever needs loosening, freeing up your potential. If the Unraveller is worked with by someone who has not first undergone and understood the power of the Grindstone in one form or another, they will swiftly unravel mentally and physically. Again, the Mysteries protect themselves.

By working with these two powers through your own life and body, *your body and mind* learn how to cope with the power. This in turn allows you to work with these powers in the depths of the inner worlds without being unduly or adversely affected by them: you are already used to them in a small way.

So let's look at the Unraveller first in its action in creation, then its action in magic, and finally its actions in our everyday lives.

4.1 The Unraveller in creation

When we looked at creation via the Grindstone, we thought about how the first breath travels energetically towards manifestation, and how one of its last filters acts to slow down and solidify that energy. It then manifests as substance: a human, a tree, an animal, a rock.

The moment something becomes physically manifest, it starts its march towards destruction and death. The Unraveller energy kicks in and programs the self-destruct mechanism in the physical substance, so everything that manifests already has its 'destruction button' ready. But that self-destruct is also a part of creation: cells are constantly renewing themselves and can only do that if the self-destruct is active: as the cell completes its task, it self-destructs and new ones are created. A failure in that self-destruct process is involved in cancer, for example. The cells just keep reproducing and not destructing.

In science, specifically in biology and genetics, we are starting to realise that when a person is born, their genome already has deviations that dictate a potential for disease and death at around a certain age (excluding accidents, murder, etc.). This is the Unraveller. Our pattern of fate and our genetic pattern are interwoven, and the weave has 'hotspots' of Unravelling energy imprinted within it. How these manifest depends on how we engage with this power.

So for example at a human level, say someone was born with a predisposition to heart attacks at an early age. They can adjust that pattern to some extent (but within limits) depending on how they live their lives: they either engage the Unraveller and the Grindstone to shift their pattern, or they do not and they are subsequently at the mercy of these powers.

Similarly, in deeper aspects of creation from a magical perspective, the Unraveller is ever-constant wherever there is creation. Wherever you find a powerful being that works on the manifestation of physical being, an angelic being for example, there is always a counterbalance of a destructive being that will break down that creation when the time is ready. This is why it is so important to work across the board with all beings in the inner worlds. Magic that focuses only on creation/good/nice is unbalanced and potentially corrupt. The same is true of magic that focuses only on destruction/bad/evil—there always has to be a balance.

This polarity of creation and destruction, male and female, light and dark, runs through everything in our world and in the inner worlds. Bear that in mind in your future studies.

4.2 The Unraveller and magic

In magic the Unraveller takes on the role of disassembling. When the Unraveller has disassembled something and completed its work, it then passes on whatever has been unravelled to the next power. That may be a power of rebalancing (such as the power we magically call *Justice*) or the power of Binding, the power of releasing, or the power of rebuilding. It all depends on the magical act that the power of the Unraveller is being used for.

How this power affects you while you work with it all depends on what magical work you are doing, why you are doing it, and how well you have attended to your own baggage. The following are examples of magical use, outcome and consequence. You will not work with this level of magic yet, but it is important to understand how it affects you and why: the work that is needed to ensure your successful engagement with this power starts during the apprentice level of training. First you work on yourself so that the power does not need to as it flows through you in future work.

4.3 Unravelling magic: effects

If the Unravelling is done to restore balance, as you work with this power, it will also unbind within you things that need unbinding or unravelling in order to restore balance. The same goes for magic that calls upon the power of Justice.

So for example if you are clinging to a job, a partnership, a way of life, etc. that is ultimately unhealthy for you, the power of the Unraveller, as you work magically with it, will pass through you and begin that unravelling process.

Don't forget that the true power of Justice is to restore balance, not to 'get justice' or 'revenge.' It is more akin to the Egyptian concept of Ma'at, which you have already looked at.

Often we fight against this restoration of balance, as it can be hard for us to see far enough into our own future to see where our true balance lies. As an adept magician you learn to trust this power, to go with the flow, but also to truly understand balance—a process of understanding that begins at the apprentice level.

When you have triggered this unravelling process in your life through magical action, it is best to simply 'go with the flow,' trust the power, and actively let go of things that are unravelling around you.

If the unravelling magic is done without a goal of balance, without the need for rebalance, then it starts a new process of events. To work with the Unraveller in a magical act where there is no real unbalance draws the magician into a new cycle that will trigger uncontrolled imbalance both in the magical situation and also in the magician themselves. If the magician does not understand the process, their attempts to restore their own balance would likely make the situation worse.

Everything you do magically passes through you before it then goes off to do its job. That is the pay-off for working with deep inner powers. Ultimately, if the magician works in an intelligent way, it gives the magician access to huge reserves of power to work with. It also serves to strengthen, mature, and enlighten the magician as they allow the deep inner powers to flow through them. This is where the tradition of magical training making you a better person comes from. It doesn't come from ritual affirmations or initiations; it comes from directly engaging with the powers of Divinity as they flow through our world.

If those deep inner powers are worked with in ignorance, it can trigger all sorts of problems that eventually destroy the magician. So you can see why it is important to know how these powers work, and also to know yourself (the first requirement of the Mysteries).

There are ways of doing magic that do not engage these powers, but it is magic that is very limited in its power resources and therefore limited in its action. That type of magic is not what this course is about.

So let's look at a practical example of the Unraveller in magical action, which will then help you to see how it could affect you magically. That in turn will help you spot where you need to look to your own life and body so that you can work powerfully and effectively with this dynamic.

4.4 The Unraveller in action

A magician is contacted by someone who has been powerfully magically bound and is dying. The magician first looks, using divination, at the wider picture, and sees a number of things. The first is that the binding is quite vicious and is done by an unbalanced adept. The second is that the binding is interfering with the fate expression of the victim. The third thing the magician sees is that the binding has been done from a place of vengeance: the victim had left a magical lodge and, being an adept themselves, had decided to set up their own lodge. Some of the old lodge members had left with the victim, which had enraged the lodge leader, who is a skilled but unbalanced person.

The magician then looks at the health of the victim and sees that the binding has triggered a cancerous predisposition in the victim: by binding the life expression of the victim, that binding magic had found a way to express through the physical substance of the victim. The self-destruct mechanism in the cells of the victim was already predisposed to stop working. The binding magic was enough to nudge that action into full imbalance: the self-destruct was inhibited, and the cells started to proliferate. The victim became cancerous and was very ill.

The next step the magician takes is to self-examine where they themselves are in life: is there something in their own life that needs unbinding and unravelling? The magician realises that their own 'day job' is becoming unhealthy for them, but they enjoy the good wage and work stability that it gives them.

Before he begins the magical process of helping the victim, he opens all the gates, talks with the inner contacts, and agrees to work consciously with anything within himself that could need unbinding. He also agrees to be willing to lose his day job if that is what needed to restore balance: he puts the option on the table and asks the inner contacts to work with him.

Then the magician gets to work. He works in ritual and vision with the victim, and engages the power of the Unraveller in conjunction with the power of Justice. He creates a pattern and magical construct, pulls the power of the Unraveller and Justice into the pattern, and then places the victim within the pattern so that the power will flow through them. The Unraveller power begins to unbind the binding magic and the power of Justice gets to work on rebalancing.

It is a long process that takes a couple of weeks, but slowly, the Unraveller starts to engage in the life of the victim and a number of things happen.

On a physical level, the victim begins to respond to the medical cancer treatment—in fact they respond very well, and their prognosis is changed from okay to good.

The new lodge group feel a shift from feeling uncomfortable about starting a new lodge to feeling very good about it, and they all get an inrush of energy and enthusiasm for the new project.

The lodge leader who did the binding starts to Unravel. The power works on everyone involved just by the nature of how it works. The lodge leader was not directly targeted magically, but as a main player in this chess game they are a part of the pattern, so the magic will also flow through them and affect them. They begin to become more neurotic, to display unbalanced emotions, to overeat or engage in behaviour that is self-destructive. As a result, the remaining lodge members pull away, and the lodge collapses.

The magician prepares to lose their job by starting the job hunting process, as they figure that is where the Unraveller will work through them. However that does not happen. Instead they get a promotion and are moved to a new area that is healthier for them. Also, something that the magician was eating that was mildly irritating their system suddenly becomes a major problem, and the magician has to stop eating it. It is one of those minor intolerances that if left unchecked can do longer-term damage to the system.

By going with the flow and allowing those changes to happen without resistance, the magician engages both the power of the Grindstone and the power of Justice in their lives to restore balance. The Grindstone is engaged through self-discipline with the food issue, and the power of Justice puts the magician where they are supposed to be.

So you can see how these powers affect everyone involved, and how through the skill of the magician, 'many birds can be killed with one stone.'

A lesser type of magic would not have engaged with the deep power of the Unraveller, but would have involved different individual magical acts: unbinding the victim and attacking the lodge leader, which takes a lot more energy and is less effective. It would also not have triggered the renewal in the life of the magician.

4.5 The personal Unraveller

So before you get to work magically with this power, you need to learn how to spot your own need for, or vulnerability to, the Unraveller, and be able to engage it consciously. This is not glamorous or exciting magical work, but it is very necessary work that you will be glad you did when you reach adepthood.

For some of you this will all be very obvious; for others of you it will not. But no matter how obvious this work may be, take the time to do it and do it properly. Because of the very personal nature of this work, do two different records of this work, one on computer for the mentor if you want to be mentored in the future (just put in an overview), and the other more personal handwritten in your personal journal. Don't skip the record keeping of this work: it is important to log it and keep it so that you can refer back to it in the future.

4.6 *Task:* Looking in the mirror

Often what we think needs releasing or unravelling in our lives can be different from what *actually* needs unravelling or letting go of, or loosening up. Because of this, you will approach this work in two different ways. This is not something that can be done in a month and then moved on from: the process starts now if you have not already engaged with this process in your life, but it will be a continuous process throughout your magical life.

Do this work immediately, and then plan to revisit this process every year. A version of this can be seen in Judaism which is known as *Yom Kippur* or the *Day of Atonement*, something you were introduced to in lesson two. It actually spans a couple of weeks each year where the person reflects on their actions over the past year and atones for their 'sins.'

Looking in the mirror is not the same process: it is a similar but more profound action (a deeper octave). Pick a time each year where you plan to think about what aspects of your life you are clinging onto, or what aspects of your life or personality need loosening and freeing up. Spend that time in reflection and meditation, and think of practical ways that you can positively engage this power in your life.

During this time also think about where the Grindstone may need engaging or disengaging in your life, and where the power of Ma'at needs to flow better through your mind and actions.

None of this is about 'atonement'; rather it is about learning to *know yourself* and to know the powers active around you and how you have responded to them. Your reflections are not about other people, but about yourself: what powers were active in your past, how you responded to those powers, and how your response potentially created weakness or unbalance within you.

Also look at how any unbalanced, immature, or unwise actions created chaos or unbalance around you (the effects upon others and upon the land). Spot them, learn the mistakes, understand what when wrong, why, and why you must not go back into that pattern of behaviour again.

Again, this is not about societal or religious morals, but about self-maturing through wisdom in hindsight, responsibility, and learning to engage your own Grindstone or Unraveller where necessary in your future actions.

For a period of two weeks after you have done your meditation, work on the process of 'Looking in the Mirror.' Choose an aspect each day and think about your personality, your everyday actions, your relationships and responsibilities, your job, your magical studies and interests, memories and past events, and any other aspect of your life that comes to mind. Think about things that may need freeing up, where you are too controlling, or clinging onto things, or where things are starting to break down and need conscious engagement to bring change. Think about past imbalanced actions or behaviour and use the power of hindsight to think about your past mistakes.

The most important aspect of looking in the mirror is to not only spot present and past imbalance and mistakes, but to actually do something about it and not repeat the same mistakes in your life. Evolution is not making the same mistakes, but learning from past ones and making new mistakes that you will learn from. Eventually the process leads you to spot mistakes before you make them, engage the right polarity dynamic, and side-step them.

Write down on a piece of paper the most personal and revealing aspects of this exercise and clip the paper into your journal (so it can be taken out if you have to submit Module III journal to a mentor). This is private to you and you alone. Then type up an overview of the experience in a way that it is okay to submit to a mentor should they ask for it.

4.7 *Task:* **Readings**

Using the same method and layout as you used in the previous lesson, look at the aspects of your life, and also of your body, to see what areas are already in the process of unravelling. They will appear in the reading as 'going away' types of cards or of separation or loss.

With the results you got from your previous readings from lesson three and the results you got from this set of readings, put the two notes together and see if they match up with what came to light during your meditations. Write down the similarities and differences.

4.8 *Task:* **The Unraveller and your astrology chart**

Look at your chart and your current transits. See where Pluto is in transit in your chart. Take note of the house it is transiting, and also what astrological sign it is transiting. If you are using `astro.com`, look to see if there is a current major Pluto transit listed in your chart. If there is, read up on it. Look at your pentagram pattern/seal and see where in the pattern Pluto lies. Because Pluto is slow-moving, it will most likely be in the same place. See what magical tools, powers, etc. it is near.

Compare everything you have found with the conclusions you came to from your meditations and readings. You should now be getting a good idea of where your weak spots and strengths are, and a good idea of what needs working on and what doesn't in your life. Once you have identified areas of your life that you feel need proper engagement with the Unraveller, write them down and set yourself tasks and goals that will allow the Unravelling and/or Grindstone power to flow through you in a practical conscious way. Keep notes on your progress.

4.9 *Task:* Unraveller ritual

In the previous lesson you designed your own ritual to connect with and invite the powers of the Grindstone into your life. Take another look at that ritual and expand upon it. Write into the ritual a second part that calls in the power of the Unraveller.

Aspects to be included in the ritual: work with the magical direction of west, work with the gates, and the inner contacts at the gates.

Work at the west altar and allow whatever needs letting go of to flow energetically into the west. Also work with a mirror in the north to look at yourself and to be brutally honest with yourself in a ritual setting (and think about why the mirror belongs in the north).

Everything you do and say will be witnessed by the inner contacts, and you will be held to it. Make no promises, *make no vows* (that is very important). State your reflection, understanding, and what you intent to do about it.

Once you have reworked the ritual to be balanced, and have practised it from memory, then it is time to do it. Do it at a new moon and take a ritual bath beforehand: a fresh start.

Write down your notes afterwards. These notes will be private to you and will never be looked at, but it is important to write them down so that you can refer to them in the future, as you will need to.

Once you have completed that task, rewrite the ritual so that it is not specific to you: ensure that it can be used by any magician regardless of age, gender, culture, etc.

Remember, this is not a psychological act, but a ritual magical act. So don't get into flowery language or showy psychological actions. Keep it sharp, to the point, and magically relevant.

Some may feel that it is early days to be writing your own magical ritual, but doing so will make you think about how ritual is constructed. No matter how much you study ritual construction, it is only by actually having to *do* it that you start to see all the subtle implications.

Do this on computer and copy it somewhere safely; it is likely that it will be used by other magicians in the future when you finally come to teach or work with other magicians in some form or another.

4.10 Study

Look into the history of the Peasants' Revolt of England in 1381. It is a classic example of the interplay between the Grindstone and the Unraveller, and how complex that interplay can be. From that time of events, a slow but subtle long-term change happened within the people, the Monarchy, and the land.

Looking at the powers flowing through an event in a way that has nothing to do with magic allows you to look at the complexity of these powers without falling into the trap of stereotypical magical or ethical thinking. You will see the weave of how good and bad intertwined to produce massive change in a society.

It also begins the process of understanding how important it is to look at things beyond magic to see the forces of Divinity in action. Some of the greatest magical wisdom can be gained from history, art, music, poetry, science, etc. that have no direct magical links. This is why many adepts read widely on subjects such as history, philosophy, geography, medicine, music, sciences, etc.

Lesson 5

The Inner Guardians

Now that you have begun the process of working with the Grindstone and the Unraveller, it is time to begin to understand the other inner powers that guard and work with the thresholds of the inner worlds. Like the previous two powers you worked to understand, I have taken away the better-known names of many of them and given them titles according to what they do.

The names that have been used in magic in the past for these beings have become so distorted in the misuse and misunderstanding of these powers that it is time to step away from those names and for the magician to learn through direct experience. Even though this is an apprentice level, it is important to learn about these powers from the outset of training, which will not only prepare you for working properly with them, but will also give you a deeper understanding of them—an understanding that is sadly lacking in modern magic.

These beings can be recognised in ancient Egyptian texts as well as many other ancient texts: once you know their function and character, you will instantly recognise them in sacred texts around the world.

So why do you need to learn about these beings? Without knowledge of these powerful beings, there is no access to deeper and more profound magic. These are the powers that work behind the scenes of creation and work at the threshold of material existence, a threshold where magic begins its flowering.

Most of them you only need to know about and read up on at this phase of your training, but there is one contact within this group of guardians that you will need to meet in vision and learn to work with (and one you will also come to meet shortly in another lesson). Relationships with the rest will flower as your training progresses.

So let's have a look at these various contacts and learn a little about them: some you will recognise if you have read ancient mythic or theological texts; others you may not. First let's have a look at the realm where they reside. This realm is called the Desert, something you will learn a lot more about in the months and years to come.

5.1 The realm of the Desert

Knowledge of the realm of the Desert had sadly fallen by the wayside in modern magic, and yet it is a key realm for any powerful magic that uses inner vision and inner contacts.

Fragments of this realm can be seen in Greek mythology, where an aspect of the Desert is known as the *Lethe Plain*—the death realm, an aspect of the Desert, which you will learn about as an apprentice.

When a magician reaches deep into the inner worlds without the heavy filters of modern magic, they invariably hit a place that seems devoid of life: a vast desert with a great crack in the earth at one end (the *Abyss*) and a river at the other end (*the river of death*).

This desert is hinted at in many magical texts, but because of the dangers that can potentially threaten a magician if they wander into this realm without preparation, little detail is written about it in texts and grimoires. This danger results from the lack of knowledge of the guardians that stop humans blundering into this realm unprepared. That is why you, as an apprentice, must go through various preparations before you step fully into this realm.

Just as the Garden of Creation teems with life, so the opposite is true of the Desert. It holds no living or growing thing. It is void of life and full of knowledge. The Desert is the home of a vast array of angelic beings that are involved in the act of creation: the Desert is where pure Divine Breath and power is formed into the pattern of physical manifestation and begins its journey into life. Stepping over the threshold of the Desert, that pattern of life becomes a person, a tree, etc.—a concept you have already briefly looked at.

The Desert also houses the collective knowledge of all beings that have manifested in our world at some time or other. It is a similar idea to an inner landscape: where an inner landscape expresses the inner form of a land or person, so the Desert holds the inner temples, adepts, priests and priestesses, and deities: the inner forms of the outer manifestations.

When Crowley was told by an inner contact that he could only access communion with Choronzon in the desert, the contact did not mean an outer desert, but was talking about the inner realm of the Desert.

This is a place where the Abyss can be accessed as well as the knowledge of the ancient temples and priesthoods, where demonic and angelic beings can be safely met on their own territory, and where, as an adept, the magician can witness the true power and beauty of the Metatron Cube in action. For a magician to safely access and work in this place, he or she must first get to know and be accepted by its guardians.

If you are a person who works well through imagining something, imagine the desert appearing as a vast, lifeless plain scattered with ancient temples, the Abyss, the river and mountain of death in the distance, and the mists that shroud Divinity on the other side of the Abyss. Mists also appear to obscure areas of the Desert that the magician is not yet prepared to step into. There is also an area of the Desert that is a 'holding area' where powers or beings that should not be manifest in the outer world at this present time are held in the sands until it is time for them to be released.

If you read the Old and New Testaments of the Bible, you will also, once you have become familiar with this realm, recognise many aspects and contacts of this place in the various writings.

So now let us have a look at the various types of beings that stand on the threshold between us and the Desert. Not all of them are guardians; some are deities or sub-deities, some are workers—many beings work on this threshold to bring final form to the Divine Breath as it manifests as a physical being. They are the weavers, connectors, balancers, as well as guardians. Let's start from the closest to us and work in from there.

5.2 The Weaver

The Weaver is a deity power, female, that takes all the strands that are flowing out of the Desert and weaves them into final form to produce a specific life.

The Weaver takes the strands from the Three Fates which have defined the length of life, the time of death, and the time of birth of the person or creature, and weaves around those key points more subtle aspects of the life that is to be lived.

For example, we learned about the energies of the Unraveller as energetic hotspots in a life: the Weaver connects those 'hotspots' into the pattern set out by the Fates, and weaves a place of birth, and key moments within a life.

At this point let me say that these images and descriptions are how our consciousness can understand and interact with these powers. In real terms, these powers are truly beyond our understanding in their full expression. As a species, we have learned to use common imagery and have 'humanised' how we perceive lot of these beings so that we can interact with them safely. The depictions we use are essentially energetic filters that allow us communion. Without these filters they would be beyond our ability to communicate with: it is a common vocabulary of concepts and images, so bear that in mind.

As magicians, we work with this vocabulary of concepts and images in order to build an interface that we can work through. This vocabulary is something that has been deeply embedded within human consciousness for millennia: hence if you find these beings or places accidentally and without prior knowledge, you will see them in the same way the ancients saw them: a collective interface built up over thousands of years.

Back to the Weaver. The Weaver appears to us as a goddess who weaves life into being. She is only occasionally interacted with directly by magicians, but she is known, acknowledged, and respected. If, as a magical adept, you wish to specialise in magical work connected to fate and the formation of nations, then you will learn to work more closely with this goddess.

Most of the ancient Mysteries around the world have their own version of this goddess: in ancient Egypt she is known as *Neith* (pronounced 'Net'), one of the most ancient deities in the Egyptian pantheon. An aspect of this power is known in Greek mythology as Athena. These goddesses are known for being warriors (so much fate is determined by war) and also as weavers of creation.

Sadly, as the Mysteries of the ancient world began to degenerate, the understanding of the aspects of these powers also degenerated. Neith became known as a weaver in a day-to-day sense, as a basket or cloth weaver. This is a total misunderstanding of the vast powers this goddess wields, and we can often, as magicians, track the degeneration and collapse of a nation by tracking how the understanding of the deities fell apart.

So if you come across a goddess of weaving and she is thought to be the patron of weavers, dig a little deeper and you find that in fact it is a goddess who is the power of the Weaver of creation. As the outermost being on the threshold of the Desert, she is very well known around the world.

5.3 The Three Fates

The Three Fates figure extensively in many of the ancient Mysteries. One is involved with taking the thread of life that flows from the Divine Breath and has been formed into a pattern of a particular expression (human, animal, etc.), the second one determines the length that life will be, and the third is the one who determines the point of death.

These three beings essentially form the birth, length of life, and death of a human. If you read up on the various mythologies from ancient texts about these beings, you will notice that over the generations, more and more powers and attributes are added to their mythology (humans do have a habit of elaborating; they cannot keep anything simple). From a magician's perspective, we work with these beings in their core, original roles as the three intertwined powers that determine the *timing* of a life.

Again, few magicians would work directly with these powers unless, as an adept, they were specialising in an area of magic that would bring them into direct contact with these beings, but all magicians need to be aware of these powers, what they do, and how they operate.

Gnosis of these beings is important, as it will help you understand the mystical and inner aspects of a life, and how that life operates in the outer world. An adept working with fate or as an exorcist would need to have a deep understanding of these beings and how to interact with them when needs be.

If we take all the mythological dressing

away, what we are left with are beings that work in a very narrow and specific way with time and manifestation. Without physical substance (a body), there is no time. These beings are the ones that sit on our side of the threshold and 'midwife' the human into conception. At a deeper level of understanding, they are the powers that flow through the stars: the powers that come together in harmony to create a measured window through which a human soul can step into conception and birth.

Their power can be looked at through astrology, through angelic patterns of conception and death, and through tarot. They decide the 'when,' and the Weaver defines the 'how.'

That does not mean that a human has a set, locked fate; a path that cannot be changed. What it means is that there are certain key points in time where 'hotspots' are active. How we are affected by those hotspots largely depends on our own choice of action.

However, I have found over the decades that there are certain patterns of fate that cannot be dodged or avoided (though some can), and these key moments in time do, indeed, seem to be set before our birth. How we react to them and what we take from them (or give to them) determines our deeper development and maturity.

This is important to understand as a magician, as it directly affects how long-term magical projects are approached, and it also affects our understanding in regards to divination when we look at longer-term events. Some are mutable and some are fixed: as we mature as magicians we learn to spot these hotspots in advance so that we can approach them in the most productive and wisest way possible.

What I have observed personally as a magician over the decades is that as far as death is concerned, there seems to be a final 'fixed' time, but there are also other times that crop up as a result of the 'weave' hotspots and also through our own actions and the actions, usually magical, of others that can potentially take us out. These we can avoid if we know how to.

So in a way, we can potentially not make it to our 'fixed' time, but be taken out earlier through different influences. But I have also observed that when that fixed time comes, nothing can dodge it. Often when I have been around magicians who have come to that fixed point in time, they feel it, recognise it, and understand it. They start to disconnect from the world around them and go with the power flow rather than fight it.

My findings over years of magical exploration tell me without doubt that these beings exist and have a direct influence upon us, but the 'known wisdom' that we have about them is rudimentary. In real terms I have seen and experienced that the influence of these beings upon us is far more complex that it would at first seem. But for you as apprentices, starting from the rudimentary understanding will suffice.

As an adept, you will interact with these beings for yourself and will over time observe their influence in the world around you. From that, you will come to gain your own personal knowledge of their power and action, which is the true way the Mysteries work: you experience the depths of the inner worlds in a way that is specific to you. That in turn matures and develops you as a spiritual, mystical being.

5.4 The Keeper of Justice

The Keeper of Justice is a power that many will be familiar with: it is a power that is still depicted at courthouses throughout the Western world. Again, this power appears to us as female and is well known to us as , like the Weaver and the Fates, it is a power that resides on our side of the threshold. This means it is easy for our consciousness to tune in and connect with this power. However, the deeper powers and meaning of this being are, like the others, often misunderstood, and are expressed in our culture in their simplest and least powerful forms.

The Keeper of Justice is not a goddess; it is an angelic force that is akin to a fulcrum. It is the centre of two opposing forces, and its job is to keep a balance between them. So for example, the Keeper of Justice acts as a narrow filter for the powers of the Grindstone and the Unraveller, and also for the deeper powers that are behind those two polarities: the Keeper ensures a necessary balance between the two, whatever level of balance is needful for a particular soul to manifest physically.

Another function of this being is to act as a gatekeeper or filter that magicians encounter when they work in the Desert realm. This being maintains the tension of energy, like a membrane, that the magician passes through as they step deeper into the inner worlds. If the magician is working towards maintaining a semblance of balance in their lives, that balance will be strengthened and assisted as they pass back and forth through this membrane.

If the magician is working in a very unbalanced way, or is very unbalanced within themselves, then passing through this membrane will either push them back out of the inner worlds or will create yet more imbalance within the magician. We see this manifesting as things so extreme as magicians becoming increasingly mentally unstable as they try to force their way into the inner worlds in an unbalanced way. Another more simple and protective way this membrane can affect magicians is to push them out of vision if their body is harbouring disease, or if they are in an energetic space that is not conducive to inner work: it has a protective action.

If the magician is, for example, infected with a flu virus but not yet showing symptoms, the energetic pattern of the virus will already be making the magician energetically vulnerable: if they gained access to the deeper aspects of the inner worlds while incubating an illness, the energetic impact of the work would most likely enable the virus to attack the magician's body more successfully.

Similarly, if the magician has some event coming into their very near future that would need a lot of energy (pregnancy, a major life change, etc.), the Keeper of Justice will not allow the magician to pass deeper into the Desert. This is to ensure that the energy reserves of the magician are kept at their optimum for what is to come.

Another octave of the Keeper of Justice is the *Keeper of the Scales*: the being that oversees the power of Ma'at in our world. In a mundane life, the Keeper has minimal interactions with a human life. If, however, that human is a magician or a priest/priestess, then the deeper that human steps into the Mysteries, the more and more the Keeper will engage in order to guide the human on a path of balance. We see this through the Mysteries of the Threshing Floor, something you will learn a great deal more about in future lessons. It is also a power that is heavily involved in the action of the Sword of Justice (the Sword of Damocles).

The deeper into the Mysteries the adept goes, the more the Keeper engages with them and flows as a governing power through their lives. This enables the magician to learn how to maintain balance within an unbalanced physical existence (all physical life is unbalanced in some way—it has to be for physical manifestation to happen), and how to govern themselves and their magical work in as balanced a way as possible.

You have already, through your previous exercises and lessons, learned the beginning of how this power flows through magic, and the deeper you go in your magical studies, the more this power will crop up in your life. If you are willing, as a magician, to learn the lessons laid before you by the Keeper and to work closely in conjunction with this power, then as a magician you will mature into your own power and learn how to wield it wisely.

The power of the Keeper not only works on the threshold of the Desert, but operates throughout creation and nature: once you learn how to recognise and understand this power, you will see it in action in everything around you. It is the power that keeps polarities tight and balanced, it maintains the flow of creation and destruction in the manifest world, and it maintains opposing energies and powers within every living thing.

So now you begin to see that the Keeper of Justice has little to do with the maintaining of cultural or moral laws that are disconnected from the deeper powers of creation. The Keeper does not judge or moralise; the Keeper simply triggers the process of rebalancing that which is unbalanced, and helps to maintain balance where it exists.

5.5 The Keeper of the Threshold

Now we are getting to the layer of beings that are not so well known in mythology and stories. The Keeper of the Threshold is the first being that works in creation that is only really known to the mystics and magicians throughout time, and was not written about much.

Whereas the outer beings involved in creation who resided on 'our side of the threshold' were often communicated with, interacted with, and were widely known, the being on the threshold and the beings beyond were reached only by priesthoods and magicians working beyond the threshold.

The culture that did penetrate the threshold and pass on pertinent information that we know of was Ancient Egypt. The early kingdoms (pre-dynastic and Old Kingdom) really knew their stuff, and as a magician wanting to learn the true depths of magic, it would be wise for you as a student to study the texts and wall paintings from these amazing people.

For many years I did not fully understand the depths of their knowledge. It was only as an adept and visiting Karnak that I finally realised just how knowledgeable these people were of the inner worlds and of magic.

The Keeper of the Threshold is a vast angelic consciousness that transforms the deep inner pattern created from the Divine Breath and gives it the *inner form* of the outer being that it will become.

The Keeper of the Threshold does not determine what those patterns will become; rather this being is the catalyst that triggers the transformation, takes the information from the pattern, and moulds it into shape as per instructions. Some cultures do depict this being, often in the form of a potter who takes raw materials and gives it shape. So if you are looking for reference to this being in ancient texts and myths, look for a depiction of a potter (the ancient Egyptians called this power *Khnum*).

As a magician, you would not work directly with this power. As a power that sits on the threshold, it is too vast a power for a magician to attempt to communicate with, and it is not a power that human magicians should attempt to work with or harness. But an awareness of this being, as a working adept, will help the magician to not make inadvertent dangerous mistakes.

5.6 The Utterer and the Wheel

Before we get to the being that you as an apprentice can meet and work with, there are two other powers found upon the threshold of the Desert that it would be pertinent for you to know about. One is the Utterer, and the other is the Wheel. If you have studied tarot, the Wheel will be familiar to you, and for those who have studied theology, the Utterer will be known to you.

The Utterer is an angelic being that operates through the element of air and works within a narrow field of action. That action is the use of sound to affect change. This angel mediates the Divine Breath of God from the inner world to the outer world.

> "In the beginning was the Word, and the Word was with God, and the Word was God."

The Utterer mediates this *Word* out into the world in various forms, the most natural expression being particular storms that effect change.[1]

Another more commonly known action of the Utterer is to mediate wisdom and knowledge to humanity. This comes in the form of revelations, inspired writings,

---
[1] In my book *Magic of The North Gate* I talk about these storms that have 'intent.'

prophecies, and the teaching of humans who are treading a path into the Mysteries. The action of this angel can also been seen through inspired music, poetry, and stories, all of which bring change to the world and to the minds of humans.

A non-mystical, non-magical example of this is something that the composer Igor Stravinsky (1882–1971) once talked about. He said:

> "I heard, and I wrote what I heard. I am the vessel through which the *Sacre* passed."

He was talking about the composing of *Le Sacre du Printemps* (*The Rite of Spring*) which premiered in 1913.

This music was particularly discordant to the ears of that time, and was described as "sending listeners to hell" and driving people "to eat ashes and fill their bellies with the east wind" (Jean Cocteau). Indeed, not only did this piece of music change music in the west forever—it also foresaw the First World War.

When Stravinsky wrote this music, he did not alter it, refine it, or edit it. His notations show no working upon the composition; rather he literally wrote it out in one draft as he heard it.

This is an example, of which in history there are many, of the Utterer speaking through a human. Don't forget that sound and vibrations are the main powers through which the angelic beings of creation work: the mediation of words is very much a secondary thing.

The Utterer was also responsible for the revelations of the Prophets, and this angelic being stands behind humans who speak with an inspired voice, a voice that changes nations.

The Wheel is fairly well known to most magicians, and is an angelic being that brings change. The Wheel constantly turns and powers the cycle of birth and death, creation and destruction, and the shifting sands of fate.

As an initiate, you will learn to spot the action of the Wheel in your life, and learn how to work directly with it to facilitate that change in a conscious way: you will learn to actively participate in your fate rather than be swept along by it. The Wheel is one of the driving forces behind major 'hotspots' on your web of fate (which you will learn more about soon).

5.7 The Noble Companions/the Noble Ones

The Noble Companions/Ones, also known as the *Sandalphon*, are a collection of angelic beings that act as guides, companions, teachers, and protectors of humans who tread the road of the Mysteries. Some teachings connect the Sandalphon to the Wheel, but they are in fact different, but similar, powers.

Like many angels, the Sandalphon are a hive being: when all the bits are brought together, you have a massively powerful archangel. What we work with as magicians appears as one angel, but is in fact a fragment of this greater being (hence they are often referred to in plural). We get a small bit so that we can withstand the communion and work with them. This is why often a single angel is referred to as 'them': they are both an individual power and a group of many.

The Sandalphon, known in Egyptian texts as *The Noble Ones*, are beings that assist in the mystical evolution of humanity. They guide us along the road of the future, and walk with us as we step into the inner realms of the Desert. These are beings that we can talk to, ask questions of, and who will accompany us as we stretch deeper and deeper into the inner realms.

They will not protect you from your own stupidity: you are responsible for yourself, for your own safety, and your own learning. They will point things out to you, show you things you would not have necessarily found by yourself, and will guide you to scenes where you can observe and learn. But they will not spell things out for you, and they will not stop you from making mistakes that you can learn hard lessons from: they are true teachers.

As a magician, as you learn and mature, your interactions with the Sandalphon will expand beyond the inner realms, and they will become more apparent in your outer life as you learn to externalise your mystical development. As you cross from doing magic to *becoming* magic, the Sandalphon will walk beside you and a subtle interplay will develop between you as learn, grow, and mature.

The first step towards developing this relationship is to meet them in vision. From that first meeting, you can then begin to work with them as you learn to step into and carefully explore the inner worlds.

Do not think of these beings as parents who will indulge you or overprotect you: they will not. If you do not tread with respect and caution in your visionary work, they will not protect you from the consequences of such immaturity.

As a magician, you are responsible for yourself, and yet if you are in true danger and have acted to the best of your knowledge and ability, they will nudge you to safety.

Building a relationship with these beings is of the utmost importance for a magician, as they are beings that can guide you into the Deeper Mysteries and will show you things that you must experience for yourself. For you as an apprentice, the best way to make this connection is through vision. For the following vision in your practical work, learn the vision first by reading it a few times. Note in your mind the key points, as they are the triggers that will put you into the realm of the threshold, and will also trigger these beings into action.

Don't worry if in the midst of vision you forget a minor detail: as long as you follow the key steps, you will be successful. Working in vision this way, alone and without a resonant adept working with you, is harder and takes longer to truly trigger power in vision. But it also makes you self-sufficient and allows you to progress at a rate that is healthy for your body and mind. So don't feel like you are a failure if at first it is difficult to make any powerful connection: it can take time and practice. Eventually you will start to feel the power shift happening, and like all skills, the more you practice, the better you will get at it.

5.8 *Task:* The Vision of the Sandalphon

Light a candle in the east of your work space, sit in the centre of the room, and meditate until your mind is still (east is the magical direction of the threshold).

Once you are still, see with your inner vision the candle flame burning. Stand up in vision, and walk to the candle flame. Bow to the powers and contacts in that direction, and then step into the flame. Bathe in the flame, which is the flame of life, and feel things being burned away from you: things that no longer belong with you. You are cleansed and energised by the flame which flows through you and all around you.

When you are ready, step forward beyond the flame, with the clear intention of stepping to the threshold that joins the inner and outer worlds.

You find yourself in a place of stillness and silence. Beneath your feet is sand, a flat desert that stretches off in all directions. Most of the landscape is obscured by mists, and you can only see a small area of desert around you.

Call out, both in vision and with your physical voice:

> "I call upon the Sandalphon, if they are willing and it is right, to allow me to meet with them."

In time, a figure will walk towards you out of the mists. The figure is tall, with long hair stretching down their backs and flowing into the sand behind them. They walk in the sand, their lower legs and feet deep in the sands of the desert.

(If they do not appear, simply wait and meditate. If they still do not appear, do not retrace your steps, simply open your eyes and finish the vision: this will keep the inner pattern of the vision going. Work with the vision every day until they do appear. Don't rush it: this works in the timing that is right and safe for you.)

As the figure comes to you, hold out your hand. The Companion 'reads' you through touching your hand and feeling your hair. If you have no hair, they will lay a hand upon your head.

The companion will indicate for you to walk with them. Walk alongside them into the mists. The mists may fade, and you may see some of the landscape of the Inner Desert. They may show you things, and if they do, take note.

Take as long as you need in vision to walk with them until they indicate it is time for you to walk back into the mists. You may not see anything for the first couple of times you walk with them: being in their presence is often sufficient to begin with.

The Companion will indicate that they are now going to leave you. Bow to them, turn, and walk into the mist with the intention of walking back into the flame of life. The flame will appear before you. Step into the flame, bathe in its power, and then step forward, stepping through the flame, through the east altar, and back into the room where you first started. Sit back down into your body, and when you are ready, open your eyes. Have your journal before you.

Before you can forget (and you will), write down what you saw, what happened, and draw out any buildings, beings, or signs that you were shown. Later, type up your notes on computer so that they can be submitted if needed.

You may have a long encounter with them or a short one. Neither is preferable; it is whatever is needful for you at that time. Do not try to force any aspect of the vision, do not try to 'imagine great things,' and do not ask them questions at this stage. Simply be in their presence and look at whatever is shown to you. Take this contact a step at a time, so that your mind and body can get used to the contact.

5.9 *Task:* **Visiting with the Sandalphon**

Work with this vision two or three times a week for a month. Keep good notes of each encounter, regardless of how interesting or uninteresting the encounter is. Do not try to filter what you have seen: it is common to see things that you do not understand or that you do not feel belong in that vision. Write everything down: some strange aspects will become better known to you as your skills progress.

Also, do not move on to another lesson until you have worked with these beings for a month. It is a crucial point in your training, and it is important that you gain the skills to connect with these beings properly and get used to working in vision with them.

If you find that nothing is happening, keep working with the vision beyond the month: it will connect, as and when it is right for you.

And remember, you see everything in your own mind and imagination: that is the interface that these, and all inner beings, work through to communicate with you. Eventually you will be able to converse with these beings, but such conversing can be a major strain on your energies (their voice carries great power), so be content to simply be with them and look at what they show you. Once they begin talking to you, then you can talk back: let them initiate the first conversation.

When you do begin conversing with these beings, don't ask silly questions that you should find the answers to yourself. And ensure that any question is directly related to your own personal development as a magician and as a human: they are not an oracle, nor are they the Utterer. Keep notes in your journal of the questions that you ask, and type them up into your computer notes.

After you have worked with these beings in vision for a month, make it a routine to visit with them on a fairly regular basis, for example once a month. Keep writing down your encounters, and also note the date, location (both the visionary location and your own physical location), and any time when the Companion appears to you in other visions unexpectedly. This will happen when they are ready to start working with you through your training.

The reason to mark down the time/location details is so that you can then run a chart to see what astrological powers were flowing around you at that time. It can be quite revealing. You would look at the chart of the encounter, and then also at your own transits for that time.

5.10 *Task:* **Stravinsky's *Rites of Spring***

Lie down and listen to Stravinsky's *Rites of Spring* (find a recording that Stravinsky conducted himself). Listen to it a few times over the month that you are working with the Sandalphon/Noble One. If you are not used to listening to classical music, it will take a few times of listening for you to adjust to the taste.

If you fall asleep, take note of any dreams you have as you doze, or any dreams you have that night. Also note down how it makes you feel, how it affects you, and how it affects the room and the land around you. You can ascertain the effects on the room or land either by your own sensitivity, or by doing a Tree of Life reading with tarot, asking:

"How does this music affect the land around me when it is played?"

5.11 *Task:* **Research**

Read up on and research the following: Meskhenet, Shai, and Renenutet (Egyptian mythology), the Norns, the Moirai, The Parcae, and also search for deities of fate in different ancient cultures. Similarly, look up Weaver goddesses around the Ancient world and in mythology.

Read their descriptions and see if you can spot where attributes have been added over the ages. Don't attempt to force any of the deities and fates into neat little boxes for your own understanding: cultures approached them in different ways, and their understandings of these powers reflect a lot about their culture and the understanding of that time.

5.12 *Task:* **Working with an image**

Once you have a good idea of the different expressions of these powers around the world, choose one of the fates and one of the weaver goddesses and read about them in more depth. Find ancient depictions of your chosen subjects (wall carvings, stone carvings, wall paintings, statues, etc.) and print out the images.

Either use the printed out image or create/paint your own image using the original as reference. Don't elaborate on the image or add things in, this is not playtime nor an artistic exercise: you are slowly learning how to transfer power into a window of contact. This is the first step for the apprentice magician.

Once you have the image you are happy with of the Fates and the Weaver, put those images in the northeast section of the room where you work magically. They do not need to be on display if that causes a problem (partner hates them, or there is no room, etc.), they just need to actually physically be in that direction of the work space.

What you are doing through these art actions is learning the first action of enlivening objects (a simple baby step), but you are also slowly introducing these powers into your work space. Many magicians have lots of images and statues dotted around their living or working space. Some do that because it looks good, others do it to psychologically connect with them or they are copying something they have seen on social media. None of those reasons are why you are doing this.

By having images of key, specific powers in your space, you are learning how to live and work in a magical pattern whereby powers and contacts have 'windows' into your life and work. As an adept, you will learn how to connect the powers of the deities, angelic beings, and contacts to images, and enliven them so that the power can connect through that image to work with you in your realm.

It acts like a window, and also like a power

filter that keeps the power levels low enough for you to operate around safely. That skill does not suddenly download into you as an adept: it starts right at the beginning of your training.

This first step triggers a deep cycle of learning: it is equivalent to a toddler learning how to draw a face by scribbling a round shape, sticking arms on the side and drawing eyes and a smiley mouth. Although primitive, it is the practice of that scribbling that enables the child to develop fine motor skills.

So, too, the apprentice magician must learn to create and live with images that have the potential to carry power. They learn to choose wisely and not randomly or through dogma, fashion, or will. Each image present in the space of a magician is there for a specific reason, does a particular job, and often is unseen or unnoticed by the uninitiated.

As the magician progresses in their studies, they slowly learn how to gently 'turn on' these images and work with them. Some will not be worked with: their presence in the life of the magician is enough to trigger change and development (the Weaver and the Fates are good examples of this passive presence).

Lesson 6

The Laws of Fate

At this stage in the module, it is time to learn about the underlying laws (dynamics) of fate. This is something that very few magical schools look into or discuss, and yet it is of paramount importance to a magician, as it affects everything you do in magic. Every magical act is governed by these laws, and both its long-term outcome and its effect on you as a magician is dependant on you operating within these laws, both for your own safety and for the safety of everything around you.

The laws of fate are a complex weave indeed, and the culture around many parts of the world (which is Abrahamic-based) is unbalanced in its modern understanding these laws. This cultural overlay is often a major stumbling-block for magicians in their training and practice, hence it is important to address this early on in the training of a magician.

The power dynamics of fate pervade everything that we do, everything around us, and steer us through many lives. Knowing how to navigate this maze, to the extent that we as magicians can know and understand it, enables us to live powerful, fruitful lives as magicians. That does not mean that we live lives free of worry, pain, stress, and disaster; rather it means that the ups and downs of life become a training ground for us, and the 'hotspots' (remember those?) do not take us out or destroy us. We become co-drivers of our fate rather than passive passengers. That shift is a major one for magicians and is a shift that truly defines us as magicians and separates us from the world of non-magicians.

There are three basic dynamics that the magician needs to know about in fate. They are:

1. The dynamic of self and one's own personal relationship with fate.

2. The family web and how we are deeply connected through blood in our fate.

3. The rest of the world.

Those three sections are very clearly defined in our fate, and each one has its own peculiar dynamic.

Before we look at those dynamics, let's first look briefly at the issues of cultural overlay that act as such stumbling-blocks for magicians.

The first is what I call the Disney sentimentality. This is a nice but heavily unbalanced way of viewing the world that has no real bearing on how the world works. It is amplified by New Age sentiment and ends up twisting our understanding of a deep, enduring power dynamic that runs through every living thing. The first thing is that nature is *not cute*. It is not cute simply because everything in nature fights to survive and fights for resources.

When a being (human, animal, plant) is well-resourced, the deeper qualities of sharing, caring, patience, and communion surface in many (but not all) beings. There seems to be a disconnect in our modern thinking: we think such qualities come from being a good person, when in fact they come from being a well-resourced being (barring mental illness or mental disorders).

A lot of destructive behaviour comes from being under-resourced, be it food, shelter, community, education, or expression. I know this is simplifying the situation, but I don't want to have to write a whole book, which is what it would take, to outline the complexity of this issue. So the issue of being under-resourced (or mental health issues) should be something in the forefront of a magician's mind when he or she comes to work on a magical project that involves the fate and behaviour of an individual.

The other mistake that is also often made in issues of fate is that if the magician means well, then all will be well. More damage can be done to a fate pattern by being 'nice' than by being relevant. Sometimes pain, destruction, being under-resourced, etc. is what is needed for a situation to move forward in a balanced way: good or bad can balance the Scales, and the magician needs to know what is needed and when.

Now you begin to see the complexity? Most of this can be navigated through divination and inner sight.

The other main issue that comes up in magic is the misunderstanding of *Karma*. It has become a dogma in the East and the West that everything is locked down in fate and you can do nothing to change your lot: it is your karma. That is total bullshit.

There are indeed tides of cause and effect that do run through fate, but they are not fixed: they flow and ebb according to how you act and react, the choices you make, and the choices of those around you. You are, for the most part, in the driver's seat of your own fate, with the inner powers of fate sometimes taking over the wheel at important spots in the road: it is a joint effort.

6.1 Self

The understanding of fate in respect to you as an individual is a complex and slowly evolving skill set that usually develops over time depending on our life experience. So for those who are reading this that are young (below 35 years old) much of this knowledge will have to be taken on trust: the true understanding of fate and its actions in the life of a magician depends on personal experience and the ability to spot and recognise the dynamic in action.

Those who are older, and particularly those who have been practically involved in magic for quite some time, will recognise much of what I am about to discuss. I don't want to sound condescending (though I probably will to some), but for most (not all) people it takes a few decades of events, challenges, and knocks before we begin to understand our fate: it was certainly like that for me, and for most people I know. At thirty I knew it all. At fifty I realised I knew very little indeed.

That recognition will help you better understand your own experiences and put them in context of fate and magic. This section on 'Self' will be a bit long, as the subject matter is complex, but I will try to keep it as succinct as possible.

Let's first look at the wider picture of fate in the life of an individual magician, and then we can narrow it down to practicalities. Magicians are *born*; it is not something you wake up one morning and decide to do.

When in the life of the magician they choose to engage in magic largely depends on their individual fate weave. Some wake up to magic in childhood, some trundle along later in life. Some feel like they have done it all before and are simply remembering, and some step into magic as total empty slates ready to be filled. But one thing they all have in common is that the interaction with magic *was already in their pattern before they were conceived*.

If magic is in your pattern, you cannot run away from it. Wherever you turn in life, it will be there waiting for you. However, magic in the pattern of an individual does not always express in ways that we would today consider a 'magical path': it can express through arts, literature, music, science, or religion. Once you work as a magical adept you will instantly recognise someone who is a magician, who is working magically, but is not 'doing magic' (remember Stravinsky?). That in turn makes us stop and think about what we define as 'magic.'

A good example of people who have magic in their fate weave but do not 'do magic' in terms of outer understanding was a person like Nikola Tesla. Tesla was a scientist, but he was also a magician in that he connected to the deeper aspects of creation in dreams and visions, mediated that contact into his work, tapped into (without realising) the Inner Library, and worked instinctively with the energies and powers of creation: he was a magician who expressed that role through physics. We can also see it in people of religion, of the arts, etc.: it is not just a matter of being inspired; that is not the same thing. It is the ability to reach into the inner worlds, mediate that power to the outer world, and in turn effect change. That is essentially all that magic is.

But with that understanding we can immediately see how such action crosses paths with the powers of fate: to act in such a way is to consciously engage with the powers of creation, the powers of life, of time, of substance; and such action can alter the vast weave of fate and creation. If you are going to engage in such activities, which is what magic is all about, you need to understand a bit about how it works so that you do not blow yourself up—or others around you.

Recognising the fate path

Some have stronger, more defined fates than others; that is the first thing to understand. A strong fate path will have very clearly defined hotspots, clearly defined actions, and these will find a way to manifest in the life of a person one way or another. A weaker fate path will still have defining 'ingredients,' but it will be less fixed and more fluid (and there are lots of variants in between).

When you are born, you will have a tool box of qualities and potentials (which can be seen in your natal chart), you will have specific hotspots in your future life path (as defined by the fates, which can be seen through divination), a framework for the soul to operate through (the body, both in genetic make-up but also in how it develops, which in turn depends upon nutrition, physical illness/accident, etc.) and you will have a set of inherited skills, qualities, and problems (from your bloodline).

All these create a framework through which the soul expresses itself in life. The soul also comes into life with its own collections of experiences and skills gained in previous or future lives (unless it is someone's first time around). Already we can begin to see the complex weave that we call fate and how intricate it can be.

So we have a picture building of a soul, a vessel for the soul, a context for that vessel, and a place in time/location that the soul and vessel can operate in. The time and location for manifestation is ultimately chosen by the soul at a deep level, and that choice is then translated by the Weaver.

How that complicated weave of fate plays out largely depends on our actions, choices, and how we respond to the events that happen to and around us. Most people are blown along their path of life in this fate weave like tumbling leaves. The magician, however, learns and then engages with the dynamic to ensure that their choices and responses upon this path are clear and are made in gnosis. This in turn allows the potential for the magician to reach to its fullest extent.

Action/reaction

Most magic is born out of a need or wish for action or reaction. Sometimes it is our own wants/needs; other times it is requested of the magician by a third party. Those actions can be anything from simple magic that is involved in healing, issues of money, relationships, protection, etc., to magic that is involved in longer-term issues to do with exorcism, the development of a group or nation, tending the land, or affecting major change that will have long-term consequences for individuals or large groups of people... you get the idea.

All those varied types of magic fall into two categories: *action* or *reaction*. Clearly defining which is which, and understanding which category one is actually working with, has a profound effect not only on the outcome of the magic but also the effect such magic will have on the fate of the magician and of all those involved.

Action magic is where the magic starts a new cycle. *Reaction magic* is where the magic intervenes in an already ongoing situation. Being able to clearly identify which is which is of paramount importance to the magician, as the outcomes will be very different for all involved. Sometimes such identification is easy; sometimes it is more subtle, and the magician should always take the time to investigate and also use divination to ascertain exactly what dynamic it is they are about to work on.

Action magic

Action magic creates a whole new cycle of events. This in turn engages directly with fate powers and also, in certain circumstances, with the powers of creation itself. Immediately you begin to see the potential for huge amounts of power to flow through a magical act regardless of the intent of the magician.

When you instigate a new cycle or triggering of fate, which action magic always does, this can draw deeply on the energy reserves of the magician and affect their own fate pattern at a deep level. The level of effect this will have on the magician can vary widely depending on the long-term implications of the magical action.

Let's look at a simple, practical example of action magic and its effect on the magician. Bear in mind that everything you do as a magician is going to have some sort of effect and you cannot dodge that. What is important to understand is that some effects are worth it for all involved, and some are not. Being able to identify the differences is a skill all magicians need to have.

Let's look at very simple, low-grade magic—which is the most commonly used form of magic. The magician is approached by someone (we will call her Helen) who wants help finding a job by using magic.

An inexperienced magician would immediately get to work and use the methods they know well to trigger a situation where Helen gets a job. If they know what they are doing in terms of magical technique, it will most likely work. But the inexperienced magician did not first step back and look at the overall situation and personality of the person.

The magician does his work, Helen gets her job, and immediately the magician begins to get tired and feel energy drained. A few months later, Helen loses her newfound job because she did not do well at it, and she was soon back at the magician's door.

The magician then either figures out something is wrong, or if they are really dumb, they repeat the magical act again. If the magician fails to learn from the direct experience, and continues to do such magic for Helen, the magician will slowly, over time, become ill and poorly resourced in their own life.

So what went wrong? It is simple magic, with good intent, and should not really cause any problems, right? Wrong.

The first mistake the magician made was that they did not investigate *why* Helen could not get a job. If Helen was a hard worker, willing to do what was necessary to find work, but was in trapped in an area of high unemployment, and they had few marketable skills, then what the magician should have done is to use divination to look and see if the magic would indeed *help her fate along*.

Notice the question was not about looking to see if the magic would get Helen a job. If the magician is good at what they do, of course Helen would indeed have gotten a job, but it may not have been in harmony with her fate pattern.

So for example, Helen could have possibly needed to move out of that area in order to start a new cycle of their fate somewhere else. The only way for that to happen is either for Helen to realise that (and some people also 'feel' it), or the other option is for fate to force the Helen's hand by blocking every avenue for work until she *has* to move elsewhere in order to support themselves.

By blindly creating a magical pattern for a job, the hapless magician stalled the fate of Helen, which in turn burned up a lot of energy, energy that is drawn directly from the blockage in that fate path: the magician.

Another example of this sort of scenario is where the client does not really want to work and cannot be bothered making the effort to find a job: this helpless victim 'please do it all for me' is a common dynamic in people who seek out magicians to help them. (Not all people who seek help are like this, but many—too many—are.) This would result in a situation where the magician does the work, the client gets the job, loses it, comes back to the magician, and the same thing happens over and over again until the magician either stops the process or becomes too weak to be effective any more.

This constant 'opting out' of personal responsibility pushes the energetic burden back on the magician, and they literally energetically carry the client along a stalled fate path.

The various fate consequences of not checking before instigating action magic can be minor or major: for an extreme example of major consequence, say a client (whom we will call Fred) was a sexual deviant, a rapist by nature. In Fred's fate path, there are hotspots along the way that would force Fred to change or face his behaviour (or would have taken him out) which in turn moves him along a path of learning and maturing. If magic had not intervened in the life of this rapist, he would have been forced, by lack of jobs and poverty, to move to another city.

In that city, the Fred would have been caught, convicted (his Grindstone hotspot in action) and through that conviction and subsequent imprisonment, he would have begun a process of facing his actions and learning both to understand and control his actions; or he may have gained treatment for mental illness, or hormonal instability (or he would have entered into a cycle of offence and arrest—the hotspot set up the conditions for evolution, but it is up to the person to respond and engage, or not.).

This in turn would have moved Fred along a fate path that could be one of maturing, or one of total degeneration depending upon how he chose to respond.

Any key hotspot in this complicated weave could have been the one that, if magic had not intervened and Fred had been forced by circumstance to move to a different city, would have saved the women around him in his present location from his attack. By using magic to keep him in a job, there is a potential for a woman to be raped and murdered in a situation that would not have happened if the magician had not intervened.

And as the instigator of that process, the magician bears the full weight of the energy imbalance. Also, the twists and turns of fate can be enormously complex, and if you stall that process through magical intervention, the consequences for all involved can be limitless.

It is not all doom and gloom, though. An adept magician would have seen all of that in a first round of readings about the client, and would have refused to do the work. It is that simple: that is the difference between the actions of an inexperienced magician, and of a true adept.

Another example of a situation in a similar vein is one whereby the magician looks at a client, sees that they are indeed doing everything they can to help themselves, and/or their fate flowers massively if they are helped to get a job. In that sort of case, the magic is done, it is successful, the client blossoms in the job, and the magician has no side effects.

The key to such action is in knowing the long-term consequences of that action, and whether that action is compatible with the individual's fate path and the paths of those around them.

And that in turn is arrived at through interviewing the client, and then doing readings to look at their fate path.

A simple interview with a client can tell you a lot. Are they stupid and lazy and just want a quick, easy solution with no personal effort? Are they drama queens that are trying to stretch beyond themselves? Are they not doing everything in their lives first to solve the problem? (That self-responsibility, or lack of it, is a big flag for a magician.)

In a world where people think they can buy anything, magic is often badly misused, and that misuse can rebound in the long-term fate of a magician. They may not feel the impact straight away, but it will catch up with them at some point.

So what has this to do with creation? Everything. One of the roles of a magician is to facilitate the fate path of themselves and others, but it is not the role of the magician to interfere in a way that would short-circuit a fate path.

The same rules apply to ourselves as magicians. It is very tempting to use the skills of magic to make our lives much easier and obviate our own fate events because we might not like them. And indeed, the magician must not be a victim of their fate; rather, they should be the drivers of their own fate. Consider it like driving a powerful car. If you are irresponsible, you can do a lot of damage; if you are sensible, you can move swiftly down a road while also being safe.

Reaction magic

Reaction magic is magical intervention in an ongoing situation, and often, but not always, where magic is already in the picture. If a magician is wise and knows what they are doing, reaction magic is the easier of the two to deal with: it is simply a matter of rebalancing scales. But even that is not so simple...

If, for example, someone has been magically bound, it would make sense to unbind them magically. Sometimes that is all that is needed. But there are times that such a hostile magical act of binding is a part of the learning process of a person, and in those circumstances you would not unbind them; rather you would work magically as a catalyst for the person to find their own solutions magically, which in turn helps them to develop as magicians themselves: the best learning is from direct experience, not theory.

As you are beginning to see, these fate twists and turns can be very complex at times, and dipping into them magically in ignorance can make life a lot harder than it needs to be. The best way I have found to step around those difficulties is to use divination in the form of readings to look specifically at the long-term implications and consequences of particular magical actions before I do them. It has taught me a great deal.

However, it is also important to develop your own intuition, understanding, and wisdom. Do not just rely on one source of information: learn to use your magical skills along with your own common sense and understanding, and also your free will of choice.

Some people reading this might not agree with me (that short-term magic like jobs/money magic causes any problems) and my answer to that is, sure—find out for yourself through long-term direct action and experience.

Now you will be beginning to understand why good tarot skills are important for a magician, and why it is important that you learn them step by step in order to be a successful, safe and healthy magician.

Guardians and guides

Before we move on to looking at fate in families and the world in general, I would just like to cover a word or two about guardians and guides. When you step onto a magical path, your fate immediately 'wakes up' and can often accelerate, which can be uncomfortable at times but is ultimately worth it.

The other thing that happens through your stepping into magic and magical training is that you become, at some point, consciously connected with your guardian angel and the inner guides and beings around you. This in turn enables you to feel, hear, smell, see, or dream them when they are trying to warn you, connect with you, or teach you. These are all inner senses, something you learned about in your early lessons.

Their job is to help you, guide you, and open doors a crack for you on your magical and spiritual path of development. They do not carry you, or protect you from your own stupidity: they do not interfere with your learning process. But they will intervene at crucial moments of danger, or at times when it is really important that you stop and make a careful decision. They may speak to you through your mind, your dreams, or you may feel them around you.

There is a lot of talk in magic of "communion with your HGA," with long and elaborate processes for opening communication lines. You do not need to do that. What you need to do is learn to be still, to be aware, and as you develop as a magician, so the communion develops naturally.

The first step for an apprentice magician is to know that 'the team' is there and that it is your job to be ready to listen, take note, and act accordingly. Often it is like a whisper at first, or a 'feeling' or instinct. If you learn to recognise that, it grows, develops, and becomes eventually a relationship of communion.

If you try to force that communion through ritual, you will potentially short-circuit the natural development of the relationship: the communion will constantly be reliant upon ritual to open the doors rather than allowing the doors to open naturally, in which case they stay open all the time. It can be more frustrating to let it develop in its own time, but trust me, it is worth it.

And when you are aware that a guardian or guide has just saved your ass, thank them. I have been saved from disaster by guardians more times than I care to admit, and the process of saying thank you, and being aware of them, normalises the process of communion at a deep level within us, which in turn strengthens it.

6.2 Fate web of the family

The relationship of fate with families is a curious thing. We are heavily interwoven with those of our blood, whether we like them or not. And it does not need to be in a direct line: childless aunts can affect nieces and nephews and pass on skills sideways down a line through the children and grandchildren of their sisters.

Ten years ago I thought I had the family fate thing sort of figured out, only to find more recently that it is even more complex than I realised. Rather than write yet more volumes on the subject, suffice it to say that blood ties are strong, and when you do magic, it can amplify them.

It does not mean that the tie is strong to every one of your family members, but it does mean that key people within your line will be oddly connected to you in strange and energetic ways: you can have what I call 'collective fate' which is fate paths of a similar nature, or ones that are dependant on each other. You may not have anything to do with these family members, but even so, the connections can run deep, and waves of fate can wash through a family line like a tidal wave.

Because of this, when you work magically it can affect family members at a very deep level. Usually this is good. When you develop as a magician, you also develop as a soul and as a human. That development spreads out through your bloodline, and those who are linked strongly to you through fate will also benefit from your development. And that also is true for past family ancestors: the magical work you do today affects those who came before you as well as those around you and those who will come after you.

This is something to keep in mind when you make magical choices. It is healthier, however, for your family to benefit as a side effect of your magical work, rather than trying to work directly on your family, something which is fraught with potential pitfalls. A lot of benefit comes from the passive backwash from balanced magic: it positively affects your bloodline, the land you live on, and also you as a magician.

And this is another thing that you as a magician will find: if you do what you are supposed to be doing magically, you will never need to do magic for money, housing, or any other minor outer need: if you do your work in the way you are supposed to, what you need will come to you through outer means.

It took me a long time to trust this dynamic, but when I finally let go of the control (I am a control freak) and focused on what I was supposed to be doing, what I needed came to me as I needed it. It is all part of the fate weave: learn to work with your fate, get on with your work, and the guardians of your fate will do their job also. If you try to control it yourself, they will step back and let you get on with it, but they are far better at the job than you can ever be.

6.3 Fate and the wider world

In this day of internet and global communication, we are constantly bombarded with events and issues that are far removed from us. As magicians there is a great temptation to step in and work magic to affect world events in some way or another. This is folly for so many reasons, and yet to do nothing goes against our instincts. Those instincts were formed as the result of our cultural upbringing, and we have to recognise when that is surfacing: we assume our caring and compassion is our nature, when in fact it is our conditioning and being in a culure that is well-resourced.

When you step out of Western culture and live in a different country, you come to hear mantras like "eezz not my probleme." This is in an under-resourced country: the people focus on what is immediately around them. Start to see how simple facts of nature have a bearing on our expressions of culture at a deep level?

What I have found is that if you are meant to do something about an event or situation that is far removed from your family, land, and community, the job will be placed before you in no uncertain terms. And that job may often not be what you expected. Cultures, people, and landmasses all have their own fate paths and patterns, and to dabble with them, regardless of good intentions, can have disastrous long-term consequences for everyone involved. And you will be carrying the energetic consequences for the rest of your life. This is not theory: I have seen and experienced this for myself many times over, and am myself carrying the consequences of my own ignorant past.

But there are times when it is within your pattern to intervene, and if so, you will know about it very clearly. It is very unlikely to happen to you before you reach adeptship, as such work involves many different skills. The basic rule, which many do not like to hear, is simple: sort your own backyard out first. Once you are capable of working further, and it is right for you to do so, you will be placed in the midst of the situation so that you can effect change.

And that is all that you tend to usually do in these circumstances: you either mediate whatever is necessary to bring balance to a situation, or you mediate change. Sometimes, rarely, you are given a specific job to do, and when that happens you rarely get to know what it is you are doing until it is over.

This is to ensure that you do not inadvertently make stupid mistakes through misplaced emotion. I have been dumped into the middle of war zones, revolutions, contested elections, and epidemics; given a job to do, and then immediately taken back out of the situation. Most of the time I had no clue what I was doing until after the fact. Then it slowly dawned on me what I was working on.

This way of working seems alien to us in a world of 'knowing' and control, but it is precisely those dynamics of our modern world that short circuit deep magic. You have to learn to trust: we are simple workers in a vast, complex weave of fate, and we need to be humble enough to just do our jobs without wanting control or to be 'saviours.' Some people see that as being weak: I would say that is someone who does not know power.

A note on the practical work

Most of the following tasks are tarot readings. The skill of tarot has a major part to play in the work of a magician, particularly when working around fate, so lots of practice is a good thing. Because you are going to be looking at various fate patterns it will take a lot of energy, and you will need to spread these tasks out over a few days: don't do them all in one day, as it will drain you energetically.

Take your time with them and maybe spread them over a week or more. Expand out from the set questions and experiment if you wish to; just keep tight records, snapshots of the readings (or write down the cards in their positions), and type your notes up on computer so that you can go back to them or compare them in the future with other Quareia magicians who have done the same exercises.

Ensure that you wash your hands well with liquid soap, salt, and water after each reading session: you do not want to be carrying around fragments of the readings.

6.4   *Task:* Fate recognition

After you have meditated for the day, sit and think about your life from birth up to this point. Think about the places you have lived, the events that have happened to you, the choices you have made for good or bad, and look carefully at how certain key points, decisions, and actions have led onto better or key things in your life. Learn to recognise where fate has swept you along, and where you have had a defining input into your fate.

This simple exercise can start a process of learning and understanding within you of how fate operates around you. Obviously the older you are, the easier it is going to be for you as you, are more likely to have had major experiences in your life that are easily recognisable (though some youngsters do have a lot packed into their short lives!). Look for events out of your control, maybe ones that you fought at the time but that you eventually realised led to better things or to learning. Look for events that were a direct result of your own decisions. Think about how different (or not) they felt.

Also think about whether there were any signals you were given that you spotted.

For example, I have been moved around (from town to town and then country to country) a lot by fate ever since I was a little girl, and sometimes I moved by my own choice. Each time this happened, before I had made any decision or an event had happened that moved me on to another home, I would find it difficult to clean my house. No matter what I did, it always looked untidy or did not feel right.

It took me a long time to recognise this fate signal, but that is what it was. At a deep unconscious level somewhere, my fate weave 'pinged' to me that I no longer belonged where I was, and that it was time to move. That 'not belonging' manifested for me as the house not feeling comfortable, and for me not being able to keep it balanced.

Everyone will have their own unique 'pings' or signs that they will discover if they look back over events. Some are common ones, and some are totally unique to the person. So take the time to look back over your life to see if any have emerged for you yet. This pondering upon your own fate path is a very good exercise for you to do. It is good to look back through your own memory before you start to look using tarot: see what you can for yourself first, and then the readings will fill the picture out for you.

6.5   *Task:* Looking at historical fate patterns using tarot

Do a search for well-known historical stories in which someone within the event had a pre-warning of what was to come: Cassandra and the fall of Troy is a famous example. Once you have chosen the event, read as much as you can about it, any small details, oddities, etc.

Now get your tarot deck.

1. First do a reading using the four-directional pattern, and ask the question:

> "What inner forces were flowing into the event that triggered the person to have a precognition of the event?"

Look at what powers are showing in the east (coming/air/forming), south (here, at their height/fire) and west (starting to fade/population/water). Write them down, and look at the information the cards give you. What is your overall first impression? Is it obvious what was coming (the inner worlds shouting) or was it a subtle power that could still do a lot of damage once it manifested?

2. Then ask:

> "How did the event affect the fate of the person who had the precognition?"

Sometimes people have a precognition of an event that will not personally affect their fate in a negative way, but which will affect those around them badly (it is a precog of service to others). Other times the precog of an event is not just a warning for everyone else, but also for their own fate as well. Sometimes they are warned to get out of the way but not tell anyone else, and sometimes they are told what will happen, and that it will destroy them personally (they are given warning of their own death within the disaster).

When this warning of their own, as well as the collective doom, is pending, it is usually a major part of their fate and it will be ultimately productive for their soul/spirit: the warning is to prepare for the death, not to avoid it. See if you can discern which, if any, of these dynamics were playing out.

3. Now do a reading using the Tree of Life layout and ask:

> "What was the ultimate outcome of this fate pattern: was it for the good of the nation/people involved or was it to destroy them?"

Go by the last card in the reading (position number 10). Sometimes disasters are ultimately to push evolution forward, and sometimes they simply destroy and compost in order to make way for something different.

6.6 *Task:* Looking at your personal fate pattern with tarot

1. If you, in the past, have had a pre-warning about something in your life, a precog of something that then happened, do similar readings to the ones you have just done. Do a reading to look at what it is you were shown at that time (your keyhole/fragment view of the event), then look at the actual event (you get a wider picture), and then do the reading to look at what the ultimate long-term outcome was/will be for you. If you have not had an experience like this, move on to part 2 of this task.

2. Now think about your previous lessons in this module, and think about the dynamics of the Grindstone and Unraveller, their actions and effects in life. Think back to times in your life when these powers may have been active in your life, either through your own engagement/actions, or through fate inflicting them upon you. If you can identify times in your life when these powers were active, think about the situation.

Then do a reading, using the Tree of Life layout, and ask:

> "This situation, what was the longer-term outcome for my fate pattern, did it help me along or did it hinder my fate?"

If the reading showed that the action of one of these powers hindered you, then do a reading using the same layout and ask why.

It may show that it was because of your own action/reaction, or it may show some force outside of you hindering your fate. Write down the readings and think about the end card. The rest of the reading shows how the outcome came about.

3. Use the four-directional pattern (with the relationship card crossing the first/central card) and ask:

> "The situation I just looked at in my past, what were the deeper and longer term powers that were flowing through my fate pattern at that time?"

It may show harsh powers, regenerative powers, ancestors, deities, etc., or a mix. What it will show, as you are looking at your own fate pattern in a simple way, is what was needful then to get you where you are now. Read it in that context.

Lesson 7

Working with your Past

7.1 Crafting notes

The Cloth

For this lesson you will need a large white piece of cloth, either big enough to act as a cover that you drape around yourself, or large enough to cover the working space of your temple/work space floor.

If you want to work in the future with a magical shield that is placed around you, choose a simple, plain white cotton bedsheet that will drape over your shoulders and that is big enough for you to wrap yourself up in.

If you want to learn how to stand upon your shield (the magical floor), then choose a king-size or bigger piece of white cotton cloth that covers your working space. You can roll it up and put it away when you need to work magic that should not involve your own fate pattern.

The Cord

You will also need a length of cord. Measure it with you arms outstretched at your sides at shoulder height: it should be long enough to stretch from hand to hand with your arms held out, but it should be no longer that your outstretched arms: any length beyond your hands should be clipped off.

During this lesson, the fabric and cord will become 'tuned,' and then in Module V you will learn how to turn them into an enlivened magical tool: the Shield.

Altars

You should also have four altars for the directions and one for the centre by now. If you have been using bits of furniture etc. in the directions, that is fine, but it is coming to the time when you will need an altar for the centre that is only used for that purpose.

The cheapest and most mobile way to do that is to get a small but tallish fold-up table, similar to the ones used for camping or for garden furniture.

Whatever you use, make, or buy, make sure you can stand before it and touch it with your hands without having to bend over, that the surface is big enough to accommodate five candles laid out in the directional pattern, and that you can put things under it.

It does not matter what it is made from, though wood or metal is best. If you are really broke, make it yourself out of scraps of wood or even cardboard. If money is no issue, do not buy some fancy wild magical altar: it needs to be simple, clear, and mobile.

7.2 On the rest of the module

Now that you have had to plough through lots of reading and not much action, the final two lessons of this module will be more doing than reading. It was important for you to get a good understanding of some of the powers, dynamics, and beings involved in creation and fate before stepping into the work that you are about to do. To dabble in your own or anyone else's fate without any understanding can have all sorts of implications, some of which you will be now familiar with: that understanding will act as a caution for you, and make you think carefully before you step into any magical act that can trigger or change a fate pattern.

Before you begin to look and work with your own fate pattern, first you must learn to magically look back over your life so far, and learn how to *time jump* into sections of the life you have already lived. This can be a very interesting magical act that, once you have worked with it for a while, will change your view on spirit encounters, your view on time, and your understanding of how time does, or does not, affect inner actions.

This "going back before you go forward" is part of a power dynamic that roots you, grounds you, and slowly begins the process of stretching your spirit out like chewing gum until it becomes more fluid and your boundaries less rigid (it is an octave of the dynamic of "going down before you go up"). This in turn allows your spirit and vessel (body) to be able to work without too much impact when you start to work forward in time: it is like muscle exercise for the spirit, while also teaching you a great deal.

7.3 Passing into the past

In this lesson, you are going to learn how to go back into moments of your life and intervene if needed.

If you think of time as a linear path, this work will tie you up in knots trying to understand what it is you are doing. Time and events are very fluid and heavily interwoven: just learn to flow through time, and don't try to take it apart to analyse it until you have worked a great deal in the methods of flowing back and forth through time. That way, when you do come to analyse it for yourself, you will be able to draw on a good reservoir of direct experience that will help you understand it in a way that you can work with.

This method uses ritual as a gateway and vision as an interface to allow your consciousness to flow back through time within your own life pattern in order to observe, interact, and commune with yourself at an earlier age. This is not a psychological act: it is an active magical act that effects change beyond ourselves.

Think of your life not as a path you walk, even though we often magically work with 'paths' as an access point to the future. Think instead of a large fishing net with shiny things dotted around the fabric of the web. Think of time as spreading out from the centre, which is your conception, and the rest of your physical life flows around, upon, and within this 'net' like water. There is no real 'back' and 'forward'; it is more like, 'over here' and 'over there.' Changes made by revisiting events you have already enacted trigger the whole net to change in a constant evolution—your past, present, and future all change.

Learning to be more malleable with your understanding of time will stop you from blocking yourself by overanalysing—just do it, and then let the impact unfold slowly. Then you can think about it, and let your deeper instincts and the guardians around you gently nudge your understanding.

In the last few lessons, you have been casting your thoughts back into various events in your life so far, and have potentially done some readings about them. This has tuned you in a bit to remembering and recalling past events, what they felt like, what was happening, etc.

Go over your notes from those lessons, and then sit and think about times in your life where you may have felt total despair, helplessness, or a great deal of pain or anguish, fear, etc.: it does not matter how far back in your life you go, even if it was early childhood.

Once you have identified a key moment in your life when you were really suffering or were vulnerable, try to remember everything you can about that event: smells, sounds, what you saw, what you heard, what impressions you have of that time. Write them all down.

Build up the image of that incident/time in your mind until you have a clear feel or snapshot of it that you recognise.

A warning

This really is not a psychological working that you are going to do. It is active magic, and if you are successful you will trigger change in your life and the lives of others who were involved with you at that time.

The warning is not about danger, but about respecting the power that you are working with. Do not instigate an action thinking "oh it doesn't really matter, it's only all in my head and no harm will come": that would be a great folly.

For example, if you were the victim of an attacker in your past and you are going back to that point, the attacker and his/her fate and actions have nothing whatsoever to do with you: they are not your responsibility, nor is it valid to do an act of revenge, punishment, whatever.

Do not misuse this technique: it is solely about you, your own fate, your own life, and nobody else's. Overcome any temptation to meddle with anyone else.

Now it is time to get to work.

7.4 Practical Work

You will need your cloth, your personal pentagram pattern (with your planets, names etc. on it) and the length of cord. You will also need a cushion and a blanket to have a sleep on.

Leave yourself plenty of time to do this work, and ensure that you will not be disturbed.

Set up your working space with the altars in the directions, and place the pentagram pattern image inside the fabric (wrap the fabric around it) and place it under the central altar. Position the cord around the central flame in a loop.

Sit and meditate until you are still and settled, and think about the point in your past that you want to work with. Throughout this working, keep that time foremost in your mind. The process of stretching starts now.

When you are ready, get up, light candles in the correct manner that you have learned, open the gates using the method you have learned, and acknowledge any contacts stood on the thresholds: throughout this ritual keep a mental focus of intent to pass into a specific time situation.

Now go and stand before the central altar. This is your fate ground zero: everything you are, everything you have been, and everything you will be all begins here in the centre of the pattern, and the flame that is tuned to the centre of the pattern is resonant with the flame that burns within the centre of your being.

Spend a little time tuning in to the central flame in the magical space, and the central flame within your own centre: they are one and the same flame. The outer flame is an exteriorised 'twin' of your inner flame. The temple space is an exteriorised 'twin' of your own magical consciousness.

Once you feel fully tuned to the centre, circle the room, starting (as always in ritual action) in the east. Stop at each altar briefly to bow, while keeping awareness that east and south are the powers of 'future' and west and north are the powers of 'past.' When you reach the north, bow, and then stay in that direction.

Be aware of the contact at the threshold of the north gate. It may be ancestral, it may be faery, a land being, or an angelic being: whatever being it is, acknowledge them and state, using your physical voice, that you intend to pass through the gates of time and work with your younger self. Ask for guidance from the Noble One, the Sandalphon who stands behind you beyond the south gate.[1] Place your hands (or fingertips if it is low down) on the altar as you need to have physical contact with the altar.

You will do the vision aspect of this work standing up with your eyes closed (to stop

---

[1] Now that you have made visionary contact with them, they are likely to turn up in a lot of your workings, particularly key ones.

you falling asleep and getting into hot water inadvertently).

Close your eyes, and with your inner vision see the gate and the threshold of the north before you on the other side of the north altar. See the flame before you, and feel your inner flame: be aware of it resonating with the outer flame in the north. Remember that point in your past that you are intending to visit.

When you are ready, see yourself step *through* the altar of the north (it is important that you do not walk around it, but pass in vision through the body of the north altar) and cross over the threshold of the north with the intention of going to a particular time in your life that you have already pinpointed in your mind.

As you cross the threshold, you will find yourself standing in mist. Keep a mental focus on that point/incident in time, and keep focus on the intent to visit that time. Once you have total focus on that intent, start walking forward into the mist. You may walk only a few steps, or you may have to walk for a while until you come to a state where the mists begin to clear.

As the mists clear, you will find yourself stepping into a scene. It may take you a little time to orientate yourself, and it may also take you a little while to recognise your younger self in that scene (we often appear different in spirit than we do in body).

If you have arrived at a scene from your past that is not the one you intended, but is still an aspect/event of your past, stay with it: you will have been directed to that event in particular because you were more needful of work at that point in time than the event you had intended to go to.

Watch the scene passively as it unfolds around you. Do not get drawn into the emotion of the situation or the memories. This can be hard, but it is vital that you do not connect emotionally with the memory. Observe yourself in that scene, observe your inner energies (which may appear to you as lights or colours around and within you), and watch your emotions. There will come a crisis point where the lights within the body seem to dip as the full impact of the situation hits your younger self. It may be in the midst of the situation, or it may be the time directly after: just stay with the scene until you see that dip. Some magicians observe it as a dip in vibration, or sound, light, colour, scent: whatever shows around and within your younger self that is fluctuating.

When you see that dip, that is the time to get to work. As soon as the dip happens, that is the deep impact in your inner energies at that time, a dip that can be dangerous for you in terms of longer-term damage, and weakens the web both at that time and in your future.

Step over to your younger self and place your hands upon their shoulders, standing behind them (always behind them). If it is a particularly traumatising event, stand behind them and wrap your arms and your energies around them. Now allow your own vital force/inner flame to brighten and to spread around and within them: share your current strength and vitality with them.

Whisper into the ear of your younger self: tell her/him that it is okay, they are not alone, that they will flower, grow, mature, and go on to great things. Tell them they are guarded: let a feeling of safety, protection, strength and endurance flow into them from you. They may or may not hear you: it doesn't matter. What matters is that the dip is rectified by filling them with strength, and letting that young spirit know that they are going to be okay and that they are not alone.

Once you feel they are more stable, step back and immediately walk away back into the mists without staying around to see how they do: it is important with past work to leave immediately after you have finished what you are doing.

Walk through the mists with the intention of stepping back over the north threshold. When you reach the gate/the gate appears, step over the threshold, through the altar, and open your eyes. You or may not feel very tired after that working: if the event was a major hotspot in your fate weave, your intervention will have taken a lot of energy.

Lesson 7. Working with your Past

But you cannot rest just yet.

Now go to the central altar with the south beyond the central altar and the north behind you, and pick up the cord. Hold the cord out so that it stretches across your chest from east to west with the ends in your hands—your arms should be out at your sides, at shoulder length, with your left hand in the east and your right hand in the west.

Close your eyes, and see with your inner vision the gates of the south. Two figures immediately step through the threshold: one is the Noble One and the other is a mature woman in ornate clothing. The Noble One puts out an arm for the lady, and they walk together to the other side of the central altar and stand before you.

The lady is Lachesis, the Measurer (also known as Decima). She closely inspects the cord you are holding, and then she pulls out a cord from her robes and measures it against your cord: she is checking that your cord is indeed the right length. She indicates to you to give her your cord. Drop your arms, and hold out the cord over the altar (careful of the flame) to her side of the flame (the flame is always a threshold).

Lachesis places her cord into your cord so that they become one and hands it back to you: now lay it back down in a circle around the central flame—your ground zero and your measure are together.

Lachesis steps back, and the Sandalphon steps forward. The Noble One bends down and places his hands upon your sheet and pentagram pattern that is under the altar. He waits as something passes into the cloth/pentagram, and when he has finished he stands up, bows to the central flame, and then steps back.

Bow to Lachesis, the fate who measures life and to the Noble One, and watch as they withdraw back over the south threshold. Once they have gone, open your eyes.

Starting in the east, go to the east altar, bow, pick up the candle, and place it on the east part of the central altar. Do the same in the south, west, and north until the four directional flames closely surround the central flame.

Now lie down and have a sleep while the cloth, pentagram, and cord are cooking—and really do try to sleep: it helps to 'fix' this action in your spirit.

Once you have rested, however long or short that time is, get up, and before you put the candles out, take the cord, the pentagram, and the cloth. Roll up the cloth around the pentagram. Now tie it with the cord by wrapping it around and around the cloth, and tying a knot. Take the bundle and hold it to yourself for a moment: it will be charged with energy. Let your body and the bundle be in the same space for a few moments.

Find a safe place to store the bundle where it will not be messed with at all (you only take it out to place it under the altar when you work on your own fate). In Module V you will transfer the images on the pentagram pattern onto the fabric. Before that time, they both have to energetically 'cook' and tie in to each other. The cord is the binding of your own personal time, and it will hold and protect the fabric and image until they are fused together to become a specific form of shield.

If you feel up to it, and feel a need for it, this is something you can repeat at other times in your past if it is necessary, but only if it is really necessary—and if you do not observe a dip in the energies, do not take any action at all, simply observe. Watching your past experiences from this inner standpoint can be very interesting and revealing indeed: you sometimes see things from a totally different point of view and can often see how an event was a necessary occurrence that guided you towards something else in your future, or gave you strength or an experience that was needful for your development.

Spend a week or two experimenting with this method of stepping into your own past. Just don't overdo it, as it can take a lot of energy. Each time you do it, simply put the bundle under the altar (so that it gets more charging) and ensure the Sandalphon are standing at the south threshold. You would not work with

Lachesis again (she worked with you just to trigger the cord). You would simply light the directions, open the gates, go around the directions, and then step through the north gate with your focused intention.

7.5 *Task:* The Egyptian Book of the Dead

Note: Don't do the following task until you have done the visionary work. Always look up after the fact, not before.

Look up E. A. Wallis Budge's *The Egyptian Book of Going Forth by Day: The Theban Recension*, on the internet, and search for text and images that relate to the Net of Souls.[2] There are some search terms listed below and a link to Budge's analysis of the text. If you use that link, search within the text for the word 'net.'

In the Egyptian understanding of the cycle of creation and destruction of life, an understanding which was considerable, they considered rebirth as a lesser existence, and something that affected the common people. The king[3] and the senior priests & priestesses of the Mysteries[4] studied and practised hard within the Mysteries to avoid the net of souls upon their death.

Just as the individual has a web/net of fate, so too does a nation and a species (and everything else): like all creation, everything is octaves of everything else. Everything in creation works along the same patterns (recycling, I like it). The net of souls is the collective web of fate, and the hapless soul upon death becomes trapped in a cycle of rebirth (trapped by the net of souls).

The king and other highly initiated ones learned how to sidestep that pattern: the king in particular, along with other major players in the Mysteries would, upon death, go through a process whereby their body and spirit was carefully prepared in order to stay upon the land for a protracted length of time while also simultaneously 'residing with the gods' (hence a mortuary temple was called 'the temple of a million years'). Some details of this process will be covered later in the next module and again later in depth as an initiate.

This is just one example in the ancient cultures of a deep understanding of the fate process, and of also the process of the passage from human to deity. When you search the texts, you are not going to find much (there is not a lot), but you will find some things. If you then search the terms in Google images, you will start to see hidden things in the images that you will begin to understand and recognise. It is not all spelled out for you: these are the Mysteries hidden in plain sight. There will be objects, stances, hand positions, symbols, and much more that you will begin to recognise from your training.

Also do a search (sometimes an image search is helpful) to look at different ancient cultures and their knowledge of patterns (like the web of fate/net of souls) in relation to weaving creation and destruction. It is known in Tibetan, Greek, and Hindu Mysteries, for example. This research is not for an essay, it is for yourself: finding aspects of the Mysteries in different art, religions and stories will trigger deep memories, and can start opening many sleeping doors within you.

Regardless of what culture a human is from, if it is a temple culture, then it also has the Mysteries, and although there are slight differences in interpretation, the core essence, patterns, contacts, and powers are the same.

This is why I keep saying to you, that as you learn and experience things, so you will begin to finally see the Mysteries all around you in paintings, poetry, ancient temples, stories, legends, etc. They don't need to hide, because you need to understand the keys to see them. When you are an adept, you will revisit the ancient Egyptian texts, and other texts from all around the ancient world, and then you

---

[2] You need to look in chapter 153.

[3] The title Pharaoh did not come to mean the head of state until the Amarna/eighteenth dynasty in Egypt: before that, they were kings.

[4] Not all of the priesthood worked within the Mysteries: some were royal officials or basic temple attendants.

will really notice and recognise many of the magical techniques that you have learned.

7.6 Search terms and link:

- The Chapter of coming forth from the net.
- Vignette—A net being drawn by a number of men.
- The Chapter of coming forth from the fishing net.
- Vignette—Three apes drawing a fishing net.
- `https://ebooks.adelaide.edu.au/b/budge/eawallis/book_of_the_dead/complete.html`

Lesson 8

Working with your future fate pattern

Again, this is less of a reading lesson and more of a doing lesson. Get out your journal notes from when you were working with the Pentagram pattern in Module II (the one you now have wrapped up in the bundle), and reconstruct the pattern by drawing it out: the tools in the hands of the pentagram, the hexagram, earth sign, your name, your planet positions, etc. Map it out on paper.

What you are going to work on is the dynamic that opposes that of the past: you are going to do the early step of working on your future, working within your web of fate. This is not about changing your future, but about learning first how to recognise the inner aspects of your web of fate, the beings, powers, and aspects that flow through it and then tune into it. This visionary ritual exercise is also about meeting your guardian angel: the tentative first step in learning how to work as a team with your guardian angel.

Because of our modern culture, we think that changing our future directly will make things better, but because of the complexity of fate, it can often make things worse. It is wiser to fully optimise what is before you by recognising it, trusting it, and simply keeping an awareness of it. That conscious awareness of the weave, what it looks like, and being aware of the beings that work through it triggers deep shifts within you that lead to you being a co-driver of your own fate and not a helpless passenger.

This method works with ritual and vision combined, and is not an easy task to do, particularly for an apprentice. But some heavy lifting is good for you. It teaches you more respect for magic once you experience just how powerful and complex (and beautiful) it can be.

This visionary ritual works far more powerfully when done with a group energy around you; however, working alone with this is better for your training in the long term. Easier is not always better, and before you enjoy the boost of power levels that group work can bring, first you must slowly develop your own strength and independence, so that you are fully self-contained as a magician and are reliant on nothing but yourself.

We have looked at how fate operates like a web (or net), and how it has various hotspots, bumps, dips, etc. Those features are the tides that push humans along the process of life. But they are also potentials as well as drivers: potentials for development, self-ruin, destruction, renewal, learning, or vanishing into ignorance. We can become victims, or we can become active participants. The magician is the participant who connects with the raw material and joins in the process of turning it into something beautiful and unique. Before you can learn to participate, you must get to know your materials and know your co-workers.

One of the most powerful magical ways to participate is not to manipulate or craft; it is to observe with intention, which by itself enlivens the potential of the weave: your observation becomes a catalyst which triggers necessary change into action.

When you come across a difficult bump in your fate weave, before you look to see whether you can dodge around it, first look to see if it is a bump that can ultimately strengthen or teach you. Often difficulties are what help us evolve, and we must step up to those difficulties, find the gems hidden within them, and flower despite them.

One way to approach this is through the magical observation of your weave in action, and the other is to commune with the beings involved, observe your outer situation, and allow your guardian angel to guide you (without obviating responsibility for your own future). Sometimes a magician would use both.

Note that direct results magic is not used: not only is that silly, but it is also weak magically. This is one of those magical situations where less is more: a slight nudge triggers a huge movement, or an observation enlivens a sluggish pattern and triggers it back into action.

8.1 Hitting the blocks in the road

Sometimes you can come up against walls in your fate path: these can manifest for the magician as literally seeing in vision a wall or block that they cannot get around, or they can manifest in outer life by having every step forward you try to make being blocked.

When you see this or it happens, or you detect such a block in the fate weave, do not take on the mentality that you have to crash your way through it. Be more intelligent: step back, look at it, see why it is there, and from what you find, you will know if you have to just sit and wait, or if you have to find a way around it.

The way to step back and look at it is to use the visionary ritual method you will learn in this lesson: you will get a much wider view in terms of energy and weave as to what you need to do.

If you are in a truly dire or overly dynamic situation in your life, doing the visionary ritual of *Viewing the Web*, observing, and from those observations, while you are still in vision and have your guardian angel stood before you, thinking of an option for life action (or choosing a path forward at a crossroads) will trigger a response.

If the option is the right one, the beings and the web pattern will light up and become fully of vitality, and you will get a favourable response from your guardian (usually in the form of a smile). If it is the wrong option, the web will dull down, the beings will slow down, and the guardian will tell you by his facial expression that the option is not a good idea.

As an alternative to working in ritual vision, sometimes simply sitting and waiting is the best option. These blocks can act as a 'stop' or 'give way' sign: they are there to keep you in a holding pattern while something comes into form. Once that form is ready for you to interact with, the wall falls away.

The other reason the wall can appear is to stall you while your 'energy tide goes out.' Sometimes for magicians, if major changes, work, or developments are on the horizon, your energetic tide goes out in preparation. The wall serves as a block to protect you from overreaching your low resources until the tide comes back in.

Sometimes the block is there to teach you how to be mutable and move sideways. As my mother used to say, "when the door shuts, a window always opens," and she was right. When you come up against a block, first look to see if there is an alternative route or action: be like water and find a channel that you can flow down.

As a magician, the way to discern what block is doing what is to engage a variety of skills and tools. The first one is your own intelligence and common sense. The second is meditation and vision, the third is divination, and the fourth is patience and a sense of trust in your guardian.

Here is an example from my own life. In 2007 I hit a major wall in my life and magical work. I lost my job and my home, I was very ill, and my magical work ground to a halt. I went in vision and all I could see was wall after wall. I saw that some of those walls were a natural part of my fate, and others had been put there by another magician in order to block me.

I had huge responsibilities (supporting children and grandchildren) and yet every resource was whipped out from under me. I had three choices: use magic to remove all of those obstacles, wait, or 'be like water.'

I sat and thought about the overall picture of what was going on. Every resource was blocked and taken away from me: something big was going on that was beyond a simple magical aggression, and it was something that was important for me to recognise, understand, and work with.

I talked to my guardian and said that I did not want to shirk any lesson or challenge, but I was so under-resourced that I could not even think straight—yet it was critical that I made the correct decision. I was too weak to observe my weave, so I asked the guardian to help me see which direction I should be thinking about going in.

The day after, I had an enquiry from a company in Huston, Texas regarding a potential job. I flew from Nashville, where I was living, to Huston for the interview. Two minutes into the interview (which was an all-day interview) I started projectile vomiting. Not a good first impression. I was supposed to conduct an apprentice ballet class for the company, and I had to run to the bathroom every few minutes to throw up. My body would not work properly, my mind was fogged, and I could not properly demonstrate my skills and knowledge in classical ballet. Needless to say I did not get the job, and I had just wasted precious financial resources to get there.

I was too weak by this time to work in ritual vision on my fate pattern to discern what was going on and what was coming, so again I talked to the guardian. I said that I had gotten the message that I was no longer to work in my art form, but that I had no qualifications to work in most other jobs. I was too weak to take off the magic upon me, and combined with my own fate events that were unfolding, it was all too much for me.

That night I had a dream about the moorland where I was born. I finally got the message, and it made total sense: I had to go home to Britain, and take my daughter and grandson with me. Every other possible option was firmly closed to me.

We landed back in Britain with nothing but a couple of bags of personal belongings, a few toys for the baby, and enough money for few months. At my age, and after a lifetime of working hard, that is not a good state to find yourself in. We were essentially homeless, penniless, we were all sick, and I felt defeated.

But the land immediately responded to me, came into my dreams, and I felt I was where I was supposed to be, however hard it was.

I also noticed that by going with the flow of change, however much I felt defeated, the action of leaving the country voluntarily had loosened, and then cast off, the magical blocks upon me: I had essentially moved into the impact, not pulled away from it or tried to remove it. That had taken the power out of it.[1] This is a dynamic I knew well, but in my addled state I had not thought about it.

I talked again to my guardian.

"What next?" I asked.

The answer I got back was another question.

"Are you prepared to work hard?"

My answer was, "I am always prepared to work hard."

The guardian asked the question again, and I answered the same. After the third time, I simply answered "yes."

I felt the shift in my pattern immediately, and knew that no matter how hard things were, they were hard for the right reasons and I just needed to suck it up and get on with it.

---

[1] Using fate tides already in action can remove or 'burn up' magical blocks or binds: this is something you will learn about later, in another module.

Lesson 8. Working with your future fate pattern

It took nearly three years for the new path to come together for me and my daughter, and when it finally did form itself, I then understood why the wall had been so severe, and why the new path had taken so long to come back together.

The energy tide needed to go right out in preparation for the very long-term, powerful, and productive pattern that was about to come back in. Throughout that time, I had to stay my hand magically and not intervene: I was clearly made aware that I would have what I needed, so long as I focused on the future. The sheer force of the fate tide had washed away many things that did not serve me well, and when that tide came back in it brought wonderful things with it that I could not have even wished for.

The outcome is that I now live exactly where I need to be and in a situation that is optimum for me: a secure, affordable home in a wild and beautiful, quiet, powerful, and magical place. And I am doing what I am supposed to be doing: writing, teaching, and magically tending the land. I got all the healthcare that I needed so that my body could get back on its feet, and through a variety of interesting fate quirks, I connected up with all the people I needed to be in contact with for my future.

My daughter, too, ended up just where she needed to be, and is now flowering as a scientist. If we had not been forced back to Britain, there is no way she would have stepped into such an education as was available for her here, and her subsequent work would have not happened. It was a very tough time for her with a small baby in a different culture and with no resources, cut off from friends and familiar things. But she rose to the challenge, took advantage of the cheap education, and worked her ass off. She, also, trusted all the powers around her.

I tell you this so that you can see how major problematic bumps should not always be avoided (and often the really important ones cannot be dodged anyhow), and how you should not be terrified if you see large difficult obstacles in your path: learn to trust.

Sometimes they are there to shift you dramatically, to change what you do, where you are, and who you are with, so that you can flower into who you are supposed to be. If I had done magic to force my future into a picture that was to my liking, none of my books nor this course would have been written (and biology would not have gotten a talented researcher). You have to learn to trust, to always be willing to do your best, and to let the inner lot pick up the slack where you cannot. I was shown the edge of the cliff, but I was not allowed to fall off it.

This is why results magic can sometimes badly stall a wonderful future: short-term fixes can close many long-term doors. The key as a magician is to be able to look, ascertain, understand, and then act accordingly. Some disasters are not vital experiences for you to go through; but some are, and you need to slowly learn how to tell the difference. So let's get to work.

If you feel you need to do this work more than once, do not do it too soon after the first time. Keep it at least a month apart, do it on the new moon, and think carefully about the timing of it: if you are working on a Quareia lesson that is involved in destruction, exorcism, or is a lesson that is energetically hard work, wait until the next new moon after such work. Even though the work is simple observation, it can be a major stretch for your energies, and it would be easy for you to burn out. Learn to respect the fact that sometimes, seemingly simple magical acts can actually be very powerful indeed, and will take a lot of energy to do (conversely, you will also find that sometimes what can appear to be a major magical working uses little energy at all).

Resist any temptation to interfere with what you see: you must observe only, learn from the observation, recognise and acknowledge the beings and your guardian, and then leave it at that.

Read through the ritual more than once and familiarise yourself with all the keys, images, actions, and aspects: ensure that you know and remember it, then do it at the next new moon once you are ready (day or night, it doesn't matter).

8.2 Task: Viewing the web ritual

Note: after the visionary ritual there is a task to draw or paint something straight away. When you prepare to do the actual vision work, make sure you have the time and materials to get straight onto painting/drawing.

The following visionary ritual relies a lot on your own deep inner instincts. Because of this you need to let that instinct and inner sense rise to the surface. This will be easier for some than others: if you tend to overcontrol and/or overanalyse, be aware of that quality within you and keep it in check. This is about learning how to have visionary experiences that, besides imagery, also trigger energetic impressions. If you are too busy trying to interpret what it is you are feeling or experiencing while in the vision, you will kill the work. Sometimes those tight qualities are needful in your life, but like all things, the magician must learn to be the driver of their vessel, not its passenger.

Setting up

You will need the four directional altars and candles (but no central one), your bundle, and your sketch of your pentagram pattern.

Place the bundle directly in front of the south altar (future), ensuring that it is touching the bottom of the altar. Place the pentagram pattern you have drawn out just south of the centre of the space (so you have the copy before you and the original wrapped in the bundle).

You will be standing in the centre for some of this work (and looking down at the pattern for reference), so make sure the direct centre is clear. Put your art materials to one side, but within the magical working space (for energetic resonance).

Part one of the ritual

To start the work, because you are going to be working with and observing deeper powers, you need to properly tune and plug in the ritual space and yourself to the Divine powers and contacts that run through magic. This brings the room and yourself to the right frequency so that the work can be done.

To do that, use the second part of the *Hexagram Ritual* from Module II, Lesson 4: light the four directions, see the gates open, visit each direction, bow to the contacts on the thresholds, then begin part two of the Hexagram ritual.

Do that visionary ritual up to the point where you step into the empty Hexagram. Bathe in the silence.

Part two of the ritual

Turn a full circle clockwise on the spot, slowly, and end up facing south. Close your eyes, and in your inner vision see the south gate and the Noble One standing on its threshold.

The Noble One steps over the threshold, passes through the south altar, pauses to touch your bundle briefly, and then stands before you and bows. Bow back (physically and in vision). The Noble One then walks behind you and places his hands upon your shoulder—or he may place both hands upon your spine, just below the nape of your neck.

Open your eyes and look down at your pentagram pattern briefly, noting the positions of the planets. It does not matter if you cannot at that moment remember which planet is which: just let go and be aware of the positions around the pattern that the planets are in.

Now close your eyes again. Remember the Noble One still behind you, and be aware of the planets' positions around your space.

Hold out your arms (physically and in vision) to the sides, and 'see' the sword in your left hand and the cup or bowl in your right hand. Be aware of the power of Divinity above you and the land and ancestors below and behind you. Be aware of the path that vanishes into the distance through the south gate, and be aware of the beings of the sword and cup by the left and right altars. All the powers are now in place, and the space is tuned.

The Noble One places his right hand over your eyes, and tells you to look through their hand: the filtered vision of an angel. All of the beings, planets, tools, and shapes you had visualised shift and change to bright lights upon a web that you are standing in the centre of. They all have a similar energy colour of light to them, and they are all around you. Now you can drop your arms.

As you look, you notice other lights and shapes that are scattered all around your web. There may be many of them, or there may be only a few. Some will have a uniform shape, and some will be misshapen. Some will have bright lights and some will have dim lights. As you look, you begin to notice faint, ethereal beings with long fingers working in clusters around the shapes and lights: these are angelic beings that are constantly working on your web (and also on the web of every living thing) in a constant act of weaving, repairing, and disassembling aspects of the web.

The closer you look, the more you see, and you begin to notice that every single aspect of the web is a vital component: if one thing was taken out, the web would collapse. You also notice that the weave hooks into, and is a part of, the path that flows out to the south and into the mists of the future.

Focus your attention back to the beings working around your web. One seems larger and brighter than the others. As you watch this being, you notice that he is directing the others, guiding, helping them, and teaching some of them how to work on your individual web. As you watch him, he realises that you are focusing on him. The being finishes what he is doing and then walks over to stand before you.

As you look into his eyes, you see something you recognise at a deep level within you: you know this being. As your understanding begins to dawn, the being smiles at you: this is your guardian angel. You now begin to understand that the interventions, nudges, whispers, dreams, and feelings that you had were translations of this work that is being done constantly on your web of fate. As the angelic being worked on key hotspots, dips, and bumps, that work translated to you as warnings, protection, guidance, and advice.

Now that you have an understanding of your guardian angel, every time this being works on a critical point in your fate, you will become aware of them and what they are doing. That in turn will help you to make better decisions when you come to crossroads in your life. Before you can try to communicate with this being (they must always initiate the first conversation), the being steps away and gets back to work.

Turn your attention back to your web, and every time you look, you will see more and more tiny aspects, weaves, beings, and actions happening: your fate is complex indeed, which is why it is usually best just to let the beings who work in your fate get on with their job and you get on with yours. The Noble One takes his hand away from your eyes and steps back. He walks around you and stands before you, smiling.

Bow to him, and he bows back. He turns and bows to your guardian angel, and between them passes a recognition and understanding of fellowship. The Noble One walks back through the altar to the south gate, and as he walks, you realise that the ground, web, and pattern beneath him lights up: he is a guiding light for your future. He vanishes into the mists beyond the south gate, and the room once again appears to you in vision as your working space with the four altars and the candle flames.

Now open your eyes. The power is still going, the beings are still working away, but you bring your consciousness back to the living, physical world.

Go first to the east altar. Place your hands upon the altar, and be aware of the web connections that flow out of this direction and their connection into your fate weave. Step back, bow, and go to the south. Repeat the same action in the other three directions of placing your hands on the altar and just being aware of the connections these thresholds have to your fate weave.

When you step back from the north, go back to the east, bow, and put the candle out. Close the other three directions also. Place your bundle back in its resting place, and put the pentagram drawing into your journal.

Keep notes of any dreams, intuitions, or feelings that arise in the days after this working, those that you feel are connected to this work and to your future.

The working you just did is simple, and yet as you get used to it and repeat it, just to observe and nothing more, it will become more powerful. At some point in your magical training you will realise that you are becoming more aware of that weave around you all the time, and of the angelic beings that work with that weave. As an adept, you will develop enough focus to be able to tune into the weave instantly, without ritual support.

If you feel a tremor or shift in the weave, you will feel it in your energy, which in turn will alert you to the fact that something is happening, or is about to happen, that will directly affect you in some way or other.

This tuning ability comes with practice, and with learning how to work in vision, not only with images in your mind, but also with feelings in your emotions, your mind, and your body: your deeper senses develop in a way that cannot really be described in text; rather they have to be experienced. But you will begin to recognise them as they develop.

8.3 *Task:* **Painting the spider**

Paint or draw (and do this as quickly as possible after your visionary ritual work so that the energetic resonance within you can pass into the picture) a picture of a spider in the centre of a web that has the bright spots upon it: the web that is your fate pattern.

The spider has the weaver power and is deeply connected magically to the weaver goddess and the angelic beings that work on the web of fate. This is why many magicians, including myself, have a great deal of respect for spiders, and treat them with care and respect. A magical house will attract spiders, and they will take up residence in directions around the house where the most energetic threat tends to come in from: they start working with you in a passive way.

If you live in an area where some spiders are dangerous, and yet you wish to work magically with them, mark out a territory. What I used to do when I lived with black widows is that I developed a routine whereby the floors, corners, and low places where they could inadvertently cause harm or be harmed would be constantly cleaned, vacuumed, and have cleaning products put on them that spiders don't like. But the high places, crevices, disused storage spaces, etc, in the house were theirs, and they were not disturbed. They figured this out pretty quickly and stayed off the floors, furnishings, etc., and hung out in cracks and crevices nearer the ceiling and roof space.

Whenever I was under threat, or a dangerous tide of energy was coming in, they would all appear and would gravitate to the north wall in the house: they guarded the death threshold, and their weaving/hunting power stopped things coming into the house from that direction that should not be coming in.

Back to the drawing. Place the finished drawing or picture in the south of your working space, either on the wall or hidden somewhere. It does not matter if it is displayed or not; however, it is important that you remember it is there, and that you keep that awareness.

The energy that is around you from doing that visionary working will flow into the picture. You are placing her in the south to focus her power on the weaving of the future—your future. It is a simple, passive form of magic: the resonant image of an old power is placed in a direction where you wish that influence to flow. South is your future path. North is protection against death.

Move her around as needs be, but only put

her in the north if you are truly under real threat, either from death magic (which will come once you are an adept and you manage to piss off enough magicians), or if there is serious illness in the house.

Simple, passive magic like this does not stop things altogether; rather these things act as filters by downing the power levels of incoming energies: they slow things down, which then gives you enough time to notice and deal with the issue.

The fact that you have met Lachesis in vision, have observed your own web, and have stood in full consciousness within the resonant power of that web, enables you to pass on an echo of that power into a picture if it is done straight after the working. It is another step towards enlivening and empowering objects fully.

8.4 *Task:* Research

Look up myths and legends to do with spiders and the web/weaving of fate. Take notes, and see what you are drawn to.

Apprentice Module IV

Death, Birth, and the Underworld

Lesson 1

Overview

Before you move on to working with enlivened magical tools (your next module), and before you also begin the process of stepping into the inner realms in any depth, it would be wise to lean about the other side of the coin of creation.

That opposing side of creation has two aspects: *death*, and *destruction*. Because they are so complex, I will address them in two separate modules. We will look at destruction a bit later in the apprentice section. In this module we will look at and work with death and the Underworld.

The reason it is so important to look at this subject matter before you get to tools, temples, beings etc. is that understanding death is a major protector for a magician, and it helps you to spot those 'death hotspots' in your weave. When you wield an enlivened magical tool, you become visible to beings and powers that you were previously invisible to.

Interactions with those beings can inadvertently trigger one of those hotspots, and although triggering one will not necessarily put you in a death pattern, it can make your life a misery as it will cause discord in your pattern. That discord comes from not knowing certain powers that are coming at you, not understanding how to operate around those powers, and not being properly rooted.

The rooting of a magician is a key element in training that again, like many other aspects of magic, is woefully lacking in modern magical training. That rooting comes from understanding death, and magically going into the Underworld within life so that you understand and are familiar, through practical magical experience, with the Underworld and the powers that flow in and out of that realm. Through the rooting action, you are strongly anchored in the foundation of your ancestors, and anchored with an aspect of yourself in the Underworld: you have to go 'down' before you can go 'up.'

You have touched very briefly on this mechanism both in vision and in ritual, but now it is time to learn this aspect of magic in more depth, both in practical and theoretical terms. Once you come to wield magical tools properly, and step deep into the inner worlds, you will then understand why you had to do this work before you came to play with cool things like swords, wands, and all the glittery things that make magic so fashionable: if you are going to do it, do it properly!

Most (not all) of today's magical training puts tools into your hands in your apprentice stage, and does not begin to teach these Deeper Mysteries until much later (and most frequently these days, not at all). I have found that to be a self-defeating folly: know the powers *before* you work with them.

Many magical systems train their initiates with these tools without the initiate being rooted, and without gnosis of what each tool truly is: what tends to happen in such circumstances is that either the work quickly devolves down into ritual drama with no power, or the magician slowly starts, mentally or emotionally, to fall apart.

The other dangerous thing that happens, particularly if the initiate is a natural magician, is that they find themselves suddenly visible to all manner of beings, some of whom aggressively challenge them, and they have no knowledge of what to do, how to deal with it, or even what it is that is challenging them.

When you learn about and then work with death and the Underworld, it changes you at a very deep level: it completes a loop of power while you are still in life. That loop of birth and death is a pattern of all living things, but when a magician completes that loop in life, in gnosis, it takes them out of the uncontrolled endless pattern and puts them on a very different path. Passing through death while in life as an Initiate is a deep visionary process, and is one that is essential for any serious magician to do. The preparation for that visionary work comes during the apprentice phase of training.

I used to throw early students into the death vision when I trained groups, but I found that by doing it too early, it had a negative affect on their progress. Now, in hindsight, I have learned to tread a bit slower with students, to get them firmly anchored in mind, spirit, and body so that when they do step into the death realms as an initiate, they are truly solid and ready for work.

These days, many magical training groups have forgotten that the death-in-life work is an actual magical act, and instead they approach it as a 'self development' psychological ritual of a 'new start.' That is all well and good, but it is not the magical death within life.

As an apprentice, you learn to connect, recognise, and work with the beings that work in death; you learn to connect and work with beings that operate in the Underworld; and you learn to grow roots like a tree that hold you firm in the face of destructive power. These skills and keys put helpers and guardians in your path, and you learn to navigate, recognise, and work with the stronger powers, beings and deeper realms in a productive, safer way.

For this overview introduction lesson, we will look briefly at the various aspects of this subject matter that will then be addressed and worked with in detail in the lessons of this module, and you will be given some reading suggestions on some of the topics. I do not think it necessary, at this stage, for you to read in depth the various heavy tomes of death and the Mysteries (that is something you can do later, as and when you feel it is necessary), but it is necessary at least to be aware of the various writings, and have a basic idea of their approach, the reason for the writings, and a general understanding of the methods used in death (from a magician's perspective) by various ancient and not-so-ancient cultures.

This in turn will prepare you for the coming lessons of this module that go into depth on the subject, so that you can get deeper into the subject matter, both in theory and in practical magical work: once you have a good basic understanding of the subject matter, you will find the coming lessons a lot easier to understand and work with.

In these short overviews, I will not go into explanations or discussions as such; rather it is just to outline the subject matter and give you chance to do a bit of your own research before you are plunged magically into the Death Mysteries.

1.1 Death in general

Before we get into the magical Mysteries of death, let's just ensure we are all on the same page, as there is so much bullshit written about death, and also so much religious programming that is warped and twisted.

The current Western religious view on death is that death is something to be terrified of, and that whether or not you were 'good' will determine where you go: either 'up,' or into holding, or 'down.' There is also an idea that if you confess your 'sins' on your deathbed, all will be well—which is not true.

Death is seen as abhorrent, and very few Westerners have ever seen a dead body. When a person dies, they are whisked away, sanitised, held in a freezer, and then suitably disposed of without further family contact with the body. This is all very unhealthy for the living and the dead.

Most modern secular thinking is that after you die, it's lights out and goodbye. On the other end of the scale is the belief that you will 'pass down a dark tunnel' and emerge in a happy landscape with all your loved ones and live a surreal life with no mortgage.

These different religious and secular views are degenerate, and they show just how low we have sunk into a magical/mystical dark age.

There is also a view of reincarnation that either plays into power games—"it's your lot to be poor; shut up and suffer"—or into fantasy—"I was Mary Queen of Scots, you know…" The number of times I have heard that is enough to give me eye strain from rolling my eyes. Moving in magical circles, I sometimes have to venture into areas that wallow in New Age fantasy. In Glastonbury, for example, the number of folks who think they are the reincarnated 'Jesus,' Merlin, Morgan le Fey, etc. is hysterically funny and depressing at the same time.

As a people we have become disconnected from the experience of death, and of the experience of the Mysteries that lie beyond it. This disconnect becomes very apparent in magicians who have not managed to step outside of this soup of ignorance, and many leave themselves prey to fake mediums, spiritualists, or seers (which are many), New Age nut-jobs, religious idiots, and wishful thinking. Some magicians and magical groups do work in death properly, but they are in the minority and tend to work under the radar.

We can also track, like many other things about the Mysteries, the evolution and devolution of death gnosis by looking at the texts, myths, belief systems, and artistic expressions of cultures. From the powerful mystical evolution expressed in the Pyramid texts, through the less balanced results magic of the Papyrus of Ani, to the degeneration in Christianity and beyond. This same evolution and devolution can also be tracked in Judaism, Greek Mysteries (before and after Greece's dark age), Tibetan, Indian, and so forth.

In Lesson 2 we will talk about death in general. We will look at the dying process from a magical perspective, track the post-death process from a magical perspective, and look into dismantling some of the dogmas we have clung to that serve only to bring difficulty and ignorance.

To help you prepare for that, look into different cultures and how they act with the body after death. Some cultures bury the body straight away, take down pictures of the dead person, and refuse to mention their name. Some cultures dig up the bones of their ancestors once a year to have dinner with them (yes…interesting). Some keep the body in the house and go through certain rites over a period of days before they are finally buried (how I grew up).

Get on the internet and find out what you can about different approaches to death. Look at different cultures, but not at New Age/modern magical death stuff, which is mostly psychology and modern constructed religious feel-good babble. You don't need to do any deep reading, just get an overview.

1.2 Death and the Mysteries

This is where death starts to get interesting. A magical understanding of death, and the ability to pass into the realm of death in order to work, is a major stepping stone for a magician. Every Mystery system around the world has, at some point or other, discovered, worked with, and then written about the realm of death. The realm of death is not a standalone realm; rather it is a part of a much bigger picture of a realm that exists within, around, and which is woven into the manifest world: it is the inner world of which the outer world is a physical manifestation.

Some ancient cultures worked within the inner realm as a part of their physical mystical life, while others strived to leave the physical world behind and step into the inner world as the 'real world.' The Greeks and early Christians were some who took this escapist approach. As an understanding of the guardians and gates of this realm became more known, the magician priests and priestesses of certain cultures figured out how to try and dodge these guardians and bypass natural spiritual evolution.

Whenever this manipulation appeared in a culture, that culture then began its descent into ignorance. The key is not to dodge, lie, trick, or bully your way through these guardians by having the right names, the right tale to tell, or the right ritual actions, but to enter these realms in a clear and balanced way so that the guardians recognise you and let you pass voluntarily.

One thing that does become apparent in virtually all of these ancient cultures is a similar attitude to rebirth: that reincarnation is for the lesser mortals. As one ancient Egyptian text put it:

> "Being trapped in the net of souls[1] is for the common man."

The key was (and is) to develop well as a magician and a human being, to become recognised as such by the inner world guardians, and to flow through the inner worlds in magical work until you have a deep soul level understanding of how balance works (this is why the Scales feature so strongly in some ancient Mysteries).

Then, when the magician dies, he or she can make a choice, a conscious choice born out of necessity, and decide where and how they wish to move forward: do they need for some reason to come back into life, or do they wish to stay in the inner realms on the threshold of the manifest world in order to work with the living, or do they need to move deeper into the inner worlds and step out of the pattern of the manifest world completely?

---
[1] Rebirth.

Not only is it important, vastly important, for the magician to learn about death in life for his or her own death, but also because of the massive unfolding that triggers as a result of that work in the magician's life: essentially it is one of the key actions that plugs you in. This is why the 'death in life' features so strongly in ancient Mystery cults, where it either shows as death visions/rituals, or a 'passing into the Underworld and traversing of the stars.' Remnants of that can be seen in the well-meant but essentially useless psychodramas around death that we see in today's modern 'Mystery cults.'

Here is a list of things to read/look up. These are just a small selection of texts from around the world: should you wish to delve deeper/wider into more ancient cultures, read the list below first, as it will then help you to spot the Mysteries in other cultures.

Browse through them so that you get an idea of what approach that particular culture is taking at that time. Some of the text and images you will now begin to recognise; many you will not at this stage of your training. Don't try to psychologise or philosophise around the texts; just let them sit with you and let the imagery surface in your mind, and compare it with what you already know. And you do not have to study these in depth—that is not necessary, and in my opinion would be counterproductive to you at this stage. Just look them over, dip in where you are drawn, and then ponder on the words.

The Tibetan Book of the Dead: The Great Liberation through Hearing in the Bardo

This is a complied book that tries to codify and organise what are essentially very different writings. When Walter Evans-Wentz came across these various writings, like every organised Westerner, he had to control it, bring it into order, and make it fit things he already knew.

So this book, which is presented as a coherent path through death, is not how it is, or was, used. Interactions between the living and the dead, and between the living and the inner worlds, are not neat and tidy, and do not follow a linear path that is easily mapped.

So when you come to look through this book, keep it in mind that these writings were, and are, used in a more fluid way (and the same goes for the Egyptian ones), and not all were used; nor is it a 'bible' of Tibetan Death Mysteries. Each area and each lineage had their own version, and in truth it is a series of scattered writings that are drawn upon.

Note, however, in the title the emphasis on hearing. Knowing what you now know about sound, utterance, and the power of the word, that will give you more insights. These texts are spoken to the body of the dead person, as the spirit/soul stays near the body for quite some time. Not only do they tell the spirit what to do, but the utterance of a Mystery also changes the web, the power, and the space around the newly dead person's spirit: it is also a form of assistance.

The Pyramid Texts

These are early texts from Old Kingdom Egypt, and display quite clearly the knowledge of how to traverse the inner realms and step from mortal life into the deep realm of the deities. The fact that they were written down—inscribed on the walls of the tomb of King Unas—tells us that Unas, the last ruler of the 5th dynasty, knew that things in his culture at that time were falling apart.

When a Mystery cult is at its height, its secrets are handed down mouth to mouth, and its magic is uttered but never written. Only when the culture or religion is on a sharp descent are the Mysteries written down and sent into the future so that they will be waiting for the next period of renewal (something that is also a feature of the Tibetan Mysteries).

We see this by the events that followed the reign of Unas: discord, conflict, and famine came as a result of the imbalance in the structure of Ma'at within the kingship. We will look into this in more depth in the lessons, as it is an important Mystery dynamic. In Lesson 2 we will look at the Mystery behind the Pyramid texts, as they are an ancient wisdom regarding magic, death, and death/life existence.

To prepare for that, as well as your own browsing of the Pyramid Texts, look up the following excerpts from the *Pyramid Texts of Unas:*[2] Utterance 224 *plus the postscript*, and Utterance 690. Once you have worked with the Mysteries in the lessons, come back to these excerpts, as you will understand them better.

```
http://www.pyramidtextsonline.com/
```

The Book of Coming Forth by Day (Papyrus of Ani)

You have already visited this text in the last module. Now you will look a bit deeper, but ensure that you have looked at the Pyramid texts first.

Whereas the Pyramid texts outline the passage of the Divine Transformation of the King, and that transformation is very dependant on the king's upholding of Ma'at in his life and spirit, the Papyrus of Ani, covering the same death/Underworld passage, approaches it more from of an aspect of magical manipulation. It outlines how to dodge the guardians, how to lie, cheat, and use magic to get past the various threshold keepers.

This Papyrus also reflects the change from the exclusive passage of the Divine King to the passage of anyone who can afford to pay the magician priests to give them the secrets and have them inscribed on their tomb walls. This is the mid-point of the descent of the Mysteries of Egypt.

Pay particular attention to the forty-two Negative Confessions. Remember your work with the Grindstone and the Unraveller, with the Threshing Floor, and the practice of reviewing your mistakes and learning from them so that you learn to self-limit in life? The forty-two Negative Confessions tell the dead person how to answer the challenges of the Keeper of the Scales, and the texts also hold a spell to stop the heart (spirit) from telling

---

[2] I am using Raymond O. Faulkner's version, but there is also a very good book on the Pyramid Texts by James P. Allen.

the Keeper that you are lying—the living consciousness will lie, but the deeper spirit (heart) always tells the truth, which is why it is the heart that is placed upon the Scales.

You start to see the degeneracy from living in balance to pretending to have lived in balance. You can track this degeneracy, and how it affected the nation and the religion, by looking at the various Mystery texts in parallel to the chaos in the nation: conflict, famine, etc.

The Book of Am-Tuat

> "He who knows these words will approach those who dwell in the Netherworld. It is very very useful for a man upon Earth."
>
> —concluding text of the Second Hour

The Book of Am-Tuat (Duat) tells the dead king about the various thresholds and guardians in the Underworld so that he may traverse them safely and ascend into the sky to traverse the sky like/with Ra.

This text first appeared as a complete work on the walls of the tomb of Thutmose III (18th Dynasty, New Kingdom) and unlike the Papyrus of Ani, the book of Am-Tuat was reserved for the king. So we see an attempt to return to the inner progress of the Divine King—and yet it is still littered with the results magic that we see in the Papyrus of Ani.

Look through the text, which tells the king what, and who, resides in the Underworld, and see what you think about what was going on in the Mysteries at that time in Egyptian history.

1.3 Working magically in death while alive

One of the things we will explore and work with at an apprentice level is working with and in death while still being alive. Although you will not step into death fully until you are at Initiate level, standing on the thresholds, observing, and seeing the beings that work in death are major parts of your leap forward in the Mysteries.

From there you learn to work with the newly dead in this realm, and also in the death realm. It is part of the work of a magician to work with the newly dead where needed and appropriate, and before you can get to that level of work, you first need to know how to ascertain if a newly dead person needs help, and when it is best to leave them to it.

Not quite on this topic, but related to everything within this module, is a short piece of writing by Plato that is very pertinent to this subject matter. That piece of writing is called *The Vision of Ayr the Armenian*, which appears in Plato's Republic. You may have already read this. If you have, then read it again in the context of the subject matter of this module. If you have not already read it, then now is the time to do that. It is not a long piece at all, but it is packed with very illuminating aspects.

1.4 The dead in the living world

One of the things that is really useful for a magician to learn about and work with is the knowledge of the dead in the world of the living. The most common ones that we in the Western world encounter are ghosts, sleepers, and ancient ancestors.

We will look at the issues around hauntings, the various problems that arise when a spirit stays around the living, and how to recognise when there is a problem.

1.5 The Underworld and the Abyss

Knowledge of and practical familiarity with the realm of the Underworld is essential for all magicians, and the earlier you connect with it, the better. Volumes have been written about the Underworld and Abyss in modern terms, but few of those tomes even begin to touch on what the Underworld and Abyss is about.

In ancient writings you have to stretch back pretty far to find a good outline of this realm, but another way of having a preview of it before we get to that lesson is to sit and look at the paintings of William Blake.

In fact, the works of William Blake are a wonderful example of magical art: he was touching into some very deep visions and realms with his work. The filter they flow through is Christian: Blake had a strong connection with the Divine as connected with via the Christian filter, and yet he considered the church and its structure to be not worth the time of day (sensible man). He was an eccentric and a visionary: for you as an apprentice magician to spend time looking through his paintings would be time well spent indeed.

The paintings will not tell you directly about the Underworld and Abyss (or the inner worlds and angelic beings, of which he painted many), but the true inner knowledge and power that flows through these paintings will touch you deeply indeed.

The lesson on the Underworld will take you on your first steps of visionary descent into the Underworld so that you can begin the preparation process that will lead to the act of stepping into death while in life: something that you will do as an initiate.

1.6 Inner contacts and inner adepts

The lesson on inner contacts and adepts will take you through the process of how these people come to step into the inner worlds in service. These people, who once lived as adept magicians and priests/priestesses, are an invaluable source of support, advice, assistance, and guidance to any magician wishing to work with any level of power. You will also learn how to work in vision with these contacts, how to connect with them, and how to access and operate through the inner structure known as the Inner Library: a central and critical visionary interface for magicians.

1.7 The Bound Ones

The last lesson in the module looks at the phenomenon of the Bound Ones, humans and other beings who are bound up and held within the Desert and the sands of death. Although as an apprentice you will not work around this issue, it is an important one for apprentices to know about: it directly links in to what you learned in the last module and will deepen your understanding of some of the powers and dynamics that flow through life and death.

1.8 Summary

Read and take notes from the suggested texts—and as I said earlier, there is no need to read all of the texts completely;[3] rather it is just a matter of getting used to the texts. It is also simply about getting more of an idea of what particular cultures were working on in terms of the Mysteries and death, and looking at how they approached them, for good or bad.

Once you have read what you need to read and have taken some notes for yourself, then it is time to move straight to the next lesson. Have your notes and the texts handy.

If you can, acquire a copy of *The Pyramid Texts*: of all the books listed in this lesson, this is the one to own in the flesh. Keep it close to you throughout this module, and if you wish to experiment with sleep/dream learning, place the book over your head (on a shelf) or under your pillow at night: sleep with the book.

This is a very old-fashioned way of working, and one which recognises that some texts, just by their sheer subject-matter, carry power and connection with them. I used to do this in my twenties when I could not penetrate the meaning of a text. I would sleep each night with the book, and slowly but surely a sort of strange understanding of the book began to surface in my mind.

It was not that I read the book in my sleep; rather it was that my spirit interacted with the energies of the book and the energies of the Mysteries portrayed in the text: I 'got it' at a deep level. It works for some folks and not others, and can be a fun experiment.

Write down any pertinent things that come to mind, any 'ah-has,' and any understandings

---

[3]Other than the *Vision of Ayr*—read that whole vision, which is quite short.

that come to you from reading the texts and looking at the pictures. Later, you can compare those understandings with what you have learned and discovered by the end of the module.

Lesson 2

Regular Death

Before we get to the Inner Mysteries, where we will look how magicians work and pass through death, let's first look at the actual dying and death process in general.

What follows here is based on my own experiences of death and from working with people who are dying or who recently died. I realise that I probably only understand about 10% of what there is to know about the death process from an inner point of view, and I do not want to write from theory or conjecture. It is important that every step in this magical path of Quareia is rooted in experience, not theory.

There is a lot of theorising written about death in magical circles. Some of it touches upon real experiences, but a lot is theory from old texts and the conclusions drawn from those texts, along with a peppering of modern thinking. But as a magician, your work must always be grounded in direct experience, and by the time you come to the latter part of your training you will have had plenty of experience, both through this course and through things placed in your path that you can draw upon.

So although I am writing from that 10% pot of experience, it is consistent experience, and working with that experience has brought profound change not only to me, but to those whom I worked with and around.

Most (but not all) death work, in magical terms, is vision work, divination, charts, and inner contacts. There is some ritual work, but not a lot: it is a process of interiorising for the spirit, not exteriorising. So the magician would not use a lot of ritual work other than to open and close gates, or to lay paths, give shelter, etc.

Let's look at the process first from the act of dying and go in deeper a step at a time. I will give practical information for you, as you are very likely to be put in a position of having to deal with someone who is going through the death process: the more you do magic, the more you are put to work.

2.1 Slow Death

The first aspect of dying we will look at is the *slow death*. This is the most common aspect of death that you as a magician will likely be prompted to work with, particularly if you are also clergy of some sort. The majority of Pagan/occult ritual and information about death tends to focus on the family left behind, but there is very little for the actual person who is on the threshold of death.

When someone is going through a slow death, for example someone with cancer, the spirit is usually already stretching itself out upon a web pattern of energy that is about *lives*, not merely this life. Remember your web of fate? There is another octave of this and that is the *web of lives*. Just as your web of fate has hotspots on it, the web of lives also has hotspots, and those hotspots are different lives.

As the body engages with the dying process, sometimes (not always) the spirit/soul starts stretching out in search of a new hotspot or life within its fate pattern that it can manifest through. This process shows very clearly in divination: the readings often show the new life and new parents lining up before the old life is completely finished. It seems to be an instinctive rather than a conscious impulse.

If a person has lived their life in a very closed-down[1] way, totally devoid of any mystical, magical, or spiritual consciousness, they are prone to be constantly seeking a new life. As the old life draws to an end, the soul desperately casts around its web of existence looking for a new life to connect into.

By "closed-down" I mean someone who is wrapped up in their own life of consuming, and is totally unaware of anything else around them. It is not about religion or being a spiritual person or a mystical person; it is more a matter of them being either *switched on* at a deep level, or *switched off*.

For example, someone who is nonreligious, non-magical, etc. but has a sense of awe at life, who is aware that their actions affect others (not in a moral sense, but in a true sense), and feels at a deep level that there is something more—that is a *switched on* person.

By contrast, someone who is only out for themselves and is totally unaware of life around them, who fills their life with what suits them best to the detriment of everything around them, and who has no problem destroying others to get what they want when they want it—that is a *switched off* person. As they lie dying, their need to get what they want—life at all costs—drives their deeper spirit to cast around for another life to slip into. And so the pattern of life and death without any conscious engagement continues.

Someone who is switched on is less likely to line up another life while they are still dying—though it does happen; or else the stretching out comes a bit later when they are closer to the point of death. Someone who is very switched on will not cast about at all: the spirit stays still, waiting, and as they pass through the death process, *then* you start to see in divination the crossroads of choosing. It can be very apparent in readings to see a person like this spending time in stillness and waiting.

Back to the dying person. Even if the person is unconscious or in a coma, *they can still hear*, either in a physical way or in a spirit way. It is really important to communicate with the dying, as most people tend to be terrified at that point.

This can be seen in a person who is unconscious or semiconscious and is hyperventilating from fear: it is a common occurrence and causes a lot of unnecessary suffering. On the medical side, this should be immediately addressed with Valium or something similar to calm the person down. From the magical side of things, this should be addressed by talking to the person using mediated utterance. By that, I mean talking using empowered magical speech.

This can take the form of simply talking to them to calm them, and telling them it is going to be okay, but doing so with the gates open behind you, the contacts or Noble One beside you, or through mediating the Divine Breath as you speak.

This is at its most powerful when you are reading out loud or recounting a sacred text connected to death or prayer. By doing this, it stills the space around the dying person, reaches the deep spirit, and calms them to a point where they are less likely to rashly jump or cling to another life in panic: it gives them breathing space.

The other thing to do is to hold their hand and allow your deeper spirit to talk to theirs. This is a good way to work if you are in a hospital room full of people and with a person trying to die peacefully amongst noise, family, and bustle.

Holding the hand of the dying person,

---

[1] And this is where I stumble with vocabulary (because I don't have one) so bear with me if I am clumsy...

while also mediating the void within you, and opening the gates in your mind while also chatting to the people around the dying person is a profound service to the dying: that takes skill and focus, but it is a great service. The chatting normalises the space for the dying person—the breathless reverent silence or whispers around a dying person can be counterproductive to a stressed-out spirit.

Normal chatting, while also conducting deep mediation across the thresholds, can make a major difference to a dying person. The reverse of this is true if the person is dying in gnosis: when a magician or priest is dying, often they need calm and quiet in order for their spirit to start lining itself up for death. Quiet companionship is a great service under such circumstances.

From the dying person's perspective, they are withdrawing more and more from the outside conscious world, and many drift in a semiconscious haze (if they are not in a coma), so bear that in mind.

One thing I have seen over and over again which I find interesting, is that many times, when a person is in a coma or unconscious, they sometimes wake up just at the point of death. If you find yourself at a bedside, just be ready for that, just in case, and be ready to hold the gate wide open for them (something you will learn later in this module).

Slow deaths of magicians, priests, and priestesses

If a magician (or priest/priestess) is dying, they should already know what they are doing and what is happening to them. What they will need, if you are in attendance, and if it is possible is this: the four directions lit, the gates wide open with the inner contacts on the thresholds, the underside of their feet anointing with consecrated oil, moisture upon their lips, and their enlivened vessel/cup in or by their right hand.

Let's take a moment to look at the 'whys' behind those ritual actions, and bear in mind that they all have a very good reason to be done. And this is why it is preferable to die at home rather than in a hospital bed, so that the ritual actions can be attended to.

First we will look at this from the perspective of the dying magician. The optimal situation for a dying magician or priest/priestess is a death that is not only medically eased (pain relief) but is also *magically* eased.

The gates should be open (the directions opened), and the gate of the west should be *widely* opened, which involves someone opening the gates, having two candles instead of one[2] to light the threshold, and the view of the death vision triggered beyond the gates.

The anointing of the feet with consecrated frankincense oil is an old and deeply powerful, simple magical action: the feet carry the person into death, and the soles of the feet are anointed to ensure that they tread unhindered over the lights upon the path that are left there by the Noble Ones.

This is not a symbolic action; rather it is a magical action. While the body and spirit are still connected (which can continue for days after death), what happens to the outer feet of the dying person affects the 'inner feet.'

If you are sensitive and have good visionary technique, then when a person is close to death, if you place your hands upon their shoulder or head and 'feel' down the inner expression of the body, often the right foot cannot be felt: they have 'one foot in the grave.'

The slow death comes up from the feet, and the inner body of the person seems to withdraw from the bottom up. Using consecrated oil[3] 'tunes' the spirit's footfall on its journey, and prevents any parasites sticking to them as they begin to journey through death (a problem that is very common in slow deaths).

Moisture on their lips is another outer action that affects the inner spirit of the dying person. There is a dynamic that happens with the element of water in death,[4] and the way

---
[2] A bit like landing lights!
[3] You will learn a preparation method later in the apprentice section.
[4] Covered in the next chapter.

this dynamic expresses to the spirit while it is still connected to the body is through thirst.

The magician will know to 'reel' in the impulses of the body at this time, and that knowing has to be at a deep, unconscious level: chances are the magician will not be very conscious, hence certain Mysteries have to be deeply embedded within the dying magician's psyche for them to activate in such circumstances: *the body and spirit have to know as well as the intellect.* And that comes from years of training and work as a magician or mystic.

The touch of moisture upon the lips, or the washing of the magician's face, triggers a response in the body which in turn alerts the spirit to what is coming and what to do. A switched off person newly arrived in death rages with a thirst that almost overwhelms them:

> "They are the souls who are destined for Reincarnation; and now at Lethe's stream they are drinking the waters that quench man's troubles, the deep draught of oblivion…They come in crowds to the river Lethe, so that you see, with memory washed out they may revisit the earth above."
>
> —Virgil, *Aeneid 6*

For a magician, mystic, or priest/priestess, the training of how to self-limit truly becomes a gift at this time, and the person knows, at the deepest, most profound level, not to 'drink of the waters.' We see this, as living people working in vision, as a river that many have the compulsion to drink from. To a newly dead person, it is an energetic impulse that triggers at a deep level, but the trained or switched on person knows not to act on that energetic impulse.

The bathing of the dying magician's face, or the tracing of water upon their lips, reminds them of this impulse, and often—particularly with a magician or a switched on person—when they are offered fluid to drink when they are close to death, they will turn away or clamp their lips shut.

This happened when my mother was very close to death and I, along with other family members, was by her side. My sister kept trying to offer her fluid, as my mother's lips were very dry. My mother, who was semiconscious, kept turning her face away from the offer, which my sister found very distressing. My mother knew what she was doing; my sister did not.

If you see this impulse in a dying person, to turn away from the offer of moisture, you know that they are clued in and the spirit knows what it is doing—you do not need to interfere.

The enlivened vessel in the hand is part of the Deep Mysteries, and is echoed in folk magic as placing a coin in the hand, mouth, or over the eyes of the dead person in order to "pay the ferryman."

The enlivened vessel (or scales) that the magician worked with magically in life will hold (just as water holds) the sum *Harvest* of that magician's life.

Remember the fragments on the threshing floor that the being of the vessel was picking through in your ritual vision work? Those fragments were your Harvest up to that point. Another way of looking at this, from a Judaic point of view, is the Book of Judgement: the sum total of your actions recorded.

The vessel, holding the energetic information of your scales, is what triggers different levels of guardians at the threshold of the death journey.[5] This is not about good deeds and bad deeds: that is a degeneration of a much deeper knowledge. It is about what dynamics of balance that mind and spirit has learned and acted upon—the balance of Ma'at within life.[6]

When the sum total of your Harvest is given/shown to the 'ferryman' or threshold keeper, it is not payment; rather it is showing the keys of your development in life as a human being. That is seen as different frequencies of energy, and those frequencies decide what level of the threshold opens for you.

---

[5] Something we will look at in depth in the next lesson.

[6] Again, discussed in the next lesson.

We will go into more depth in the next lesson on this particular subject matter, so let's get back to the person who is on the threshold of death.

At the point of death

At the point of death, if you are with someone at that point, your job as a magician is simply to *hold the space* in a clear, balanced, and powerful way.

Often this translates in practical terms to having to appear normal amidst a crying family while doing your magical work silently in your head and through your hands.

And sometimes the point of death is not pretty. Sometimes death is fairly peaceful, with only a few tremors of the hand, or 'stoking'-style breathing just at the point of death. But at other times it can get messy, with vomiting or diarrhoea at the point of death.

When this happens, your job is not to react, but simply to continue doing what you are doing. Let others worry about the mess of the body as you facilitate the separation between body and soul.

If you are at the beside of someone who is dying, particularly if it is a slow death from something like cancer, it might be an idea to gently warn the other family members that it could possibly get messy: we do not all have TV-inspired deaths.

2.2 Upon the threshold of death

At the point of death and shortly after, the dying person often has a slight recognition of the gates opening, and they perceive this as seeing light, or even seeing beings (who often cross-dress from the minds of the dying). More than once I have been at the point of death with someone who could speak, and they invariably became aware of the inner world as they died.

I have found that immediately after the death it is as though the soul/spirit steps into a place of silence briefly: in vision this shows as if they have vanished, but it is short and temporary, like the resetting of a clock.

But I have also found that the body still continues to hear after death—which sounds bizarre, I know. The spirit and body do not fully separate straight away: it seems for many (but not all) to be a slow processes of disengagement that in our terms of time seems to happen over a few days.

This must be taken into consideration when you are around a newly-dead person: they still hear you. The spirit of the person often has an aspect that stays close to their body for a few days, and I have no idea how this mechanism of hearing in conjunction with a dead body works, only that it does in most (not all) cases.

In the time between death and burial or cremation, the spirit often goes through a period of 'visiting' the people they were strongly connected to in life. Some people have a strong enough focus to be able to bridge between the non-physical world and the physical world to make their presence known. Other times they simply visit and then leave without being able to let you know they have visited you.

In my family, these visits do tend to bridge the physical and non-physical, and this often plays out through the blowing of light bulbs. When someone in my family who was close to me dies, they sometimes turn up in my house (and the houses of other inner-sighted women in the family) and all the light bulbs blow, one after the other. It can get rather expensive. My nephew's favourite action with his mother (my sister) was to visit and blow the TV up: he died in particularly difficult circumstances, and he continued to visit her for some years on the anniversary of his death.

This strong energetic output while trying to communicate, besides being very spectacular when witnessed, also gives us a little insight into the energies the dead can operate through: electrical things tend to be an easy and favourite way for the dead to try and signal their presence. Whether this is intentional or not, I don't know.

Because of these varied factors, learning to speak to the newly dead, both with your voice and your mind, can alleviate a lot of suffering, fear, and confusion not only in the newly dead person but also in the people around them. Often the dead person just wants you to know they still exist and that all is okay.

Some newly dead do not go through this, and seem to have stretched out so far during the last phases of their illness that they simply vanish deep into death straight away. Others, often magicians, immediately walk off into death with gnosis and purpose, often only visiting one or two people briefly to say goodbye—and some do not even do that.

When a properly prepared magician steps into death, they immediately drop all connection to the living world and move forward without looking back. That can be a painful thought for the living, but it is the healthiest of all actions for the dead. Again, we will look at that in more depth in the next lesson.

From a magical point of view, for the time between death and funeral/burial/cremation, the living magician who is assisting in this death has a few things they can do to assist the passage of the dead.

One is to keep a space fully tuned, with gates open, flames going, and the magician's ritual tools out so that there is a temple space that the dead can come into.

This enables them to communicate with you in a more controlled way (through vision), but also gives them a holding place where they can stay, settle themselves, and prepare for the deeper walk into death. It also gives them a balanced space that is governed by Ma'at where they can go through their own life reassessment process before they step completely over the threshold.

But once the burial/cremation is done, the gates should be closed, the lights extinguished, and the dead soul should not be encouraged to hang around. If a soul chooses to hang around and not step further into death, it must be purely their own decision, and not one enabled by the living magician.

2.3 Religious aspects of death

Some religious ritual patterns for death can be very helpful, and some are totally useless and only there for the people left behind. A Catholic high requiem mass, for example, will often trigger the opening of the gates and ensure the dead person goes through them, often with a ritual firm hand just to make sure.

Some religious rituals, for example in Tibetan Buddhism and some other forms of Buddhism, talk to the spirit of the person to ensure they know what to do and where to go: reciting of texts reminds the spirit of what they had learned in life, and reminds them of the path that now needs to be taken.

Some people traversing death (and we get this report back from near-death experiences also) 'see' or encounter religious figures like saints, Jesus, prophets, etc. These are the beings that work in death, and they will often cross-dress from the mind of the dead person in order to connect and communicate with a frightened and traumatised soul.

I have watched numerous times in death situations where a being, usually angelic, approaches a newly dead person, and as they get closer to the person, they transform into a human, usually dressed in a religious personality of some sort or other. Though I have also seen an angelic being transform into a heavily-breasted young blond girl in order to entice a comatose testosterone-fuelled teen into death (it worked: the teen died at that point as I was observing in vision).

Religious and mystical texts either guide people through the death stages, or they give the mind something to cling to (imagery).

When people who are switched off die without any religious, mystical, or inner reference point it is often messy and traumatising for their spirit, and also for those left behind. However, I have seen very peaceful transitions done by people who are atheist scientists, who nevertheless understand the dynamics of energy, consciousness, vibration, and frequency: they are essentially understanding the Mysteries from an entirely different perspective, but it is a deep understanding nonetheless: they are switched on. And that understanding facilitates them through the death process.

2.4 Energetic clinging

This is a particularly distressing problem that happens in death and around death, and something that as a magician you really need to know about. This can happen around a slow death or a quick death.

The factors that trigger energetic clinging are being switched off, being terrified, and being used to not taking responsibility for oneself (again, the skills and maturing one acquires in life come in very handy at death).

A person who dies unwillingly and who is absolutely terrified, and who is used to grabbing what they want, will instinctively *grab* for the nearest living human and cling to them. This creates an immediate and powerful energy drain upon the living person who is being clung to, and in some cases can drag them into death also. We see this as a sudden death in someone who is close to a newly dead person.

When we die we revert to our unguarded selves. If the unguarded self is a mess, then this mess will come to the fore at the threshold of death. So a selfish, clinging person who is dying is very likely, upon death, to try and cling to someone near to them.

However, energetic clinging can also happen when the death is sudden, unexpected, or the spirit does not immediately realise what has happened. The instinct is to reach out and grab—a bit like grabbing for arms as you fall off a cliff. In this case it is not done out of selfishness, but out of sudden fearful instinct.

This has happened to me a few times, so I tend to tread carefully around dying people I do not know.

A few years back, when I was in the States, I was driving through a junction and a motorist to the side of me slammed his brakes on for some reason and a motorcyclist ran straight into the back of him at quite a speed. The motorcyclist was catapulted off his bike and he went straight through the windscreen at the back of the car.

It all happened so fast, and I was trying to focus on the cars around me at the intersection, which was suddenly thrown into chaos. I saw the biker, his head stuck in the back window of the car beside me, and I instinctively went into the void as I pulled over.[7]

The ambulance and police were called. There was nothing more to be done, and standing around staring was not a good thing to do. People had gathered, and everything that could be done was being done. I was also tired and was just at the start of a long illness, so I drove back off after leaving witness details.

As I drove, I got more and more weary. And it was not a natural weariness: it was the feeling I have learned to recognise and know as the product of something seriously dragging on my life force.

I staggered back to where I was staying and got into bed. It took me a little while to realise what was happening, and it was only when I noticed that my heart was racing and that I was not only shocked but terrified—and yet this was *not my own emotion*, that I realised I had picked up the biker as I drove past his moment of death. His spirit, in the sudden panic, had grabbed at the nearest thing he could: me.

It took me a few hours to disengage him properly, but I essentially had to calm him down and then frogmarch him into death.

Knowing about this dynamic is really important[8] for magicians, as the deeper you go into magic practically, the more you become visible. It will be only a matter of time before you are *grabbed*, particularly if you work in a hospital or with the police, or anywhere where sudden death can occur. Knowing how to recognise this when it happens, and how to work with it and get yourself untangled, will get you out of danger. Then you need to

---

[7]This is why it is important to practice these basic magical actions so they become instinctive responses, not conscious actions.

[8]Yeah, I know, I say that a lot.

know how to pick up the pieces of your own shocked body and spirit: the energetic impact of such a grab can have strong implications for your health.

I address inner and outer methods of putting your body back together at an inner and outer level in depth in my book *Magical Healing: a health survival guide for magicians and healers*. This might be a very useful book for you to have and read, as among other things it has invaluable information within it about how to maintain your body from magical and energetic impacts, which is subject matter I will not address in this course.[9]

You also need to know, as magician, how to keep an eye out for this happening to others, and to know exactly what to do and how to do it quickly in the event that someone else has been grabbed in the middle of a death situation.

2.5 Death Parasites

When a person is dying slowly, particularly and most commonly when they are old, there is a major possibility that energetic parasites will have infested the weakened person and will be feeding off of their energy. The parasites will keep the person alive so that they can continue to feed, with the result that the person is held close to death in a weakened state.

This is something to keep a sharp eye out for when you are around someone who is dying—and if you spot it, you will need to clean the dying person up energetically so that they can let go and die in peace. When this is the case, the death usually comes swiftly, often within hours, of the magical clean-up work.

There are also types of parasites that cling onto the newly dead and prevent them moving deeper into death, and feed off of the emotion/anxiety of the dead person. When the dead person has fully detached from their body, the emotion shifts its energetic form and becomes less about chemical bodily reactions and more about deeper spirit issues. The parasites cling to the energy outputted in its various forms in order to feed, and this prevents the spirit from moving deeper into death (and rebirth, if that is where they are heading).

This is one of the reasons, wherever possible, to keep the space of a dying or newly dead person clean energetically, and to keep the gates open: that prevents any parasites either getting near or keeping hold of the person.

2.6 Quick deaths

Quick deaths have a very different dynamic from slow deaths and tend to be slightly less traumatic. We have already looked at what can happen with a quick death (the motorcyclist), and often, when the death is very sudden and unexpected (accident, massive heart attack), the spirit is catapulted away from the body.

Within a few days in our time frame, the spirit seems to reorganize itself and either draws close to the body or close to someone they are deeply connected to.

Sometimes, if the trauma is great and the death was very sudden, they often do not at first realise they are dead. The spirit will be in a major panic, and they will thrash around energetically until they come to understand what has happened and what they need to do.

Often, particularly when young adults die suddenly, they will not accept death and will try very hard to cling to the world of the living. In these cases, the magician has to spend time talking in vision with the traumatised dead and giving them horizons in the death passage. Once you 'see' it in your head, they also begin to see it, and will eventually set off under their own steam.

So often when someone dies these days, they have no religious, mystical, or cultural pattern for their consciousness to operate through—so you have to provide it for them, both ritually and in vision. Some spirits do not need this and seem to get themselves pretty well organised, and all they need is a 'good job' pat on the back.

---

[9]I have already written about it and put it out there, so there is no need to do it all again.

This is also very true of children and babies: they very rarely need any help at all. It is as if they remember, as they have not lived a long life that will fill up their spirit with new patterns: they remember and get on with it quickly—and often painlessly.

2.7 Comas

The last thing I want to cover briefly before we move on to practical work is the issue of comas. There are lots of different types of coma, and people respond very differently from a spirit point of view. There are comas where the spirit is no longer there but is stretched already into death, still connected lightly to the body by an energetic umbilical cord, but they are beyond coming back into the body. There are some comas that are not connected to death at all, and there are some comas where the person is no longer there and something else has stepped into the body and is trying to operate it.

When a person is in a coma and their body is beyond real repair, often the spirit will stand upon the threshold of death, unable to move forward into death as the body is being kept alive artificially; or else they don't wish to continue living in a body that does not work, but they are also scared of death.

There are also times when the spirit is starting to move towards death but a parasite is keeping the body going, which in turn makes it difficult for the spirit to really move on.

Working with people in comas is a fascinating experience, and is a major service to all concerned. The first thing for a magician to ascertain is whether the spirit/person is still properly anchored in the body and is 'there,' or if they are on their way out, or have already gone. This is done via visionary work on the threshold of death, and also by going into the vessel (body) of the person to see who or what is still there.

More often than not, the person is still there but unable to operate the body. Under such circumstances it is a simple waiting game, and the magician's job is to ensure there is nothing else in the body with the person and vying for residence. Parasites are the most common squatters, and whatever the magician finds in there, he must remove in order for the spirit to have full, proper residence.

With the use of functional MRI's, the incidences of switching off life support to people who are still 'in' are becoming less frequent.

I remember when I was a little girl and my mother was working on a ward of people with head injuries and/or who were in comas. (Her speciality was in infectious/tropical disease, but as the call for that grew less in the 1960s she moved sideways in her work.)

She told me of a situation once where she, her fellow medical students, and doctors were gathered round a coma patient. The person was being reviewed for turning off life support and the consultant had come to the conclusion that the person was brain-dead.

My mother could feel the person still in their body, trying to look out. She had a twenty-four hour window to figure out what was going on before the person was going to be switched off.

She poured over his medical records and also looked up his drug regime in detail. He had been brought to the ward after a bout of meningitis (her home territory) and had fallen into a coma just as he was winning the fight with the infection.

She noticed he was on a drug that in a very small number of people could cause total paralysis. She discussed it with the consultant and asked if they would take him off the drug and wait forty-eight hours to see what happened. After a battle of egos, the consultant agreed. The patient woke up within twenty-four hours.

It was not her medical expertise that first led to that recovery; it was the fact that as a natural psychic she could 'feel' him alive, in panic, trying to communicate.

Few people have such natural psychic ability, but a magician trains to be able to do essentially the same thing: talk in your mind to the body and see if there is still a person trapped in there. The moral of the story is: always check the lights are truly out before you go disconnecting someone.

For many people, though, the prognosis is not so good. And that is where the magician comes in. The job of the magician is to trigger change: that change could be the patient waking up or the patient dying. And the hardest part of that job is to not get involved with the emotion of the situation: the magician should always remain neutral.

That is why, as an apprentice, you spend so much time learning to be still, learning about the balance of powers, the balance of influences, and about your own Harvest. Emotion rules our culture and causes untold damage out of good intent.

Without going into detail, which will come later in your training, with most comas the magician works with the body and also with the spirit in vision during the death process. The body is first checked and cleared of all parasites, is harmonised and balanced, and then the magician goes into death in vision to talk to the spirit. If the spirit wishes to let go, the magician asks if there is anything that the spirit wishes to convey to the family, and then the umbilical cord is cut. The cutting of the cord does not cause an immediate cessation of life; rather it triggers the body and spirit's own disengagement process. The spirit is then shown how and where to begin the walk into death.

When a magician who knows what she is doing does this, death usually follows naturally within twenty-four hours: the heart gives out or just stops. This can bring to an end a long cycle of suffering for both the spirit and the family.

In one such coma case I worked on at an intensive care unit, the message that the spirit wanted conveying was that if he could not be who he was, then he did not want to come back into consciousness.

The man had been in a coma for around a month and they wanted help reaching him. I went in vision into death and found him, but could not get him to communicate with me. He visited me in my dreams that night and conveyed his rather cryptic message.

I was not sure what it meant, but I thought it had something to do with the very strict family he lived in. When I conveyed the message (and it must be done word for word; *never* interpret) the father burst into tears and nodded.

The patient had massive brain damage that I was not told about (they thought I would not work on him if I knew how bad the injuries were) and if he had survived, he would have been totally paralysed or worse. I went back to the hospital the following morning, worked on him to 'line him up,' and he died that night.

This is a difficult area of magical healing to work in, and it is very likely that few of you will follow that specialisation in magic, but having a rudimentary understanding of the dynamic is important should you at some time in the future be put in the position of needing to try and reach someone who is deep in a coma.

2.8 Task: **Astrology**

When we look at a chart, we not only look at the natal planets and the current transits, but we also learn as magicians to look at the 'sigils' that the alignments make, particularly when it comes to specific events that we are looking at. This can be particularly helpful when looking at a death chart.

When we look at a death chart, we are not looking at the person's astrology; rather we are looking at the planetary influences at the point of death. The death chart will tell us a lot about the timing of a person's death, and whether that death was their true, final, appointed time, or whether they had died during a hotspot.

If a spirit is properly attuned, is magical, mystical, or a priest in the real sense of the word (in true communion with Divinity), then we will see the spirit using the optimum time to pass into death.

This is very well demonstrated with the death of Pope John Paul II. Regardless of what we think of religious leaders, this man was a true priest in every sense of the word, and died at a time when the planetary alignments over Rome were in a position where the gates were wide open.

We can see this clearly in his death chart, which was cast for the location and time of his death. Look at the following chart, and see the four directions open and the planetary gates held open:

John Paul II
Radix
Rome, Latium, Italy
2005-04-02 21:37:00 [+02:00]
Latitude: 41°53'41" North
Longitude: 12°29'2" East
Apparent Geocentric

Sun ☉	13°09'14" ♈	Cusp 1: ♏	07°25'02"
Moon ☽	23°30'41" ♑	Cusp 2: ♐	06°10'32"
Mercury ☿	05°38'51" ♈ R	Cusp 3: ♑	09°38'00"
Venus ♀	13°50'06" ♈	Cusp 4: ♒	15°30'54"
Mars ♂	09°27'15" ♒	Cusp 5: ♓	18°25'05"
Jupiter ♃	14°04'39" ♎ R	Cusp 6: ♈	15°31'41"
Saturn ♄	20°31'12" ♋	Cusp 7: ♉	07°25'02"
Uranus ♅	08°45'40" ♓	Cusp 8: ♊	06°10'32"
Neptune ♆	17°00'29" ♒	Cusp 9: ♋	09°38'00"
Pluto ♇	24°30'10" ♐ R	Cusp 10: ♌	15°30'54"
North Node ☊	23°27'38" ♈ R	Cusp 11: ♍	18°25'05"
Chiron ⚷	02°29'26" ♒	Cusp 12: ♎	15°31'41"
Asc As	07°25'02" ♏		
Mc Mc	15°30'54" ♌		

Figure 2.1: Pope John Paul II's death chart.

See how clearly the gates are shown, and how many of the planets are down below his horizon—all the activity is in the Underworld. This is a very poetic way of reading an event chart, but it gives you a clear view of patterns of power in action.

A magician's death chart will either show the four gates, or a great triangle.

2.9 *Task:* Death chart practice

Using the free chart drawing facility at astro.com, choose ten people, either known to you or public figures, where you can get the time, date, and location of the death, and run death charts for them.

Look at their charts, the shapes of the lines generated from the planets' positions, and see what sort of patterns were around them astrologically when they died. Take computer notes: using Word or something similar, embed the charts and write your observations, ideas, and what you know of the person, and compare what you know to what the chart reflects. Keep the file, as it may need to be submitted later.

2.10 *Task:* Tarot and death

Using the same ten people, you are going to do a series of readings to look the state of the spirit/soul of the person at the point of death, and then also track them through the early stages of death. You will use the four-directional layout, and also a new layout that is more focussed on the inner landscape of a person.

Four-directional readings

For the four-directional readings, the first card (centre) tells you about the state of the body itself at the point of death; the four directions tell you the influences that are flowing around the spirit of the person at that time as the gates open; and the final card that crosses the centre card tells you about the power/contact that the person is having a direct relationship/contact with at the point of death.

The question you will ask for each person is:

"Show me this person at the point of their death, and show me the inner power influences that were flowing around them at that time."

Write down the card positions of each reading and your conclusions. When you have all ten of them, compare the readings to the death charts. Look at the planetary influences at that time and compare them to the four directions in the readings, and see if there is a correlation between the planets, the houses they are in, and the powers flowing out of the directions. Don't try and do all of the readings in one session, as it would tire you out. Spread them out over days.

The Inner Landscape/Desert Layout readings

This is an abridged version of a larger layout that gives you more details as to the passage or state of a spirit and what influences are flowing through their situation, where those influences come from, and where the spirit is going.

You may have worked with this layout already from my books, or it may be totally new to you. Either way, it is a key layout for magicians, and you will learn a lot more about it in this course, and also work with it in its full expression.

Learn the layout first, map it out on paper, and have the map at your side so that you can work with it. As with all new layouts, fix the layout in your mind as you shuffle so that both you and the cards know what pattern it is you are reaching for. It is a magical layout that is very versatile and can be used for all sorts of magical questions: it is not geared specifically to death readings, so bear that in mind as you interpret the positions.

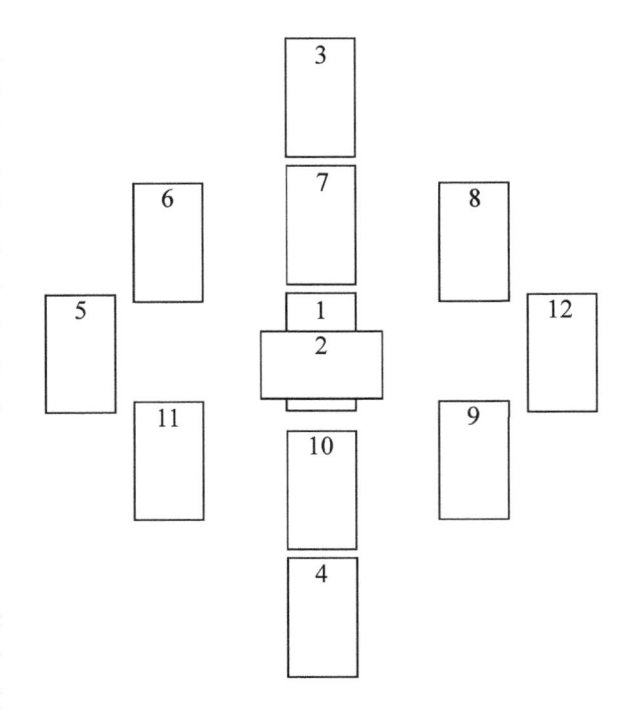

Figure 2.2: The Inner Landscape or Desert Layout.

Position meanings

1. The first position is the body or land.

2. The second position, that crosses the first, tells us what power or people dynamics we are currently dealing with.

3. The third position tells us what is coming in the long-term future, a pattern that is still being formed in the stars. If resolution is on its way, but will take some time, then that will show here; however, if the problem is going to be prolonged, then that will also be indicated here.

4. The fourth position shows us what has already passed away down into the depths and will not be returning any time soon.

5. The fifth position shows us the gate to the past: this is the threshold of what is now in the immediate past. Whatever is in this position of the threshold has the potential to return at some point in the future, but for the moment is considered past.

6. The sixth position is the current pattern of fate or action that is playing out: that could be a struggle, a cycle of magical work, a period of renewal, etc. This is the path you are currently on, unless you do something to change that path's direction.

7. The seventh position is hardships and difficulties that must be overcome. On the current path (indicated in the sixth position) there are bound to be hardships, difficulties, and barriers that must be overcome: these are shown in the seventh position, and must be endured if you are

to continue in the fate direction you are currently travelling.

8. The eighth position shows what is coming directly into your landscape from the inner worlds. All magical attacks, inner contacts, work programs, inner support, deities, etc. will show here.

9. The ninth position shows you what influence in your inner landscape is potentially affecting your home/family surroundings or vice versa. If there is a haunting, bad energy, or difficulty in the home environment it will show here.

10. The tenth position is what is falling away or starting to go into decline. If you have defeated something, or it is starting to leave your body or fate path, it will show here. It is travelling towards the gate of the past and will finally vanish into the depths. If, however, you do not meet the challenges that appear in the seventh position, then any difficulties that show in the tenth position will come right back to challenge you until you get the message.

11. The eleventh position is dreams and sleep. This position tells you what your deeper unconscious mind is dealing with, and what is happening to you in your sleep.

12. The twelfth position is the way ahead, and tells you the immediate outcome to your question. For a longer-term outcome, look to position three.

Do the Desert layout for each of the ten deaths you are looking at. The question you will ask for each person is:

"Show me the death of person X, their point of death, and what happened to them as they went through the death process."

This spread will show you how the body dealt with death (1 is the body, 2 is their relationship with death). The reading will also show you their short-term movement into death and how they are handling it (6); it will show you what they have to overcome in their journey (7), what inner, deeper powers are flowing to them from the inner worlds, i.e. angelic, or human or priesthood guidance (8), what effect the family left behind is having on them (9), what is falling away from them/what they are letting go of (10), what they are dreaming for the future (11), what their short-term future is—is it resting, balancing, cleaning up, or are they struggling, or looking to jump back into life (12)? Position 3 will tell you whether they are going back into life (and may show what sort of life), or it will show if they are going to step into the inner worlds to be a contact, or if they are going to rest.

As with the charts, write it all down, and then compare each reading to the other readings and the death chart of each person.

Take your time to ponder over each person, and look in depth at the little details. If something confounds you, put it to one side and go back to it later.

This process of charts, readings, and conclusions should take you three weeks to a month, which gives you time to do the readings, look at the charts, meditate on each person, and let the story slowly unfold for you. Also take note of any unusual dreams or encounters at this time, as some of it may filter through your dream world.

Lesson 3

The Magical Mysteries of Death

Now that you have a basic background idea of death, it is time for us to look a bit closer and find out about some of the deeper mysteries that surround death. As you will have seen from the Egyptian texts, constant rebirth was/is considered the lowest common denominator, not only in the Egyptian Mysteries but also in the Buddhist Mysteries.

You will find, as you expand your reading list further over the span of the course, that many of the ancient and not-so-ancient Mysteries have the same core to them. That is because they are expressing what is there, not because they are copying or sharing.

The writings of the various versions of the Mysteries around the world, particularly when it comes to the subject of death, usually have two layers to them: one for the everyday person and one for the initiates/priests/magicians. The one that is aimed at the common man (a switched off person) tends to be simplistic, moralistic, and full of threats. A deeper layer of such writings also hides profound aspects of the Mysteries that someone who is both switched on and has knowledge of the Mysteries (through direct experience, not academia) will spot and can learn from.

It is the common, moralistic writings that tend to become popular and well-known to the various populations, and many of our world religions are based upon those moral writings and stories. Initiates of the Mysteries often reject those writings or dogmatic systems in search of something else: an initiate knows in their very depths that there is 'more.' And there is.

But it is wise to understand that the outer writings aimed at the common man serve a multi-fold purpose: first to ensure some societal boundaries, but also to bridge the common man from being switched off to being switched on. They either get it at a deeper level, or they stay switched off and follow the shallow moral code slavishly.

This is important for magicians to understand, as, for an adept working in the depths of death and dying, knowing that bridging aspect helps the magician to work with the dying person in their 'reality' and not the reality of the initiate.

If a religion connects a person to a sense of Divinity, to a sense that even slightly approaches balance, then it is a religion that is serving that person. If the religion locks down the dying person (overly dogmatic), then there is nothing that the magician can do to change that—all you can do is to hold the space.

Before we go on to look at the Deeper Mysteries, let's first look at religious dogma and how it affects the passage of the soul through death.

3.1 Religion versus the Mysteries

Most religions have a version of heaven and hell, of judgement, of helpers, and of the angel of death. In the past, before more advanced education was the norm, this gave a switched off person a compass of behaviour that was easy to understand and follow.

But most religions in their everyday sense have degenerated to the point that they simply express as manipulation and encourage the devolving of personal responsibility, along with having a 'God' who is humanesque and parent-like. A person within a religion learns to manipulate the system for their own ends, and devolves responsibility for themselves to a 'higher power.'

For example, if a person wants something, they will pray to a saint, to God, or to a religious symbol. The mantra of "it's God's will," or doing something "in God's name," or blaming God when things go wrong, are all degenerations and serve to switch the person off even further.

The summary of all religions is: be good and you get to have an easy life after death; be bad and you will burn. And if you say sorry at the end, or pay enough money into a religion, you will be saved. Within that unbalanced, dogmatic view, there are fragments of cause and effect, and of the Mysteries themselves, but they are so far buried as to make them almost unreachable.

For people who gain a good education, and who tend to be thinkers, they look at this pattern, they see how silly, empty, and degenerate it is, and they walk away from it. Some eventually delve into the Mysteries, but most do not. This is the human melting pot that the magician confronts when they work in death.

So why did it get like that? Human nature. Working within the depths of the Mysteries is hard work indeed. Very few people are drawn to such work, and even fewer are able or willing to withstand the hard work.

3.2 The Death Mysteries

So let us have an overview of the Death Mysteries, and as we go through it you will start to see the roots of certain dogmas and beliefs, see how they have developed out of context, and how they have developed in a degenerate, manipulative way.

At this point it is pertinent to point out that that however much an adept learns about these Mysteries there will always be aspects of them that we cannot understand, grasp, or even find. What we have as magicians and mystics is a small section of understanding; nothing more.

First I will briefly outline the steps within the Mysteries that deal with death, and then we will look in more depth at key aspects of them.

Bear in mind that the imagery in these steps is how the living, conscious mind perceives energy dynamics: on the side of the dead person, the imagery is more a matter of processing energy, emotion, power, and balance. The deeper into death the deceased goes, the less they perceive in terms of imagery and the more they perceive in terms of energy responses. The images are our interface for recognition and understanding.

3.3 The steps of the process: a brief overview

The first step of a person when they step onto the threshold of death is to begin the process of disconnection from their body, and their spirit stays in our world for a brief time.

We have already looked at this. Suffice to say, this is the stage where the newly dead can influence the physical world and reach out to the living. However, for most people this period is fairly brief.

The vast majority of the newly dead begin their 'descent into the Underworld' fairly quickly, often at or just after funerals. In life, we perceive this as 'down'; in religion it is often termed as 'hell,' and subsequently fills many with fear…or the more adventurous with curiosity. We will look in depth at the Underworld and the Abyss in the next lesson.

It is at this stage of the Underworld that the process of 'awareness of self' begins. In some Death Mysteries, this is depicted for us as the newly dead walking across a desert towards a river in the Underworld, where some cross the river, some stay at the side of it, and some attempt to avoid going deeper into death by immediately grabbing for a new life: unconscious reincarnation.

For those that do not immediately grab for new life during that walk, a deeper process triggers for the person which is the process of *the Scales*. The desert is the Inner Desert; or to be more precise, it is an aspect of that vast inner territory that adepts learn to operate within for lots of different reasons.

The triggering of the Scales is sometimes depicted in Mysteries as the opening of the Book of Judgement, or of facing judges, or a literal weighing of scales, or crossing a bridge over a river, or being confronted by demons with sharp pointy things. The outcome of this process defines what stage the spirit moves on to next: deeper into the Underworld, back into life through rebirth, etc.

So far this all sounds very neat and tidy, and yet the reality is far more complex. For instance, spirits that are deeply disturbed can often be observed, while in the Underworld, suddenly being absorbed into a deity, or becoming trapped in the sands of the Desert. Some stay in the Underworld, trapped, until they find manipulative ways to access the living, manifest world. Some descend deeper into the Underworld and a few pass through the Underworld and into the Abyss.

For some who descend into the Underworld, there comes a point where they emerge from the Underworld out into the stars and go through a process where they either choose web patterns of fate within the stars that they can step into, or they learn to navigate around those webs and complete the journey of the stars, which brings them back to a centre point.

Reaching that centre point is one of the goals of an adept of the Mysteries: it brings the spirit in direct, face-to-face contact with a vast angelic being. This process is depicted in many different ways in the Mysteries, but the dynamic is the same.

From that centre point, the adept chooses either to move deeper into the depths of Divinity (depicted as heaven, which is a total degeneration of the idea), to stay in the inner worlds in gnosis and in service, or to step into life in full gnosis in service, or to step into the Underworld. For the adept, all of these options are conscious decisions that have specific reasons attached to them. The key point being that nothing is moved towards from impulse, desire, fear, or any other emotive or manipulative reason.

So in a moment we will look at these key steps in detail from the view of a magician. Most of those keys can be read about in various Mystery texts around the world, but few who look at them intellectually actually understand what it is they are looking at as they browse through these texts.

Just before we get to those keys, let's look at why it often goes so badly wrong for people, or why they cannot access the keys properly as they traverse through death. The understanding of these problems will help you to understand the keys better.

The majority of people who travel through death as a spirit either approach it blindly (no religious map), or in dogmatic ignorance (the dogmatic map), or with a focus on manipulation (using spells/magic to dodge the guardians). All of these approaches fail and can sometimes result in intense suffering for the spirit (not the suffering of hell's damnation, but the suffering of being stuck and not knowing a way out).

If the spirit approaches death blindly (no religious map), then the deeper instinct of that spirit leads the way. The success or failure of that approach largely depends on the balance of the person in life.

If the spirit approaches death through religious dogma, the spirit quickly learns that such dogmas are for the large part meaningless in this realm (as you will see when we get to the keys).

As for the manipulator, this is often the spirit of a person who followed a magical path, either through ritual magic, tribal magic, or folk magic. They sometimes get a bit further in and then are confronted by the degeneracy of their action. That confrontation is often aggressive for the spirit and deeply counterproductive: they get stuck with no way forward and no way back, and potentially have a nasty-looking being with sharp knives following them around.

When people make these mistakes, sometimes the process of death itself unfolds them, and the deeper aspect of their spirit emerges and propels them forward. However if that deeper aspect is very unbalanced then the spirit experiences many difficulties that could have been avoided.

The one point to remember in all of this, before we reach the keys, is that there is no moralistic or punishment/reward dynamic involved: the process of death is one of finding (or not) balance. That balance is an energy harmonic that allows the consciousness to flow freely and to interact with its environment in a conscious way.

So let us look a bit closer at some of the key aspects of death, and the Mysteries of death. Through that understanding, not only can you help yourself, you can also help others.

3.4 The Descent into the Underworld

The Descent into the Underworld is a purely natural action that creates separation between the dead person and the land of the living.[1] This natural impulse is sometimes mirrored by the living in the action of burying the dead.

We call it "Descent" because in our living worldview, density, age, and the layers of the past are 'down' deep in the land. This is mirrored in the inner landscape of the Desert, as we see the past as being down in the sands, and the future as being up in the stars. As the body decays and becomes part of the dirt and rock of the earth, the spirit too, on its initial journey, moves into this vast processing system. For the spirit it is less a sense of 'down' and more a sense of 'forward.'

This stepping away from life triggers a deep inner response, and that response is the first major key of the Mysteries. A major part of the learning process within the ancient Mysteries was geared towards preparing the spirit at a very deep level, while in life, to respond appropriately to this response.

In the early development of most Mysteries, that in-life preparation was about changing first the individual's behaviour, and then their knowledge and understanding. That deep shift over a lifetime enabled the spirit to move through the death process with ease and in a conscious, active way.

As the Mysteries began to degenerate for one reason or another depending on the culture, that process of deeply shifting over a lifetime turned into the rote learning of a series of spells to dodge the process, and finally a series of dogmatic threats, scary stories, and hints of great 'rewards.' Both of these degenerations resulted (and still result) in spirits having great difficulty in death.

The first trigger response from the inner world for the spirit in the death process is known by a number of names, the most common one being *Judgement*.

Many spirits do not get this far (to Judgement), as many rush impulsively back to life before ever properly entering the death process. But in this lesson we are focusing on those who do manage to step forward and onto the Deeper Mysteries.

3.5 The River and Judgement

The River and *Judgement* are the first and most important keys; and of all of them they are the ones most badly misunderstood and misinterpreted, both in religion and in the modern study of the Mysteries and magic. On average, fewer spirits get to the Judgement point in the death process; many dive straight back into the

---
[1]The whole process and understanding of the Underworld is pretty involved, hence it has its own lesson (coming next).

rebirth cycle in an unconscious, impulsive grab for life at any cost.

That is one of the reasons that many Death Mystery writings talk about the Death Mysteries in terms of "not for the common man." This is not a class discrimination; it is merely an observation from adepts of the Mysteries: many people do not even get to the door of the Death Mysteries.

The River stage of death is depicted in ancient texts, and can also be observed in vision as people in a desert running towards a river and drinking great quantities of its waters. That is how we the living 'see' this process. From an inner point of view, what is happening is that a switched off person, driven only by instinctive impulse for life, reaches out for an energy that will *blind* the spirit from its memories, allowing it a clean slate free from the pattern of the last life. This in turn enables the spirit to lunge forward unconsciously back into life, so that the cycle begins all over again.

Those who value life at any cost see this wiping of their slates as a boon, a great way to get back to where they want to be. Ghosts who cling to the material world and their past life/family/belongings, try hard to not be drawn to the river: once they have drunk and forgotten, they are cast back into a new life.

For those who have trodden the path of the Mysteries in some form or other, such unconscious lunging blindly back into life is seen as an undesirable action that will lead to more blindness and less advancement into being one's true self.

This first step is written about in virtually all Mysteries in the form of the warning:

> "Do not drink of
> the River of Oblivion."

"Men, driven on by thirst, run about like a snared hare; let therefore the mendicant drive out thirst, by striving after passionlessness[2] for himself."

—Ch 24, *Dhammapada*

---
[2] Not driven by emotions or impulse.

The initiate learns first to be aware of their deeper impulses in life, and then to turn those impulses into a conscious act of choice. Through developing that conscious ability in life, it becomes second nature in death. The adept or mystic reaches this first threshold and makes a conscious choice that is not dictated by desire or emotion.

If the adept chooses not to drink of the river, or not even to wash their face, they move forward deeper into the realm of the death aspect of the Desert. This is where they reach the key of judgement, also known as the *Weighing of the Scales*.

The choice of the spirit to step into judgement is a conscious one, and is a decision made by a mystical or adept spirit who wishes to progress deeper into the Divine Mysteries that can only be reached through the passage of death. It is a decision that involves a great deal of danger for the spirit, and is a choice that is not taken lightly: hence the training in life.

If a spirit does not feel ready, or knows that they are not ready to move forward into Judgement, as they still have work to do on themselves and in the world around them, they will not drink of the River: they may wash their face in order to rid themselves of the memory of their physical image, which if left may pull them backwards rather than forwards. The adept would then step into the next life, while still retaining a deep memory of what they learned.

Those who feel they are ready forge forward towards Judgement. Those who feel they have enough magical skill to manipulate their way through the process will also, foolishly, step forward.

A wise adept/mystic knows what submitting to the Judgement of the Scales entails: potential annihilation is the worst case scenario (the Second Death). An unwise adept or mystic will try to manipulate their way through this process, only to be potentially caught by the guardians beyond the threshold. The spirit that decides it is ready for Judgement makes a clear decision and then steps forward. This is depicted in the Greco-Roman Mysteries as the Bridge across the River (the Bridge is a being of the Scales, not an actual bridge).

3.6 The Key of the Scales

This is the major step, the major filter that decides where and how the spirit of the dead person moves forward in their journey.

In Egyptian texts this is depicted as the *Scales of Ma'at* weighing the heart of the dead person. To the Egyptians, the heart was the seat of the soul/spirit and is shown as being placed upon the Scales of Ma'at and weighed against the white feather of Ma'at. If the heart weighs less than or equal to the feather of Ma'at, the guardians will part and allow the dead person to begin their deep journey through the inner processes of death and renewal.

So what is it that is being weighed? This concept is where a lot of degeneration of wisdom has happened in religion and the Mysteries over time.

In most of today's religions, and also in some magic, what is perceived as being judged/weighed is the life deeds of the individual in relation to the morals and cultural norms of a particular society. Sometimes those morals/norms cross paths with balance, but most often they do not.

There is also a get out clause in many religions nowadays, that if you 'confess', or pay money to a shrine, or go on holy war, etc., then you will be judged lightly. That is not the case.

These get out clauses developed within religious systems as a method of control and manipulation. So people feel they can behave badly and then make up for it: it plays to the wish of people to have their cake and eat it.

For the magician, the process of balancing the scales is a lifetime of evolution and development. We are driven by our hormones, by our bodies, by our relationships, and by society, and each of these things gives us both difficulties to overcome and also excuses: "it was not my fault."

As a magician progresses, it becomes less about struggling to 'behave' in a certain way, and more about coming to know yourself, taking responsibility for yourself and your own actions, and realising that development of the spirit is all about "the buck starts and ends with you."

> "By oneself the evil is one, by oneself one suffers: by oneself evil is left undone, by oneself one is purified. Purity and impurity belong to oneself, no one can purify another."
>
> —Chapter 12, *Dhammapada*

We have already looked into this process in a previous lesson, so I do not need to go over it again. That process slowly changes how we live, how we act, and how we treat everything around us, and it is that adjustment in how we exist as human beings, how our deeper responses change, that is weighed.

It is not about actions or lack of actions; it is the deepest part of us, how we are on a day-to-day basis, both consciously and unconsciously, that is placed on the Scales. How the Scales react defines what then happens to the spirit.

As an aside, there is a stunning example of a deep mystery of adept service that is found in Old Kingdom Egypt, a dynamic that began to fall apart by the time to kingship had reached king Unas. The dynamic was this: the king was also a priest (sacred kingship), and the king worked deeply in mystical magic to take on the role of *Scapegoat* and "Heart upon the Scales" for the nation and the land.

While the king worked with total balance (Ma'at) for the good of the land and the people, and kept himself balanced, the nation and the land would all collectively enjoy the benefits of the king's balance.

This takes us back to the Sword of Damocles hovering over the head of the king. The king had to tread a very thin line of self and behaviour, constantly striving to be in balance, self-aware, and in harmony with the land. By doing this he took on the burden of the spirits of the people, and the whole nation and land benefitted from this kingship of

Ma'at. In return, the king enjoyed the help and assistance of all the deities.

At the end of his life he would be placed before the Scales: it was not a choice the king had. By taking on that role he submitted to the lesser judgement in life which would ensure that upon death he or she would be immediately placed before the Scales to finish the job.

This worked well for a few generations of kingship, but soon human nature reared its ugly head and we got to a king who thought he could dodge his way around it. The moment the king steps off that very thin line, the sword falls, the connection to the land and people is cut, the deities withdraw their support, and chaos ensues.

We see this pattern over and over again in Egyptian history, with successive kings trying to reestablish that balance. But every time human nature crept in or the rules of Ma'at were manipulated, the sword would fall once more and the nation would be plunged into war, famine, etc.

If you read the following clip of text from the Dhammapada in the context of Ma'at and not morals, you begin to see the dynamic within this text:

> "All that we are is the result of what we have thought: it is founded on our thoughts, it is made up of our thoughts. If a man speaks or acts with an evil thought, pain follows him, as the wheel follows the foot of the ox that draws the carriage."

It demonstrates so clearly that the thought, the first impulse, that only you know, is the root of the balance or imbalance of the spirit. The action follows the thought and creates a good or bad effect.

Modern religions judge upon effects; the Mysteries realise that the Judgement is upon the spirit itself, and that is founded in the thought impulse.

This theme of sacred kingship, and the failure or success of the sacred king, is found repeatedly in Egyptian and also Biblical texts. It is also probably at the root of the role of Jesus as the saviour of mankind: he takes on the suffering of the people, acts in balance, and descends into the Underworld in order to release those in suffering.

It is also very possible that it is this dynamic that is behind the tales of Solomon the king. The more you look at Biblical text and the ancient texts and stories from the Near and Middle East, the more you begin to see this role in action.

The other and very important ancient aspect of the Mysteries that the sacred kingship shows us as magicians is the most forgotten one: as adepts we are all potentially those sacred kings and queens.

In Egypt this was ritualised and formalised, but it is in fact a natural magical dynamic that does not need one to be a king or a queen to practise—and nor does it *make* one a king or a queen.

It is a dynamic that wherever there is a person (usually an adept, priest/priestess, or mystic) who is fully immersed in Ma'at and lives within the narrow boundary of Ma'at, so too will you find a land or part of a land (where the person lives) that is healthy and balanced, or is moving towards balance.

How you are affects everything around you. The energetic frequency that you generate by living within that dynamic affects the Divinity within substance all around you: that frequency triggers rebalance and regeneration actions in whatever way it needs to express in order to bring balance.

3.7 The Second Death

If the Scales tip against the spirit being weighed, it is cast aside and torn apart, or is hacked at. This all sounds very final and not very pleasant, but it is the risk that the adept or mystic takes.

The Scales are a major step, so to speak, of the spirit, which is why so many in death choose not to invoke it but rather choose to step back into life without the potential benefits that the Scales can bring.

The Second Death, where the spirit is totally composted, is something I have little understanding of, and is possibly connected to the idea of the soul first being cocooned and then bound into the Underworld, something we will look at in Lesson 8.

The closest I have seen, apart from the 'cocoons' which may have been what I was observing and didn't realise, was something I saw in vision when working deep in the Desert. I wrote it into a chapter in my novel *The Last Scabbard*.

I had requested and triggered judgement in life (the Lesser Judgement, a bit like an exam pre-run) as part of my role as an exorcist. I did not do it lightly, but I realised that my work was taking me into very deep and dangerous waters, so I needed to make a decision: either stop that work, or surrender to judgement.

I needed to surrender to judgement, as the work I was doing in service as an exorcist was at a critical point and I could not just drop my responsibilities; but to continue working without a Scales assessment would have put my life in danger: by submitting to the Lesser Judgement and surviving, the adept then enjoys greater support and help from the deities.

So I triggered the process and stood before the vast being that 'weighs the Scales.' As I stood there, I realised another spirit was standing at the side of me. I had no clue who or what it was, and was prevented from looking at the spirit. A 'sword' came out of nowhere and sliced into the spirit next to me, and the spirit vanished. I started to get a bit worried, and then the sword came down on me. It hit me in the shoulder very hard, and I fell out of the vision.

Looking back, years later, I began to wonder if the spirit that vanished had undergone a Second Death and had ceased to be.

I also understand now why the sword hit my shoulder (and physically injured me). I was not really ready for Judgement: I still have blind spots and unbalanced parts of myself that I have slowly become aware of, and I now know how much more work I have to do in order to lighten the spirit to that of a feather (huge mountain to climb). Putting myself up for Judgement at that time was both necessary—and was also folly. It was one of those moments where you look back in time and think...moron...

But the process did speed along my self-reflection process, and since that day I have become more and more aware of what I need to do to work towards the Greater Judgement, if I truly want to opt out of the continuous cycle of life.

3.8 Fooling the Scales

In ancient Egypt (yeah, them) as the civilisation developed and the temples gained more power, manipulations crept in. This manipulation can be seen very clearly in the Egyptian funeral texts (Papyrus of Ani) where spells abound that attempt to dodge, manipulate, bind, or lie to the guardians and the Scales.

One spell in particular works upon the heart of the deceased spirit and forces it to lie or be silent on behalf of the dead person. When the heart is placed upon the Scales, it is depicted in Egyptian texts that the spirit has to undergo the forty-two negative confessions: declarations of the heart that tells what sins they have not committed.

There are spells in the text which force the heart to lie in order not to be judged harshly. This is a degeneration in so many major ways: not only does it not work, but it shows just how badly this society had degenerated. It had gone from the sacred king upholding Ma'at for the whole of society, and in return having the help of the gods (and the help of the Pyramid texts to guide the king through death). The process was for the king and the occasional high priest/priestess only: not from class distinction, but from necessity.

To live a life of Ma'at and be immersed in the Mysteries is a hard life indeed. Very few can be expected to live such a life, so in practical terms, it was left to the king and the occasional magical priest/priestess to live such a life for the good of all. As the society degenerated, two things happened. The vast magical power that flowed in harmony with Divinity and the land was cast aside (too much hard work), and a lesser, though still very powerful magic of manipulation, bargaining, and binding replaced it. This immediately caused an imbalance in the Ma'at of the land and the nation.

The second thing that happened, as a result of that magical degeneration, is that the rich aristocrats wanted their chance at passing by the Scales and moving deep into harmony (heaven). So they paid priest magicians to work with artisans to paint the spells on the walls of their tombs, so that their spirits would have all the spells ready in order to dodge their fate and judgement. Of course it does not work, but hey, if a corrupt priesthood is offered enough money, they will tell you anything. I think also that the Mysteries had begun to degenerate to a point whereby the priesthood believed such behaviour would work.

3.9 The walk of the knives

Once the Scales have been dealt with, the spirit begins its walk through the Desert towards the Abyss and to Divinity beyond. If the spirit weighed badly, the blade would fall. If the spirit weighed a bit off but not enough for a Second Death, nor enough to pass deeper into the process, then the blade would cut into the spirit to disable, but not enough to destroy.

This is depicted in Egyptian funeral texts as demonic or Underworld deities who carry long, sharp blades and cut into the spirit as it journeys through the Desert. Some spirits are cut deeply and some are not.

When I was a young woman and working in vision in death, I would work within a landscape of desert, river, bridge over river, plains, mountain, and mists beyond. I worked with that visionary system for many years until I realised it was only a fraction of what was actually there.

The Bridge is the Scales (the bridge is a being, not a structure). When I was working in this vision and was learning about it as I pushed deeper and deeper into the vision, I noticed that many who crossed the bridge (and some did not cross, but vanished in the middle of it: Second Death?) and began walking towards the mountain had bits dropping off of them. At the time, and for years later, I thought they were just dropping their attachments to the life they had just left behind. As the years went by, I realised that they were having their bits sliced by the guardians. These were spirits preparing to climb the mountain who had gone through the Scales, and what I was seeing was the result of that judgement: they were sustaining injuries that were triggering the process of Ma'at so that as they went forward (to life or whatever) they had these injuries not to punish, but to trigger an awareness and understanding of their imbalance that they then could work with.

It then dawned on me that as a young woman, I had done something terrible in ignorance and arrogance. When I worked in the death vision, I got it into my head that a major job was to assist people across the bridge so that they could go back into life. I noticed that multitudes of people simply sat at the side of the river and I became evangelical about hauling them over the bridge, sometimes kicking and screaming.

It was only in the last few years that I got to see and then realise a dynamic that I was interfering with: if a soul crosses the bridge under its own steam, when it is ready, it may or may not trigger the Scales on the bridge depending on what that spirit is doing. Some pass over the bridge and continue without triggering the Scales, and eventually go back into life. Some trigger the Scales by themselves as they pass through this stage of death.

But by forcibly putting people on the bridge, or pushing them towards it, I was obviating their own natural process and also triggering the Scales for every spirit I pushed onto the bridge. I do not know why it triggers the Scales if a soul is forced; only that it does. I was horrified when I was finally able to see this: the implications of my actions were far reaching indeed.

Which takes us back to the Mystery wisdom: you are responsible for yourself. Everything starts and ends with you. Everyone has to walk their own path and take the consequences of their own path upon themselves. By forcing people over the bridge I had interfered with that process: I was trying to sort everyone else out instead of minding my own business and sorting myself out.

The old maxim that people should not start Mystery training until they have reached forty began to make more and more sense to me. Before that age we are too dumb, too full of hormones and everything else that goes with that (ego, emotion, impulse). And yet I have learned far more from my mistakes than I have learned from my successes. So it is a two-edged sword, really.

3.10 The face of the angel

Once the spirit has crossed the plains of the Desert and overcome many challenges,[3] it comes face to face with a vast angelic being *whose face shines with the light of Divine Being.* That is to say, an angelic being that is a direct mediator of the powers of creation and destruction: the angel of glory.

This encounter is a deep mystical version of 'looking in the mirror.' The spirit is given a brief look at Divine Being and also of their true self at a soul level. This enables the soul to make a choice, and it is this choice that adepts of the Mysteries strive for, and thus work hard to learn the powers of the Scales in life and death. You see, life is not the be-all and end-all, or the 'true existence'; it is more like going to the gym to get strong and fit.

Those who have been through this process once or more remember it at a deep level and strive in life not only to repair and renew the 'cuts' they received, but also to pass on guidance (but not help) to others in order to point the way. We see this throughout history as magicians, mystics, priests/priestesses who spend their life pointing the way through texts and teachings. Or they simply write/paint or express their experience so that others may have a step upon the road.

[3] In the Greek Mysteries that is depicted as a mountain that must be climbed.

The experience of looking into the face of the vast angelic being triggers a deeper understanding of their eternal self and what it is they need to do. Once they have settled on what they need to do, the angel opens up a *Vista* of options that would facilitate that process.

3.11 The Vista

The *Opening of the Vista*, in magical terms, is something that happens when the spirit is shown a variety of options that are open and accessible to them in order to do whatever it is they need to achieve. This could be a life or series of lives, and often the spirit is shown a variety of lives. Or it could be passing into the inner worlds (inner temples, for example) in order to work as an inner contact; it could be rest in the arms of a deity power that holds the spirit in sleep for a while; it could be service in the Underworld; or it could be, if the spirit did not sustain injury from the blades and is therefore complete, the option of the *ladder of angels*, which takes the spirit into a deep, Divine state of balance and union (going home).

The choice is for the spirit to make, and as soon as that decision is made all other options close off and the spirit falls into the option that they reached for. If the option was life, the angel withdraws and the spirit falls into life.

This action is a much higher and vastly more powerful dynamic of the one that you learned a little about in the last module when you stood in the centre of the web of lives/fate and looked around that web for hotspots or lives. This is the same mechanism, but at an infinitely more powerful level.

What fascinates me is that I have often come across this mechanism in action not only in deep vision, but in people who remember this process at a deep level. They will dream it, taste it, feel it: a deep part of them remembers, but the everyday consciousness tries to suppress the memory (for good reason). As the person gets older—and I have come across this not only in priests/priestesses or adepts, but also in seemingly everyday folks—they slowly remember more and more fragments of the event. Of course there are always the silly people who read about events like this and then loudly declare that they remember in total, that their spirit was the spirit of Cleopatra/Jesus/Buddha/whatever, and that they were sent back on the earth to be a messiah (what, another one??). Those you can discount as just being nuts.

I remember a conversation with one person, who wasn't magical or religious but was a deeply profound human, after they had surgery (which can sometimes trigger deep memories). About a month after the surgery he had a vivid dream that not only was powerful, exhausting, and terrifying; it also 'woke him up' and changed his life forever.

He dreamed of standing before a vast, shining face, and beyond the face was a parade of many lives. He was missing a foot and a hand (action of the blades?), and felt a total failure. But the angel smiled and nodded towards the parade of lives. He looked, and saw a life that pulled at him deeply. He fell towards it and woke up with a bump. There was nothing untoward in the dream, but it shook him to the core: his spirit recognised and remembered.

He came to me to chat, as he was still shaken days later and could not understand why. I told him about the Death Mysteries process and when we came to the Opening of the Vista, his face lit up. He said he remembered, and he also remembered what it was he needed to do to feel complete—and off he went. He left his job and travelled half way round the world to go work on the top of a mountain with a tribal community. He never told me what it was that he needed to do, and as I moved around we slowly lost contact.

This act of remembering also brings me to another aspect of the Death Mysteries, and that is reincarnation. So let's have a look at the many twists and turns that are relevant to the Mysteries.

3.12 Reincarnation

Reincarnation is something that happens either unconsciously or consciously. I do not mean that in a sense of remembering past lives, but in a sense of whether it was by conscious choice of the spirit (at the Vista) or whether it was an unconscious, impulsive grabbing for life.

The unconscious reincarnation is something that virtually everyone has an idea about, but the conscious action of reincarnation is not so widely known. It has come to the public's attention in the last few decades through the actions of one particular spirit who chooses conscious reincarnation: the Dalai Lama. Whether or not we think his actions have been of use is irrelevant—the fact remains that here is a soul that chooses to come back and live within the same pattern over and over. My personal opinion is that such action is degenerate and counterproductive for so many reasons, regardless of the good intent of the spirit. And as I write this lesson, the Dalai Lama has announced that he (or the line of consciousness that flows through him) will possibly not be coming back. Wise choice.

Many in the modern world get very hung up on reincarnation and devolve into a fantasy world of past lives—this is just silly. It does not matter who or what you were in another life; what you do, how you evolve, and how you move forward in *this* life is what is important. Memories are truly fleeting, and can serve only to weigh us down.

One thing that has become apparent to me over the years is that sometimes spirits choose consciously to come into life to rebalance themselves by serving in a life that triggers a rebalancing for a wider group of people or a nation. Sometimes these lives they step into are not pleasant, or they step into a fate role that will result in them being a hated person. I came across this purely by accident many years ago. I was teaching a group different tarot techniques, and we were looking at deeply unpopular political figures.

Once we had looked at their current situation, we then looked at their whole life pattern, and finally at their deeper spirit. One particularly nasty politician[4] who has caused immense suffering through his warmongering caught my attention. His outer life showed a story of destruction. His deeper self showed a profound soul in service. I was deeply shocked.

Once the class was over, I delved deeper into investigating this. Sure enough, this vile warmonger had a great and balanced spirit, and had consciously chosen to step into the fate pattern of destruction in order to bring balance and change: he was a soul in Divine service.

Subsequently I came across more of these people, and it really changed how I viewed people in general. I did not wholly trust my results, so I asked other adepts to look as well, without telling them what to look for, just to check out the deeper spirits of a group of people. They came back with the same results and the same sense of astonishment.

Sometimes it takes destruction to bring regeneration, and the key players in that destruction, often reviled, are sometimes (not always) profound spirits who stood at the Vista and agreed to take on the burden of such a life in order to bring balance to themselves and everything around them. Divine service indeed. To knowingly step into a life pattern that brings intense suffering and destruction to others, to be hated and reviled, is a sacrifice indeed.

Rather than write reams on reincarnation, which is not really necessary, there a documentary on YouTube which I strongly suggest you should watch. The link to it is in the practical work section.

It is a documentary of the work of a clinical psychologist in Australia who has dedicated his life to researching this phenomena. It is not a silly New Age film; rather it is the practical results of a large clinical psychology research programme. It was so shocking and outstanding that this documentary was banned from many TV stations around the world by film censors under pressure from the church, who felt that it challenged things just a bit too much.

3.13 Summary

Because the main body of this lesson is about the first steps of learning about these Mysteries and this is an apprentice section, there will be no visionary work attached to this lesson: it is far too dangerous for you to wander off into these Deeper Mysteries. But knowing about them is important for your progression, even at this early stage of training. That knowing triggers deep changes within you that will surface in your more advanced work, and at that point it will be time to delve a little deeper in a practical sense.

In the meantime you can explore for yourself through research. I will not set you specific research tasks for this lesson; it is up to you to decide how much more you wish to look into this. If you do wish to research, then look at depictions of funeral imagery in ancient texts, and go back over the ones you have already looked at. You may well spot more things now you know a bit more of the Mystery. Also look at visionary paintings by past mystical painters, and wall paintings in various temples.

3.14 *Task:* Observing

Watch the following documentary on YouTube:

    www.youtube.com/watch?v=p9IZFw6qIX4

3.15 *Task:* Finding

By now you should have your scales and they should be somewhere in the west part of your house or working room. Now it is time to find the feather. This is not something you can buy, or go to someone who keeps birds and get one: you have to come across it yourself, out in nature.

Over the next couple of weeks, go out for walks (in nature if possible) and as you walk, mull over in your mind the concept of the

---

[4]Still living, so I will not name him.

Scales, the Judgement, the passage of the spirit through death, and how the way you live potentially affects that process. As you walk and think, keep an eye out for a white feather. It must be pure white, and must be either on the ground already or falling down to you in the air. It cannot have been placed somewhere by human hands.

When you find it, place it upon your scales. Do not place it in the cup of the scales (the trigger of Judgement) but place it at the top of one arm of the Scales (where the chain of the cup and the arm of the Scales meet—thread it into the chain). By placing it there and not in the cup, it serves as an indicator that you are beginning to walk within the Death Mysteries and are striving to learn and evolve, but you are not yet asking for Judgement in life, nor are you ready yet to have Judgement in life or death.

Once it is there, just leave it there. Always keep your Scales where they cannot be knocked or tampered with. They are slowly, magically, becoming an exteriorisation of your evolution of Ma'at, of balance, and of your Harvest.

Over your years of magic, you will energetically bond more and more with the Scales, and you will work with them magically as an adept. Should they ever become damaged, simply repair them and put them back where they belong.

Don't move onto the next lesson until you have found your feather. It seems like such a simple thing, but there is a powerful magical action behind this, and having the feather you are given by the land fixed to your Scales before you go in vision deeper into the Underworld (next lesson) is very important.

3.16 Task: Reading

Read the following passage below (*Aeneid* extract from Chapter 6) which is about the Death Mysteries. Read it a few times so that some of its more hidden meanings can come to light in your mind. It is the Greco-Roman version of part of the Death Mystery.

Revisit *The Vision of Ayr the Armenian* from Plato's *Republic*—you should have recently read it. Read the section about the passage of souls flowing down to the land and Underworld, and others flowing up into the stars. This passage of souls is the spirit in conscious choosing where it needs to be next. It is not the spirits of the switched off, but the spirits of the switched on as they choose the next place from the Vista and go to where they need to be.

Extract from Chapter Six of *The Aeneid*—Virgil

And, just before the confines of the wood,
The gliding Lethe leads her silent flood.
About the boughs an airy nation flew,
Thick as the humming bees, that hunt the golden dew;
In summer's heat on tops of lilies feed,
And creep within their bells, to suck the balmy seed:
The winged army roams the fields around;
The rivers and the rocks remurmur to the sound.
Aeneas wond'ring stood, then ask'd the cause
Which to the stream the crowding people draws.

Then thus the sire: "The souls that throng the flood
Are those to whom, by fate, are other bodies ow'd:
In Lethe's lake they long oblivion taste,
Of future life secure, forgetful of the past.
Long has my soul desir'd this time and place,
To set before your sight your glorious race,
That this presaging joy may fire your mind
To seek the shores by destiny design'd."

"O father, can it be, that souls sublime
Return to visit our terrestrial clime,
And that the gen'rous mind, releas'd by death,
Can covet lazy limbs and mortal breath?"

Anchises then, in order, thus begun
To clear those wonders to his godlike son:
"Know, first, that heav'n, and earth's compacted frame,
And flowing waters, and the starry flame,
And both the radiant lights, one common soul

Inspires and feeds, and animates the whole.
This active mind, infus'd thro' all the space,
Unites and mingles with the mighty mass.
Hence men and beasts the breath of life obtain,
And birds of air, and monsters of the main.
Th' ethereal vigor is in all the same,
And every soul is fill'd with equal flame;
As much as earthy limbs, and gross allay
Of mortal members, subject to decay,
Blunt not the beams of heav'n and edge of day.
From this coarse mixture of terrestrial parts,
Desire and fear by turns possess their hearts,
And grief, and joy; nor can the groveling mind,
In the dark dungeon of the limbs confin'd,
Assert the native skies, or own its heav'nly kind:
Nor death itself can wholly wash their stains;
But long-contracted filth ev'n in the soul remains.
The relics of inveterate vice they wear,
And spots of sin obscene in ev'ry face appear.
For this are various penances enjoin'd;
And some are hung to bleach upon the wind,
Some plung'd in waters, others purg'd in fires,
Till all the dregs are drain'd, and all the rust expires.
All have their manes, and those manes bear:
The few, so cleans'd, to these abodes repair,
And breathe, in ample fields, the soft Elysian air.

Lesson 4

The Underworld and the Abyss

With an understanding of fate and death under your belt, it is now time to learn a bit more about the Underworld. In texts it is mainly touched upon in relation to death, but it is much more than that.

The Underworld, in its deepest, most abstract form, is the *compression of manifestation*. As consciousness crosses over the threshold into manifestation, the body that houses that spirit/consciousness begins its long march to destruction and breakdown. We talked briefly in the module on creation about how the Divine Breath issues out an energetic impulse that, as it moves towards manifestation, is slowed down by the beings that interact with that energy so that it can manifest.

That same action of slowing down continues throughout the physical manifestation until it becomes so slow and dense that it eventually ceases to be a vehicle for living consciousness: the spirit releases and the body/substance composts, finally becoming dense substance. We see this in geology and archaeology, and from a magical perspective we call this process the Underworld.

If we look at it from a different angle, we can also see this process in action in the Inner Desert: the realm where nothing lives. This is the back room of creation and destruction, and the template for time, manifestation, and destruction is held in the Inner Desert. When you stand in the Inner Desert in vision, 'up' is the future, the desert is the present, and beneath the sands is the 'past' (the Underworld).

If we look at the Underworld from the point of view of our physical existence on the earth as magicians, the Underworld is beneath our feet and is the realm of ancient deities, ancestors, the death landscape, the sleepers, and vast beings from the distant past.

Magicians access this realm for many reasons: working in death, connecting with the ancient powers of the land, working with ancient deities, ancient temples, and our distant, long gone relatives of humanity. There is also another very important reason why magicians work with this realm: it is an anchor. One of the dynamics you have already begun to learn about is the energetic balancing that occurs for a magician if they go into the past before they go into the future, and if they go 'down' before they go 'up.'

Magicians also learn about the various types of beings that can be found in the Underworld, beings that are often treated with fear and revulsion, usually because of a lack of knowledge and direct experience. What some call demons can be accessed through the Underworld and the Abyss, but the term 'demon' is laden with misunderstanding, fantasy, and fear.

We will look at demonic beings (along with

angelic beings) a bit later in the apprentice section. Suffice it to say that although these beings are dangerous and should not be lightly messed around with, they are not 'evil.'

The whole concept of good and evil that has been promulgated by some more recent religions (Christianity, for example) is designed to steer you away from danger, but it has also instilled a simplistic duality into the minds of generations which only serves to cut people off from the deeper aspects of creation and destruction.

So let us have a look at the different layers of the Underworld, what one would expect to find there, and how a magician would work there. Then we will look briefly at the Abyss, a connected realm that links directly into the Underworld. In this lesson you will also visit the Underworld in vision to begin your first real connections with this realm, but you will not be going down the Abyss just yet: to access such a place needs knowledge and skill to keep you from destruction—it is not a place to play in.

4.1 Threshold of the Underworld

The first layer of the Underworld is the threshold between the living and the dead. It is also a layer that appears in the inner landscape of a land, and is the place where the dead, the living, faery beings, and land spirits all interconnect and intersect.

This is the layer of the Underworld most known to various types of magicians and which is worked with to access the faery realm, recent ancestors who have remained connected to the land (rather than gone in to rebirth), and to access the first layer of older deities.

This aspect of the inner realm is very interesting and is a space where magicians are very active. If a magician wishes to learn about the land around them, its fairly recent history, or about the faery beings and land beings that are all around us, the magician would work in this threshold place.

It is pretty close to our own consciousness, therefore the rules of safe engagement are very close to the rules you would apply in your everyday physical life when you are in a place unknown to you.

The threshold of the Underworld can be accessed through the inner landscape of the land: they overlap and are of one another.

In this crossover space, we find faery beings, land beings, ghosts, recent ancestors, and all manner of different beings.

You have already begun to work in the inner landscape, and if you move into the inner landscape with intent to interact with this crossover threshold, it will open up to you. We will spend a bit more time looking at this crossover place and the beings within it (mainly faery beings) in another lesson.

Faery beings are not nice little sweet things with wings: they are strange, powerful beings with a twisted sense of humour and no particular love of humanity. But once the magician earns the trust of these beings and learns to work sensibly with them, they can become powerful allies in your life and magical work.

If in your work as an apprentice you cross paths with one of these beings, be very honourable, honest, straightforward, and respectful—regardless of how you are treated or approached by them. These beings will test you, harass you, or try to beguile you to see what your deeper self is like. They will watch how you treat the land and creatures around you, how you interact with the land, the elements, animals, birds, spiders, etc., and they will form their opinion of you from how you act towards everything around you.

The difference between land beings and faery beings is the difference between a reptile and an ape: one is much closer to us than the other in terms of consciousness. Again, this is something you will learn more about in lessons to come, and is not something you need to be dipping you toe into just yet.

The other type of beings you are likely to come into contact with in this threshold space are the *sleeping dead*. Basically, there are two different types of sleepers that you will encounter upon the land and in this realm: working sleepers and waiting sleepers. A *working sleeper* is usually an ancestor that is deeply (tribally) connected to a land area, and went into death, sometimes ritually, with the intent to work as an interface between the land and the tribe. The incidences of these sleepers are getting rarer as archaeologists dig more and more of them up.

Not every ancient burial is a sleeper; it is often just a body. But sometimes they are, and if you wish to work with an intentional tribal sleeper, you need to know the rules of engagement: something you will learn fairly soon. Most countries have some sort of intentional sleeper present upon the land, as this was a widespread practice in many different cultures.

Another type of ancestral consciousness you will potentially come across in this threshold space are the *waiting sleepers*. These are people who upon death believed that they had to stay asleep in the land until the time of judgement arrived. This is particularly common in pre-twentieth century Catholic communities. The religious pattern was so strong in the life of the person that upon death they immediately fixed themselves to their body in burial and simply stayed there.

One way to spot this in a culture is where the idea of cremation or exposure of the body to the elements is abhorrent. In the Catholic communities, it was felt that keeping the body as preserved as possible would enable them, upon judgement, to rise in body and ascend to heaven. In terms of the death realm, they would not really appear, or only appear in that realm briefly as they held on tightly to their bodies in the belief that this would guarantee them a place in heaven.

As an aside, but one very relevant to you, there is a strange phenomenon that I have observed that is probably the fragmented root of this belief. Over the last few years I have observed waves of 'Judgement' flowing over the land of the living, and other people who are sensitive have also been picking up on this. It seems to affect those who do pick up on it, triggering an impulse to either magically engage with the Lesser Judgement in life, or triggering an unconscious impulse to 'clean up their act.' In the northern hemisphere it seems to trigger once a year, and over the last few years it has gotten stronger and stronger.

I became very curious about this, as so many magicians from around the world were contacting me about this experience, and were seeing what I was seeing. So I decided to investigate further.

I worked in the inner realms to try and watch this impulse as it flowed out onto the land, and asked a being standing beside me what the hell was going on. This was an angelic being, a type very close to humanity (a Noble One) and therefore easy to converse with.

The being showed me cycles of this type of event happening every few thousand years, usually when large parts of humanity had become 'rotten.' Essentially, what the being conveyed was that as a nation or group of nations devolves (which is a natural progression in most nations), the people engage less and less with any mystical, religious, tribal, or magical patterns. Some who are removed from such patterns still live in relative balance for generations, and some do not.

The groups that do not live in balance tend to react in a particular way in death: they are fearful and immediately grab for another life without going through the process of the Scales, or even attempting to evolve towards that process. When there are large numbers of people circumventing this natural process, it causes a deficit, an imbalance of some sort, which in turn automatically triggers a deep energetic response.

That imbalance seems to be the result of not enough people going through the natural progression in death, which in turn results in too many living humans in general (if they are not going through the full death process, which slows them down), and too many that are deeply unbalanced: the species becomes self-destructive. That response is, to put it bluntly:

"If you will not come to us, then we will come to you."

The process of balance through the Scales flows out of death and into life instead, and affects every living thing. I asked the being to show me the process, but what I was shown didn't really fully translate for me: I didn't fully get it and still don't. But I will outline for you what I did understand and what I observed, so that you can ponder over it for yourself.

What I was shown was waves of energy sweeping over the land, and the humans it flowed over seemed to be deeply affected by it. Some were affected physically, and some were swept into death. Some whom I observed seemed to recognise what was happening and intentionally engaged in the Lesser Judgement process, and in those cases, the wave of energy seemed to enliven them.

As I write this,[1] we are currently in a phase of this 'wave.' Just from chatting lightly to the local villagers where I live, I have found that many are having sleepless nights, some are feeling a sense of doom, and others are furiously spring cleaning. Interesting...

I have been working with the self-assessment process, as have other magicians I know, and the energy does seem to get up behind that conscious engagement.

It is not a wave of 'God's punishment'; rather it seems to be a very natural response to the state of our species at this time. We really need to get away from this dualist and simplistic religious dogmatic thinking that infects everything that we do as magicians.

Observing this process, and also thinking about it, it makes me wonder if this natural response/process is behind some of the Biblical stories that run along similar veins, and also the ideas of the Essenes, who felt that Judgement was at hand.

The Essenes felt that they needed to prepare for Judgement and therefore had to live their lives in a particular way. If we take the religious dressing out of the picture, what we are left with is a group of people who were picking up on this wave of the Judgement process and tried to live their lives in a way that would positively engage it. But as always with everything connected to humanity, dogmatic thinking quickly moves in and the process begins to fall apart.

And in that, I think, is a major lesson for us at this time in our own history: do not try to box, organise, and systematise too much. We all need some structure, but there has to be fluidity in thinking that allows the consciousness of an individual person to connect fully with these inner impulses in their own way. That translates to *walking your own path in gnosis*: we are truly unique as individuals, and what is the right approach for one may not be the right approach for another person.

Back to the Underworld. (By the way, these little diversions are intentionally put into these lessons so that they cannot be easily found by those simply dipping into the text out of curiosity. What an apprentice can take away from these texts is vastly different to what a casual reader will understand.)

4.2 The first layer of the Underworld

The first true layer of the Underworld is where you find deities that are still active in the outside world, deities that are connected to the Underworld in terms of death, destruction, the cycles of species, etc. It is also the layer where the magician finds access to the realm of death.

This is also the realm where we find the ancient dynamic of prophecy: going into an Underworld cave to meet an oracle or goddess who heals, curses, or prophesies is an ancient pattern indeed.

In most ancient cultures in the northern hemisphere, we have many examples of stories of Underworld goddesses who sit at the first layer of the Underworld and interact with the living world. The goddess Sul in Bath, England is a prime example. She is also

---
[1] September 2014.

known as Sulis Minerva, and was a goddess of cursing, blessing, and healing. Glastonbury in England is another place that is an ancient entrance to this first layer of the Underworld.

Sadly, these days fantasy has overtaken reality in regards to Glastonbury, and it abounds with Merlins, people dressing as faeries, and various women play-acting in a generic 'goddess' community.

Glastonbury is an entrance to the realm of death, to the Underworld, and to the powers that surface into our world from the Underworld: the power of destruction. These days it is covered with a crust of commercial messiahs, wannabe 'wizards,' and tons of escapism.

One way to sidestep a lot of this type of 'crust' that seems to cover the Underworld, and one of the major keys to working with this realm and the deities, powers, and beings that inhabit this realm, is to work with the beings without attaching 'names' or dogmas to them.

One way to do this, and it is an ancient way of working, is to work with and connect with the beings as they appear, without all the dogmatic dressing, and to not work with 'known names' but to address them in relation to their function.

A goddess of the Underworld is just that. She does not need the names that humans have given her, nor the dressings that they have attached to her.

Before we move on, let's just look a bit closer at these different goddesses of the Underworld, as you will be soon meeting one.

4.3 The Goddess in the Cave

The Goddess in the Cave is an ancient expression of the female deities that reside in this first layer of the Underworld. It is a visionary interface that I have used with students for decades as it is so stable and predictable. It is not 'one' goddess that is connected to when magicians work in vision with this being; rather it is the female deity of a particular land that is contacted.

Overall, though, the interface is the same throughout the northern hemisphere (I have no idea if the same pattern exists in the southern hemisphere) and that is to say: cave, goddess, pool or river of water.

It seems to be a particular pattern that allows the individual female deity of a particular land to interface through. So for example, if you have been working with the goddess in the cave on your own land for a while and then move to another country, it is likely that the same visionary pattern would work, but the actual being you meet, while still being a goddess, is different. They are heavily interwoven with the landmass, and seem to be expressions of the female power within that land.

By using the stripped-down interface, the magician is able to use that pattern to connect with the goddess in the land where they are and work with them without having to resort to using names/dogmas or human constructed patterns.

It is very much a fashion these days to take goddesses out of their natural environment and shoehorn them into a modern role which is often far removed from who and what they actually are. And while some goddesses do *travel* i.e. you can connect to the exact same goddess regardless of what landmass you are on, there are many who do not travel. The usual rule of thumb is the deeper in the Underworld they reside, the more likely they are to travel. This is for a lot of reasons which we will cover later in another lesson.

The reason the magician connects with these 'Goddesses in the Cave' is that such a connection helps to open up a lot of the Underworld for the magician, makes it more accessible, and also can afford a deep level of protection: you work for her, she will work for you. The work trade-off changes somewhat according to where you live and what exact power it is you are tapping into. And even within your own land, there are various layers of these goddesses.

For example, where I live there is a layer of this cave goddess that is very specific to the valley that I live in. If you go just a few miles down the road, she vanishes. But if you go a little deeper into the first layer of the Underworld, where I live, you hit another layer of goddess that is specific to the island of Britain, but does not appear, for example, in the USA.

So it would seem we are connecting with various frequencies and more surface expressions of a deeper power, and it is that deeper power that we will look at next.

4.4 The Deeper Underworld

Once you pass through the first layer of the Underworld and continue moving downward, you come to a deeper layer of the Underworld where ancient powers reside and are still accessible to the magician.

These realms work very much along the lines of *as above, so below*, in that the patterns and layers mirror each other. Just as the magician reaches 'up' and finds primal deities, mediators of Divinity, angelic beings, etc., so the Underworld, too, has its own mirrored layers. The Deeper Underworld and the powers that reside there mirror the deeper powers of creation that flow into manifestation.

In practical terms of an apprentice and initiate, that means finding and being able to work with powerful deities that once were widely worked with in the ancient world. Although some of these deities still have a presence in their temples in the manifest worlds, their roots and deeper selves reside in the Underworld, anchoring them as they bridge between the past and the present.

The ancient deities, and also the roots of the ancient temples that are still partially or fully operating in the manifest/surface world, create a bridge between their outer existence in the surface world, their original outer structure in the Underworld, and their inner templates in the Desert. The surface world is a fulcrum for them, and the power flows in a constant stream from the inner world, out into the surface manifest world, and then flows down into the Underworld.

This constant stream of energy creates a highway for power and consciousness to travel along. We as living humans can flow into the inner realm as magicians to access the inner temple, and we can also flow down into the Underworld to reach the patterns of its original existence. This pathway of power is also utilised by spirits, and this is demonstrated, for example, by the *Vision of Ayr* that you read in Plato.

These pathways can be utilised not only to access these powerful deities and their temples, but they are also highways to realms that these temples and deities are connected to and plugged into. So now you can begin to see how knowledge of this realm is so vital to the work of a magician. They are more than just realms in themselves; they are also highways to the depths of creation and destruction itself.

Rather than ramble on for hours about this realm, it will be easier for you to just visit it in vision, passing through the layers and going into an ancient temple to stand before one of the very powerful goddesses that reside in this deep realm. This interaction will trigger the creation of your deep tap root that will anchor you in the depths of the Underworld in order to prepare you for the work to come in the future.

Before you get to that practical work, I want to also outline another major aspect of this subject matter for you (though it will not be something you visit or work in for quite some times in your studies, for safety's sake), and that aspect is the Abyss.

4.5 The Abyss

There has been quite a lot written about the Abyss over the last century, but most of it is vague, or is written from a place of 'not knowing,' where the writer draws on other texts and forms a theory based upon them. Others have written about the Abyss, inspired by Crowley, and place personal psychological meaning to the Abyss and the magical act of crossing the Abyss. Still others deny it altogether as they have not had any experience of it, and the writings they have read make no sense to them. There are some modern writings out there on the Abyss that actually do tackle it from the writers' direct experience, but for the most part, much of what is readable and truly is about the Abyss can be found in ancient and mystical texts.

It is not that magicians don't know about it: many do but they choose, for good reason, to be silent about it. I thought long and hard about how best to approach this for the apprentice section, as I have written about the Abyss before, which has helped some people but has also triggered truly disastrous experiments in others. I came to the conclusion that it would be wise to give the apprentice an overview, with the appropriate health warnings, so that the apprentice at least has a basic understanding of what it is, why it is, and how it works.

Later, in your adept level of training, you will learn how to work in the Abyss and how to cross the Abyss, and most important of all, why a magician crosses the Abyss, what it does, and what effect it has on the rest of your life. Too many people play around magically in and around the Abyss, and the result of such curiosity and experimentation tends invariably to result in death or mental illness.

So what is the Abyss? Moving away from all previous writings, the following is what I have discovered through decades of magical visionary work.

My earliest encounter with the Abyss was as a young magician. I was working down in the Underworld in ritual vision when a being appeared and guided me down a tunnel which opened out over what appeared to be a vast crack that ran through all the worlds.

Something within me knew what it was and what I had to do. I knew that what I was about to do could potentially kill me, but I also knew deep inside that it was something I needed to do. I had to step off the cliff I was standing on, and put my trust in my own soul and in Divinity. I crossed the Abyss by stepping out into the nothing and not falling, but reaching the other side. It changed my life in every way possible.

After that event I spent years exploring and discovering the Abyss, and then more years of working in service both down and up in the Abyss. I finally had to stop working in the Abyss when I hit the menopause, as my body could no longer handle the huge physical and energetic impact that such work involved.

So now let's go over what I found, so that you have a good idea of what it is we are talking about.

As an aside, for a time after my first experience, I did not realise that what I was working with was the Abyss—it was only after lengthy discussions with Jewish Kabbalists and mystical visionaries that they finally drilled into me what it was I was doing and looking at.

In retrospect I was very lucky to survive unscathed: I was very young and foolish, but I was also well grounded and was working deeply with the Noble Ones. I think I owe my life, or at least my mental health, to their attentive guidance in those early years.

4.6 The Highway of the Abyss

The Abyss is found in the Inner Desert and appears to us in a visionary context as a vast, seemingly bottomless crack in the earth. If you look up (it took me some years to realise that there is an 'up' also) the crack also runs through the 'sky': it is a separation that runs through the whole pattern of the Desert.

The other side of the Abyss appears misty: the knowledge of what lies beyond is obscured with mist. If you look down the Abyss, you will see ledges and tunnels, and sometimes you will also see beings looking back at you. If you look up, it tends to be obscured by mist: most of the time you are only able to see the Desert (our own time) and down (our past).

And that brings me to the dynamics that flow through this place: up is future, surface is now, down is past. What is coming into formation (life, substance, time) flows down from above, and also concurrently from across the Abyss (Divine utterance across the Abyss): those two streams of power meet on our side of the Abyss and immediately filter through a pattern which begins the process of shaping something for creation (something you will learn a lot more about in the Initiate section).

When something is breaking down, it stays in the manifest world and sinks into the Underworld. If it is a power or energy or being/soul that should not be coming back into manifestation, it sinks deeply into the Underworld and finally passes into the Abyss. The Abyss is a place where manifestation is suspended: beings sleep here—or are bound here—to keep them out of the circulation of physical life or the manifest world.

When a being (or species, even) is or becomes very imbalanced to the point of being overly destructive, it is withdrawn from the cycle of birth/death and is essentially put into storage. (This also makes me wonder if this is where the 'Second Deathers' go.) The beings found down the Abyss are not just humans pulled out of circulation, but also many other types of beings that are destructive and seriously out of balance, or simply do not fit in the pattern of life any more.

Very ancient deities can be found sleeping or even bound into the Abyss, as are demonic beings, i.e. beings that are solely destructive and no longer have a role in the composting/necessary destruction process in life, along with the consciousness of ancient dangerous diseases, the spirits of ancient sentient beings that have been taken out of the loop of creation (like some dinosaurs, for example)—you get the idea.

The layers of the Abyss that are nearest to our layer of the Desert (fairly recent past—last few thousand years) have beings that are not fully locked down or sleeping, but they cannot leave the Abyss. These beings can be worked with in times of major crisis, as they hold ancient knowledge and have excellent guarding skills.

However, a magician who does that really needs to know what they are doing and have a very good reason for doing it. If one of these beings bridges through a human (hitches a ride) and into the manifest world, our world, they can do untold damage: as it is with disease, so it is with these beings. If they have been out of circulation for a few thousand years and are suddenly inadvertently released back into the world, we have no natural immunity to them. The consequences of that can be horrifying.

The Abyss has a vast angelic being that is essentially the 'doorkeeper' of the Abyss. For some reason, some magicians seem to think that this being is a demon...no it is not, it is just a vastly powerful, non-fluffy angelic being that keeps and guards the threshold.

When as magicians you come to learn how to work with the Abyss, first you will learn to work with this keeper, who will ensure you do what you are supposed to do and don't do what you are not supposed to do.

On the other side of the Abyss is the source of Divine Breath: the Universal Power of Divine Being. The other side of the Abyss is the realm that has no time, no structure of manifestation; it is a place beyond creation, a place of eternal being, and is the source of the impulse that crosses the Abyss and begins its journey into creation and manifestation.

Heavy stuff indeed! So let us get back to the topic of the Underworld and on to the practical work.

4.7 About the practical work

The practical work in this lesson, for the most part, will be visionary work.

It is important—really important, for your own safety—that you do not step out of the boundaries of the vision and go off exploring on your own. When worked with correctly, this visionary work is perfectly safe and will give you more information on some aspects of the Underworld than a pile of books could. However, if you step outside of or over the thresholds outlined in the vision you are very likely to injure yourself: this is where the apprentice has to be a responsible adult and not a curious, foolish teen.

The act of doing these Underworld visions will trigger the establishment and growth of your own 'tap root' that will seat strongly in the Underworld, giving you a strong foundation and anchor for your future work.

It will, for some, also trigger the slow process of 'remembering' for those of you who have stepped into the inner worlds in other lives. If this triggering happens, do not get hung up on it and start to identify with that remembering. You do not make a big deal out of your childhood memories, and these are the same. They are past: remember, and then move on.

Advice:

Do these visions when you have time to relax or sleep afterwards. Plan ahead, and ensure that you have plenty of time to process the vision work through your sleep and through your body. After you have been in the Underworld, eat something solid that will ground you. Do this every time you go into the Underworld, as it will help your body deal with the impact.

Have your journal to hand in the room with you so that you can take notes as soon as you come out of vision. Always write up your findings, impressions, and consequent dreams, and also note any bodily effects afterwards, or strange happenings around you. Write them in a computer log so that they can be submitted.

Like all other visions on this course, learn the key elements and steps to each vision before you attempt it. Read it repeatedly, like a story, until you are familiar with each part of the vision.

Then—and only then—if you wish, record the vision so that you can listen to it as you work and have it guide you.

If you do record it, make sure you put in the breaks of silence where you are doing something (like climbing) that will take a bit of time. Do not add anything to it, do not embellish or dress the vision in any way. It is a specific map to follow, not a psychological pathworking.

4.8 *Task:* **First Vision—The access to death through the Underworld**

Before you start the vision, open the directions, see the contacts on the thresholds, and then sit before the central altar with your back to the east, so you are facing west with the central flame before you. Do not lie down for this work: it is very important that you stay awake.

Meditate for a few minutes to still yourself, and when you are ready close your eyes and see the central flame in your inner vision. Hold the clear intention that you are going to go into the Underworld to visit the threshold of death.

As you watch the flame, an entrance to the land beneath you opens up, and the flame falls down into the Underworld.

In vision, stand up and look down the hole that has appeared in the room. It will be dark, and you will just be able to see the light of the flame in the darkness. You will also see rough stone steps leading down into the darkness, and they curl around the hole to form a stone spiral stairway.

Step onto the first step, holding your hand to the wall for support, and begin to climb down the steps. Even though it is dark, you will be able to just see enough to climb safely down.

Climb down and down, moving deeper and deeper into the darkness. Take your time and run your hand over the rough stone walls as you climb down, feeling the stone, its moisture, and the occasional tree root. Eventually you come to an area where there is a floor, and an entrance covered in fabric and moss.

Pull the fabric to one side, and step into a cave that seems to be dimly lit by a light of its own and which has a pool of water in it.

The water seeps out on the far side of the cave, vanishing down a dark tunnel, and the wall on the opposite side of the cave has a large stone high-backed seat that is naturally formed out of the rock.

Upon the seat sits an old woman who is asleep. Her long hair grows into the rock beside her and down into the floor like roots.

Lesson 4. The Underworld and the Abyss

Around her, upon her lap, in her arms, and tucked into her clothing are many creatures and birds, also fast asleep. You also begin to notice the occasional human also sleeping on the floor beside her and curled around her feet, and in the edges of her long cloak that spills out onto the floor.

Tiptoe quietly towards her, as you intend to pass by her and into a tunnel that leads deeper into the Underworld.

As you get closer to her you recognise her: you have already met her, given her a gift, and honoured her. When you draw close to her, lean or kneel down and touch the hem of her cloak to honour her: this is the *Mother*, the goddess who holds the threshold between the living land and the Underworld.

As you touch the hem of her cloak, she opens one eye and looks at you. Bow to her and ask her permission to pass beyond her and into the tunnel of the Underworld.

She nods her permission, closes her eye, and goes back to sleep.

See the tunnel that leads into the darkness, and as you step into the tunnel, you realise you are walking in ankle-deep water.

Walk along the streambed and listen carefully for any sounds that you may hear. Take your time walking down this tunnel.

The tunnel eventually opens out in a vast cavern that holds shallow water and ancient trees growing out of the water. The place is lit with strange green light that flows from the trees, the water, and the very air in this strange place. This Underworld is the head of the River of Death that flows through the Underworld and emerges in the Plains of Death.

Wade through the water, walking among the trees, and as you walk, sing. The trees are the guardians of the river, and the thing they love above all else is the sound of singing. Single lullabies, childhood songs, or simply hum as you weave in and out of the trees. Take your time walking through the forest.

Should you develop a thirst as you walk, *do not drink of the water at all*. Be disciplined and continue walking.

As you make your way further into the Underworld Forest you begin to see a faint light that grows brighter the closer you get to it.

As you emerge from the forest you see a large opening, an entrance of the chamber you are in, and it opens out onto a bright, sunny desert where the waters of the Underworld come together to form a river.

Do not step out of the Underworld cavern; do not step over the threshold of the cavern into the desert. Stay within the cavern, but draw close enough that you can see the desert, the river, and everything in that landscape.

As you look out over the desert, see the river flowing from the cavern, and see it flow into the desert and off into the horizon.

See people gathered by the river, and look closely at the people. Some will look 'different' energetically: they are the angelic beings that work in death and 'dress up' to appear human in order to connect with humans more easily.

Watch for other beings coming and going; watch what the people do, how they are, how they are reacting, and what actions they take, if any. Take as long as you need to observe.

When you are ready to leave, step back and turn around.

Look at the vast cavern with the Underworld Forest and all the water, and look around the edges of the cavern. You will see, off to one side and partially hidden, a rough stone stairway that climbs up the side of the cavern and vanishes up into the darkness.

Climb onto the stone stairway and ascend to the top of the cavern. Take your time and watch your step as you climb.

Once you reach the top you will find a tunnel with yet more stairs leading up. Climb those too, with the intention of returning to the surface world.

As you climb those steps, you will hear voices or mumbles, and the stone walls of the stairwell begin to turn to compacted earth and tree roots.

Climb slowly, and listen as you climb: there are various voices one can find in this space.

Some are ancestors in the land; some are faery beings. Do not try to connect with them, just be aware of them as you climb.

As you climb, you begin to see light up above you. Climb towards that shaft of light, and you will find yourself emerging out of a hole in your working room. Climb out of the hole and as you step out of it, the hole closes up and all that is left is the central flame burning in the centre.

Before you open your eyes, go over in your mind everything you saw and experienced. Ensure you have recalled the memory, and once you are clear, open your eyes and write down key words or notations in your journal that will remind you once you come to type up the details on computer.

Always, whenever you do involved visions like this, have your journal before you and write down notes as soon as you come out of vision, as often visionary contact fades in the memory much quicker than ordinary memories do. From those notes you can then type up in more detail and keep it in a computer file.

About the vision

This vision took you down through the cave of the goddess; this is a place you can visit often if you wish, to go be there, talk to her, sleep, wash, learn, and observe. When I was a young magician I visited her often and learned a great deal from talking with her, from watching, or just being there.

From her cave you moved into a slightly deeper part of the Underworld, which often appears as a partially submerged underground forest: the head of the river Lethe. This is also a place you can work regularly to observe (nothing more) as spirits of many different species pass through on their journey in and out of death. There are quite a few different rivers that flow from this place, but simply stay with the one that you have worked with and now know. Don't try to over-organize it in your mind—it is tempting to decide what rivers flow out of this place and what their names are (there are quite a few ancient texts about this place). That is a bad road to go down early in your magical training: learn to keep an open mind that is about direct experience, and don't try to map these realms. They will eventually reveal themselves to you directly over time.

The threshold between the Underworld Forest/Cavern and the Plains/River of Death is a good place to go and observe. You can watch the dead as they go through their various processes, and also observe the angelic beings that work in depth from a safe distance. Do not be tempted at this stage in your training to step over that threshold. Be patient, learn to observe, and learn to rein in the curiosity or impulse to step over into the death realm.

Notice that you did not return the way that you came. This is slowly introducing you to a very interesting dynamic in visionary work whereby you always have to take your time going to a realm, letting the body, mind, and spirit adjust to the different energies, and also ensuring that the right steps take you to the right place. But coming back sometimes you do not need to take such a convoluted route. You needed to go through the Cave of the Goddess to trigger her protection, but to get home from the Underworld, you simply go 'up.'

So now let us move on to the second vision in this lesson, which is to go deeper into the Underworld and connect with the very ancient and powerful goddess power that resides there.

Notice that in this lesson you are connecting with goddesses and not gods: you are learning about the power of the vessel before going on to learn everything that the vessel contains. There are male powers also in the Underworld, of course, and once you have learned one side of the coin, then you will learn the other and balance the two together.

4.9 *Task:* Second Vision—Accessing the root ancient temples

This vision takes you down into a very ancient layer of temple culture so that you can interact with the consciousness still residing there.

As an aside, these ancient temples are also found in the Inner Desert: the Underworld version is on our 'side of the fence,' the remnants of the physical manifestation of the temple. And the temple found in the Desert is the remains of the inner construct of the same temple that is found in the Underworld—the Inner Desert version is the back room, so to speak, of the physical temple.

The more you work in the Desert and the Underworld (and upper worlds) as the course goes on, you will find that mirror images of places, beings, and people appear not only in the various realms, but also in the Desert.

To access the manifest history or future potential of a place or being, you go to the realms that hold the outer pattern. To access the timeless inner construct, spirit, or consciousness of a place or being, you go to the Desert.

Over the span of the course, you will learn carefully how to access these different realms individually and eventually learn how to work with them together. But to stay solid, safe, and sane, you need to learn, visit, and interact with these different aspects in slow, careful steps.

This next visit is a key step in that process. This specific ancient temple that you will be visiting has roots far back in human history, and over the millennia has become a composite made up of different temples that worked with the same power. This composite action happens to places and also beings when there is a vast span of time where they have been or still are active. So for example, the powers you experience and interact with in this temple will be recognisable when you then go to visit (in the flesh) some of the still-standing very ancient temples that worked with the same deep goddess power.

It took me a while to figure this out. After working in depth for a few years with these places, and then going to an ancient temple site, I immediately recognised the power signature and aspects of the building. But then I went to an ancient site of the same power but in a different land, and the same thing happened. It took me a while to realise that over time, as the inner aspects of the temples sink into the Underworld, those that were working with the same power fused together somehow and became a 'root' temple.

In the vision I will not name the goddess you are going to work with, as there is more than one name for her. But once you have worked with her, you will recognise her in slightly different forms, and one of those forms will gravitate to you in your magical work.

The other thing to understand about working with this deep temple is that this particular vision is the one that really roots you into the Underworld and gives you a powerful anchor to work with. The deeper you go 'down' in your practice, the further you will then be able to go 'up' in your ritual visionary work.

4.10 The vision

Prepare yourself in the same way that you did for the previous vision, but for this vision sit with your back to the central altar, facing north. The ground will open up the same way, but this time it will be the north flame that falls down into the Underworld.

In vision, follow the flame in exactly the same way, and take the same route through the cave of the goddess and through the Underworld Forest. When you get to the forest, walk through the water again with the intention of going to the deep, ancient temple of the goddess in the Underworld. (Your clear intent and focus allows the entrances to appear in the vision—the beings know from your intent where you want to go.)

As you walk through the Underworld Forest, keep a lookout for the temple guardian. This guardian can appear in many different forms, but you will know them when you see them. When you find the guardian, bow, tell them who you are, and ask permission to enter into the deep Underworld temple of the goddess. The guardian will look at you, and you will notice that they have quite a few eyes around their form that open and look at you in detail. The guardian will see that you have already worked with the goddess in the cave and are therefore suitable to access deeper into the Underworld.

When the guardian is happy with what they see (that you are who you say you are) the guardian will either point you to a hidden entrance, or they will take you by the hand and lead you to an entrance you would not have seen had you not been shown it. The entrance will have water from the forest flowing into it, and will most likely be partially submerged.

Get into the water and dive down under the water, swimming forward towards a light that will have appeared. You will swim under the entrance and emerge in a tunnel with low light and lots of ancient paintings on the walls of strange-looking demon guardians.

Stand up in the water and follow the tunnel, staying within the shallow water, and look at the paintings as you walk. As you follow the tunnel, you will notice that the water is starting to get deeper again. Continue to walk until it has become too deep, and you can no longer see anything in front of you. At that point, dive back down into the water, swimming forward underwater again towards a light.

When you reach the light, swim up to the surface and you will find yourself in an underground lake with stone steps at the side that you can use to climb out. Once you are out and have stood up, you realise you are standing at an entrance to a vast stone temple with a doorway so big you can barely see the capstones. It looks like it was built for giants.

Pass through the entrance and walk into the rectangular outer court which has huge columns on either side of you. As you continue, you see a slightly smaller doorway before you with vast wooden carved doors covered in strange signs and symbols, faces, and shapes. Place your hands upon the door so that the door can feel you. After a moment, the doors swing slowly open and you feel like you are propelled forward with an invisible push from behind.

You are pushed into a vast inner sanctum of the temple. It is cubic in shape, with a ceiling almost a hundred feet high. At the far end sits a vast statue upon a throne. The statue is of a black lioness goddess seated upon a stone throne, with two bronze doors between her feet and a bowl of fire before her. The power emanating from this statue is so strong that it takes your breath away. Take a moment to simply stand in its presence and let your mind, spirit, and body adjust to the power of this goddess.

Slowly walk to the feet of the statue and touch them lightly with respect and recognition. As you touch the foot it moves, and you realise this is not a statue but a living being. You step back, and the doors between her feet open: out walks a priest or priestess of this temple, and they stand before you. Bow to the priest/priestess, tell them your name, who you are, what time you come from, which land, city, and that you are there to make connection with this ancient place. Tell them that you are studying as an apprentice in magical training and wish to learn.

The priest/priestess may talk to you briefly, and try to remember what they say. The contact then points down to your feet and asks you to take off your shoes or socks. Even if you are physically sitting with nothing on your feet in this vision, see your everyday footwear on you in vision, and take them off until you are standing on the stone floor in bare feet. Feel the sense of your skin on the stone. Feel the temperature (hot or cold?) and feel the energy of this place through your feet.

The contact then points up to the roof. Be aware of your upper body in the surface world while you are still standing in the Underworld. Imagine your upper body in the surface world and your feet/legs in the Underworld: get a sense of stretching between the two places. Take as long as you need to in order to get this sense, and don't worry about the visuals—simply recover the feeling or sense of this stretched position: your feet upon the stone in the Underworld and your body in the surface world; imagine it as if you were standing up.

Once you have a sense of the stretch, now bring your focus back to the contact and the goddess before you. The priest/priestess tells you that this ancient lioness goddess is vital for the northern hemisphere of the earth: she is the guardian and protector of balance, or Ma'at. She is fierce, destructive, and yet compassionate and healing: whatever is needed to bring balance.

The contact reaches out and gets a hold of your left arm, and begins to draw out a small number of shapes, sigils or hieroglyphs on your skin. It will be a fairly simple shape or shapes, and work very hard to see them *and remember them*. Once that is done, the contact leads you back to the foot of the statue and asks you to once more place your hands upon the foot of the goddess. Keep your hands there and feel her power: it is a very specific power that has a very distinct feel or sense to it. Remember that feeling or sense.

When you are ready, remove your hands, bow to her, and step back. Kneel down and look at the floor. It is dusty. Write your full name in the dust, the name you were born with. In the dust you see a small but very sharp blade. Pick it up, cut your finger, and drip a few drops of blood on your name written in the dust: you are leaving your unique identity at her feet, deep in the Underworld.

Once you have done that, the great goddess moves, leans over, and places her hand by you in order for you to step up onto her hand. The priest/priestess bows to you and tells you that you can come back here as often as you like simply to be in the presence of this power, to root yourself, and also to come here if you wish to learn about your own need for balance: the priesthood here will place within you the knowledge that you need in order to facilitate that balance. That knowledge will then appear in your mind unbidden when it is needed.

Step onto the hand of the goddess, and hold on as she holds you up to her face. Feel her lion breath upon your face; see the endless stars in her eyes, the sharp power of her teeth, and the softness of her fur. She looks into your eyes and blows gently over you: the breath of the goddess. She then holds you up, higher and higher to the roof of the temple, where you see a small opening to a stair well cut into the stone. Climb onto the stairs and ascend without looking back.

As you climb, you come to a break in the steps which you recognise as the stairway from the Underworld Forest to the surface world. Keep climbing up and up until you emerge back into your work space, and step gently back into your body.

Before you open your eyes, once more remember the shapes that were drawn upon your arm. Once you have a sense of them, open your eyes and draw them in your journal.

Once you are finished and are ready to close the work space down, when you come to stand before the northern altar, before you blow out the candle, stand for a moment in silence with your eyes open. Be aware of the sense of your feet upon the stone, deep in the Underworld before the goddess, and your upper body here in the surface world. From now on, every time you still yourself to light the first candle in the ritual space, do this brief meditation of your feet on the stone in the Underworld and your body in the temple.

4.11 *Task:* Working with the symbols

The shapes that were written on your arms may very possibly become working shapes for you in the future. For some, simply having them written on their skin in vision is enough; for others the images will be useful in meditation or to use as seals in work related to that specific goddess power, or they may be shapes that directly mediate power to you for you to work with. They can also be 'marks' left upon you that will identify you in other realms and mark you as "protected by the great lioness goddess." These are magical working marks. So you need to learn what to do with them

The first step is to write them in your journal and then redraw them over and over until you can draw them from memory, accurately.

If you cannot work out what the shapes were and cannot retrieve the memory, don't panic. That also happened to me years ago. Many years later I saw them on a temple wall in a ruin that I was exploring while on holiday. The wall was full of different symbols but two, very insignificant ones, suddenly lit up and I remembered.

A year later it became very apparent to me what they were doing on me, why they were there, and what they did. They had been asleep up to that point, and then they suddenly leapt to action. So just go with the flow.

Once you have a clear image of them in your mind and can draw them with ease, then you need to do a series of readings to find out what the next step for them is. If you get no clear readings and cannot interpret them properly, just give it time for the dust to settle, and then revisit the reading exercise in the future.

But do not skip over this task of doing the readings. Not only is it important to know what to do with the symbols, but you must practice your reading skills regularly: don't be put off from lack of skill... it does not drop out of the sky, it comes with practice and focus.

4.12 *Task:* Readings on the symbols

Use the Tree of Life layout for the following questions and write up each reading on your computer log.

"Are these symbols already active in my energy field?"

"Do I need to do anything with them at this point in my training?"

"Do I need to draw them out and place them near the north altar?"

"Can I use them as a protective seal (on a talisman, or on a door for example)?"

"Should I just leave off working with them for now and let them surface later?"

If all the answers are negative, then you simply wait and move on in your studies. Not everyone works with these signs; simply having them on your inner pattern is enough.

And always with magic... *if you are in doubt, wait*. Do not take a magical action if you are not clear about what you are doing or it does not feel right. Learn to work with your instincts.

4.13 Summary

There are many different aspects to the Underworld, and in magical terms you have barely scratched the surface. These vast realms can take lifetimes to learn about in full, but the key aspects that you have learned about in this lesson will give you a good, simple, but very powerful foundation to stand upon as a magician. The Cave of the Goddess, the threshold between the Underworld Forest and death, and the deep temple are major elements in magic, and before you go on to learn about any other aspect of working in the Underworld (or the Abyss) you need to have a strong solid connection to these places.

4.14 *Task:* Practice

Go into both visions each week for four weeks. (You should still be doing your daily meditations too!) Get used to going in and out of these places, learn to observe, to acknowledge the contacts, and be respectful of the goddesses you encounter there: these are ancient and very powerful beings, so watch your manners. They are not figments of your or anyone else's imagination, and they operate in very different cultural ways to what we are used to. Respect is a major thing for these goddesses, and any disrespect will potentially be met with aggression (which will affect your physical as well as mental health).

The priesthood contact in the deep temple will probably be willing to guide you gently in how to be around these goddesses, but do not treat that contact as 'support' or badger them with questions, or ask them to do things for you that you should do yourself. They will immediately close down on you, and "sorry" does not cut any ice in this place.

Your job is to learn to get in and out of these places, to learn how to be there and observe only (no work *at all*), and to learn how to stretch yourself (feet in the Underworld). Do not try and skip ahead in your actions by exploring or pushing boundaries in this deep place—you will regret it.

4.15 Goddess

You may, after working with these visions a few times, come across an image or a statue of a goddess that triggers the same sense/feeling of the power of the lioness goddess in the Underworld. Do not go searching for one, but should one cross your path, take her home and have her in the north of your working space.

You do not need to do anything special (it is best and safest at this point just to let her be) other than find a space for her, cleanse the space with frankincense smoke, and occasionally burn frankincense before the image.

This is about tuning, clearing, and establishing. There is no deity worship—you are a magician, not a priest. But there is a deep respect, honour, and awareness of her presence. Rather than thinking in religious terms, think in terms of having a very old professor with old-fashioned ways of doing things sitting in the corner of your room. You would make sure they are happy, listen to them with respect, and treat them with the honour they deserve: she is the elder of all elders.

Lesson 5

The Living Dead

Now that you have a better idea of the death process in general, it is time to take a closer look at the people/spirits that do not go through the usual death process but stay connected to the physical world for one reason or another. Not every spirit that stays attached to the living is a 'ghost' or in distress, or is dodging the whole death process.

As a magician, it is important to know the difference between who is choosing to stay and who is stuck or clinging to the living world, so that you do not inadvertently haul someone into the death process against their will. It is also important for a magician to know the difference between a real ghost and something else: most hauntings are "something else."

A lot of magicians these days have very little understanding of these phenomena. As a result of that innocent ignorance, all sorts of problems can kick off in a house where magic is being worked with. So this basic background knowledge can become invaluable should you inadvertently trigger a pissed-off being or get an unwanted lodger.

Also, you will find that the deeper you get into magic, the more you will be placed in situations where you have to deal with these types of issues. It is a matter of the universe saying "oh good, you have switched on, now go solve this problem!"

This particular subject can be very difficult for a lot of apprentices, as the film and TV industry has used 'ghosts' as a major theme in movies to shock and horrify people. Add this to numerous old stories and taboos around death, and what results is generations of people in the West who are terrified by the very idea of a ghost. Our TV station listings are crammed full of B-rate movies, docudramas and psychic questing programs that play on fear and rely on pseudoscience to try and discover ghost activity.

Trust me, if you had real ghost activity, you would know about it. You would not need an instrument to measure a change in electromagnetic fields or anything like that—if a ghost wants your attention, it will get it.

Let us first have a close look at the 'ghost' phenomenon: what ghosts are, what they are not, how ghosts get your attention, and why. If you are a magician, particularly if you are also sensitive or psychic, then as soon as you start to work magically in a space you will light a beacon in the inner worlds. Many things come to investigate, and ghosts are one of them.

5.1 Ghosts

A fair number of people, upon death, tend to want to touch base with the living they have left behind to let family members or friends know that they still exist and that they are okay. I have already talked about the visits that tend to happen in my family, particularly when one of the women dies, and the resulting blowing of light bulbs.

These are the most common forms of *haunting*. They are harmless and all they require is recognition, conversation, and then moving on. Sometimes these visits manifest as aromas, noises, 'feelings,' or electrical disturbances. This is a time when the living can say goodbye and the dead can move forward knowing that they will be remembered, and that they have been acknowledged as still existing. This period of disengagement with the living is usually short and fades off after the funeral rites.

Sometimes a spirit will hang around a little longer if they have specific things they wish to convey—and they will try very hard to get attention. A quite dramatic and humorous example happened once when I visited a friend for a discussion.

My friend had recently lost a work colleague who had died of cancer. We were sitting chatting about life in general when the room started to feel a bit strange. I asked how the kids of the dead colleague were coping (they were fine) when suddenly my friend's cell phone launched itself off the fireplace, across the room, and landed at his feet. We all sat stunned in silence for a moment: the dead colleague was trying to tell my friend that he wanted to talk to him.

This is a good example of a spirit trying to get attention and get a message across. The phone being launched, as opposed to something easier, was the only way the dead person could say that he needed to talk.

My being in the room triggered and bridged the contact. When a natural psychic (or a magician who is psychic) is in a space, they generate a slightly different energy to most people. That different energy can be utilised by the dead to enable them to try and bridge a contact: we are like batteries, and we are also very visible in the inner worlds.

For some magicians who are not natural psychics, this phenomenon of different energy can develop as a result of magical training and practice, whereas others, like me, are born with it. We must learn how to work with it, or else we would plagued by it (and it tends to run in families).

From early childhood I was followed around by newly dead people, and that also happened to my eldest daughter when she was little—she is also a ghost magnet (I used to have to evict them out of her bedroom so that she could get to sleep). In our modern culture we see this as extra-ordinary, weird, and something to be dramatic about, but in fact it is a perfectly normal phenomenon. It is not that people like us are weird or special in any way; it is more that we are people who have not 'forgotten': I feel it is a normal survival mechanism that most of modern humanity has filtered out through the evolutionary process. In effect, we are throwbacks.

Through finding someone who can pick up on them, ghosts are able either to get a message across or just to have recognition of their existence. Once they have achieved that, they begin to relax and not panic so much—our culture has no pattern or mechanism of understanding for the newly dead: they have no compass, no idea of how to behave, of what to do, or any idea of what is going to happen to them.

The kindest thing a magician can do under these circumstances is to not whip out some equipment to prove that they are there, or to banish them, but simply to acknowledge them, ask if they need help (communing in vision is an easy way to find out what they need), and let them know they can hang out with you for a while until they feel ready to move deeper into death.

There are various things that you can do as a magician to help the dead (outlined in the next lesson). The basic rule of thumb for how to behave as a magician is: if it finds you, do the work. Don't go chasing after it or looking for jobs. Modern ghost hunting clubs and TV shows cause so much distress in the newly dead, and they only serve to perpetuate nonsense as fact. But if a dead person turns up at your home or you trigger one somewhere, then you need to deal with it. There are various ways of doing that, which we will look at in the next lesson.

Some cultures have a place within their society for these newly dead people: some Buddhist temples hang wind-chimes outside the temple for the dead. If a ghost is lost and distressed, they hear the chimes and seek refuge at the threshold of the temple for the night—a bit like a homeless shelter for lost ghosts.

Problems really start to occur when you have a true haunting of a spirit that is not newly dead and that is trapped in this world, or is clinging furiously to life. This causes all manner of problems, not just for the living but also for the dead: they become exposed to the danger of composites, something we will look at in a moment.

If a magician walks into a problem situation, it is wise to know first what it is you are dealing with. We have looked at the newly dead, which is pretty straightforward. Now let us look at the longer-term dead, and other types of haunting events that are not always human spirits.

5.2 Recordings

What people generally think of as hauntings are actually a mix of a many different phenomena that can be caused by a dead person, a faery or land being, a composite, a demonic being, a parasite, or a *recording* (a situation where a certain event in time has become recorded or impressed upon a building or a place).

The phenomenon of a recording is the simplest type of haunting, so we will look at that first and get it out of the way. Sometimes these recordings are volatile events where the energy becomes impressed into substance and keeps replaying over and over again. They are sometimes triggered into replaying by the moon's cycles, astrological events, a sensitive person visiting a place, or a sudden burst of energy caused by changing the structure of a building. Often they appear as seemingly unimportant events which, for some reason or another are recorded and play back over and over again.

There is a very famous account of one of these recordings in the ancient city of York in Britain, a well-documented haunting in the cellars of the Treasurer's House. Here is a clip from an article about the hauntings:

> Workmen repairing the cellars in 1953 reported seeing and hearing a group of Roman legionnaires marching along, though only visible from the knees upward as though marching behind a low wall. Later excavations discovered a Roman road running beneath the cellar floor, at the very spot of the apparition. Were these the ghosts of the 9th Roman Legion who went missing without trace?
>
> www.jorvik.co.uk/treasurers-house/

These types of recordings are mostly harmless and serve only to shock people when they experience them. There are no dead people involved: it is simply a scene from the past that keeps replaying. These types of hauntings cannot be interacted with, as no dead person is actually still there, and they are easily identified by the fact that the scene never changes, and the apparition cannot be interacted with. They cause no harm and are really just a curiosity.

If there is more than one of these recordings in a building or space and they constantly replay, then it is very likely that the land is seated upon an energy vortex or anomaly that causes certain events to be recorded and impressed into the building. If it is an energy anomaly, then there is nothing you can do about it and it will continue to record events through time.

5.3 Faery or land spirit haunting

This is actually the most common occurrence that people mistake for a haunting. They are also often described as poltergeists. The more that land is gobbled up by houses, towns, businesses, etc., the more the faery and land beings of an area are going to surface or clash with local inhabitants. In fact, a fair percentage of what people think of as violent or aggressive hauntings is in fact these beings.

This type of 'haunting' can manifest as poltergeist activity (throwing stones, moving things about, scratching people, pushing people down stairs, etc.). The thing that marks them out from other non-human hauntings is that land or faery beings do not try to get into the heads of the occupants living in the space: they will attack a person, but they will not attempt to move into a person's body or mind.

There is usually a combination of factors that trigger this type of event, and those triggers tend to be:

location

+

particular human

+

the behaviour of that human

The location aspects tend to include things like having a well, waterway, or spring under or very close to the house, and/or the house being built upon a particular faery spot or over an inhabited stone outcrop, an active fault line, or a nearby cave.

The particular human aspect that triggers such a haunting is often a high-testosterone male living over a faery-inhabited spring, a psychic female child hitting puberty (massive energy output), or someone who is mentally unbalanced.

The human behaviour triggers tend to be a male being violent, a psychic teen meddling in occult games, construction workers adding to a building or rewiring a house, the house's owner disrespecting a local faery site, or a person living in the house who is very hostile to nature in general.

When these elements (and there are more, but these are the most common ones) come together, it triggers a hostile response.

The activity of faery beings is very clear in some hauntings, such as the Bell Witch in Tennessee. A lot of fantasy has slowly been added to that story, to the point that I was extremely sceptical of the whole situation until I actually went and spent some time in the area around the old house, the local graveyard, and the cave area. As with all these stories, it is sometimes hard to spot the truth buried under the fantasy, but this story had enough specific aspects that are known to be connected with faery activity that I had to go and take a look for myself.

The noises, slapping, pinching, throwing things around, pulling off bedding, touching people and then talking out loud to them are all signs of a powerful faery contact, and not of a ghost. Of course, these stories are then embellished with fantasies like levitating, being stuck to a ceiling, vomiting porridge, and all the other visuals that Hollywood loves so much.

When I visited the spot it became immediately apparent as soon as I got close that this was a very active area energetically. That was the first real clue: this was not just centred on a house, but a whole area. After spending a day in the area and feeling the beings there for myself, it was very clear that this was no haunting.

What happens with these situations is that when a being gets disturbed or has its territory invaded, or is awoken from a deep sleep by human activity, or when a line of land/faery beings become hostile to particular types of humans on their territory, then they surface and start trying to attract attention.

While faery beings do not operate in the same emotional paradigm as humans, and do not live to the same social rules that we do, they are not usually just hostile for no reason: they are often willing to communicate, adjust, and negotiate a little if the humans are willing to respect them and take them into consideration.

Usually though, because of the humans' fear of haunting, which is what they think the contact is, the humans' response to the first contact (sounds, tapping) is full of fear and aggression (often followed by lots of religious ranting and prayers). This in turn triggers an aggressive response, and it usually degenerates down from there.

In Iceland, when it comes to the Huldufólk (Icelandic faery beings), the people in general have learned to communicate with these beings, or at least take them into consideration when it comes to building projects and major changes. They are treated respectfully, so the incidents of aggression are kept to a minimum.

Knowing what it is you are dealing with is fifty percent of the problem already solved, as you can then act appropriately, without fear—and with such an approach the problem usually becomes a non-issue. However, where a being has been awoken, is hostile, and is connected to a particular aspect of the land that the house is standing upon, then unless the occupants are willing to drastically change how they live in the building and understand that they are essentially interlopers on someone else's land, the violence will continue indefinitely. Houses built upon springs and wells are particularly prone to this.

5.4 Parasites and demonic beings

These are the types of hauntings that tend to be most depicted in movies. And yet they are pretty rare, particularly in countries that have long-established civilisations with religious centres. Places that have fairly recent human communities (only a few hundred years old), like the USA and Australia, are the most common places where these events occur.

And the one thing that really marks them out from all other types of hauntings is that these beings *get into the heads and bodies* of the people who are victims of the hauntings. Sometimes the beings get into the fabric of the building itself, but more often they move into a human and begin a process of possession.

These beings are often not locked to a particular place, and if the person moves out, they will move with them, hounding them often to death. Of the two types, the parasitical being is the more common of the two, but saying that, the line between what is a powerful parasite and what is a demonic being is a thin one. The only real discernible difference between the two, and one that we can often pick up on as magicians, is that a parasite infests for its *sustenance* whereas a demonic being infests in order to cause *destruction*.

We will look at demonic beings in more detail later, in the Initiate section, particularly in light of their potential for destruction: there is a lot of misunderstanding about what is or is not a demonic being, and religious programming has so overtaken the Western psyche that sensible discussion is virtually impossible. But knowing the difference is of vital importance to a magician in order to ensure that a situation can be properly dealt with. Religious ranting at a parasite will do nothing, but cutting off its food supply will. Cutting off a food supply to a demon will not work, as it is not their attractor: a totally different approach is needed (and religious ranting does not work on them, either).

So for this lesson we will concentrate on the parasitical element. Parasites are usually the cause of a haunting when there has been a very nasty incident which drew them there in the first place: a violent rape that brought death, a murder, a mass murder, seriously mentally ill people who are violent, or a concentrated disease outbreak—the attractors are usually violence, sex, and/or painful death.

The particular aspects of the energy released by these occurrences provide a major feeding station for parasites. Once the meal is over they will sometimes wait until more humans come along, and if that human or humans do not display behaviour that feeds them, the more intelligent parasites will badger the humans or break down their resistance until they can get into their heads and push them into behaviour that feeds them.

A good fictional representation of this sort of situation is presented in the film *The Amityville Horror* (2005 version). The film itself is fiction, but it had some good consultants for the film who knew just how these beings can behave. They are often mistaken for demonic beings purely because of their power and ability to manipulate the minds of humans, and their ability to affect physical objects in the house. If you wish to watch a good depiction of this sort of incident, watch that film (and then have a salt bath afterwards—read the warning lower down in the lesson and take the advice!).

Bear in mind that it is a Hollywood movie with all the accompanying shock horror dressing, but the baseline theme and the way it is presented regarding the mind of the male in the story is spot on. Also the point made in the film, that the problem originated with a mass murder, is spot on: those are often the original feeding attractor.

A *parasitical haunting* will present itself as slow changes in the personality of one or more occupants and a heavy feeling in the house that builds at certain times of the day/night and which also changes with the moon's cycle.

The changes in the person will take the form of either sexual or violent presentations, or both, or sudden unexplained suicidal tendencies.

As the parasite feeds more from the mind of the victim and gets stronger, or moves closer in to feed (or more parasites move in), the parasite will be able to use any surplus energy from the feeding to affect physical change in the house: shutting down the electrics, setting fires, dropping or smashing things, throwing weapons, psychically raping the women or children, strangling people, etc.—anything that generates a lot of fear. The more fearful the people, the stronger the parasites get, as they feed on the emotion.

At this stage in your training it is unwise to learn how to deal with this, or even how to look at it properly as a magician, because you do not have the skills and tools to deal with such a dangerous situation (and trust me, large, clever parasites are far more dangerous than real demons in a one-to-one situation: most of what people think are demons are in fact these types of parasites).

You will learn in the Initiate section how to deal with these beings, but for now it is important that you do learn to recognise them in all their different forms.

Often a parasitical haunting is not quite so dramatic, but it still has the same elements: the victim has changes in their thoughts and behaviours, the house is affected or things in the house are being tampered with (one of the clues that it is not just mental illness in the victim), and other people who stay in the house start to exhibit the same odd behaviour.

As with all types of body infestations (bacterial, fungal, etc.) there is not a simple cure, but the right approach will first weaken, then disable, and finally purge such an infestation from the house or family. Demons, however, are another matter entirely, hence they will be looked at later.

5.5 Real long-term hauntings: dead people and composites

Now we get to the actual real hauntings, which are one of the rarest events. They do tend to happen in clusters of specific areas, as the energy or a land area plays a major part in the ability of a dead person to remain present for long periods of time after death. Also note that wherever there is a properly tuned sacred place (cathedral, synagogue, Hindu temple, etc.) it is very rare to get a long-term haunting.

A real haunting of a dead person is either just the dead person themselves (the rarer of the two), or is something known as a *composite*, which is more common.

A composite is where you have a dead person who is also infested with a parasite, or the 'shell' of a dead person that a parasite has completely moved into (and has pushed the dead spirit out of the shell) and which it is operating as if it was the dead person.

When a long-term dead person (with no parasites) stays in this world, they are either trapped/bound to this realm by something or someone, or they have serious issues and are badly out of balance. There is an easy way to tell if they are simply stuck here, in that their apparitions are often expressions of suffering, of being unable or unwilling to move forward out of fear, or they just prefer to stay and hang out with the living. All of these are ultimately unhealthy and need working with, but such spirits are rarely, if ever, destructive or violent.

If there is a specific thing that is binding them magically, all that needs doing is to unbind them and let them go. If they are not moving forward by choice they must not be forced: they need time and help to come to the right decision themselves.

When I was a young mother, the house where I lived had an elderly man in residence who had died some years before. He could be heard walking around the house at night, checking on the children or standing in the corner of their bedroom watching over them.

At first I was freaked out that he might harm the children, but once I came to know him, I discovered that he simply wished he'd had children when he was alive, and wanted to make sure that the girls would be safe.

During the daytime, if someone came into the house who he didn't like or who he perceived as a threat to the family, he would throw things about: books would fly off shelves and hit people, and his favourite trick was throwing pot plants. It became a problem, as babysitters would not come to the house, neighbours would not cross the threshold into my house, and visitors were sometimes assaulted.

At that time (I was twenty-two and clueless) I did not know what to do, so we moved house. But looking back, he was right about every person he perceived to be 'bad.' I eventually learned the hard way that those people he attacked were indeed not good people. I should have listened to him better. I revisited the house many years later, (same neighbours still there) and he is still there, watching over the kids in the current family.

With what I know now, I should have talked to him, shown him how death worked, and how he could travel through death and back into life if he wanted to have a family for himself. He was stuck in a Christian mindset of only one life and desperately wanted the experience of raising his own children. The role of the magician in such instances is to open the Vista for them, show them that more lives are potentially there, and that it is a natural process, not one to be scared of. Then they usually move forward.

If a long-dead person is aggressive, they are often like terrified, wounded animals and need the magician simply to show them the way forward and then to keep the space tuned to stillness to give them healing time. Then they usually move forward under their own steam.

Occasionally you get nasty, aggressive spirits who were just total nasty assholes in life and they are terrified of going into death and onto judgement. Many people who behave very nastily in life think that death is the total end, and that they can be as destructive as they want. When they die and realise they still exist, they panic, and in that panic the deeper nastiness and manipulative personality comes to the fore.

When there is such a situation, you should not force them, as you short circuit their own development. But you can limit them by boxing them into a corner and constantly keeping the space tuned to stillness. Open the gates and let the inner beings deal with them.

If they come to a realisation that they have to move forward and there is no other option, then they will begin the process of self-examination. This in turn allows their step into evolving, which is a major service on the part of the magician. Cutting off their access to other parts of the house so their actions towards others are severely limited, and keeping the space tuned so that no parasites can latch onto them and make the situation worse, are the best options. But they is not always possible.

Sometimes, if the spirit is very destructive to the living, particularly if children or the elderly are being affected, then you have to detach them from the building and take them to the plains of death and leave them there. The key is to try everything possible first to get the spirit to move under its own steam, as that way they have a chance at improving. But when the living are under threat, then it is time to intervene. The main thing to remember with this sort of situation is that such spirits are rarely dangerous, just bloody annoying.

Remember, at this stage of your training, this is outlined for your information only: it is not yet time for you to dive in and work with any of these more difficult situations

I once had to drag a spirit into death after a particularly nasty haunting in New York. A Mafia type had died suddenly and was angry that his wife had inherited all of his wealth (he was divorcing her when he died). He harangued her night after night until I intervened and hauled his ass into death.

The woman was terrified, sleep deprived, and at the end of her tether. Catholic priests had tried to help, with no success, and I was the last resort. I was not sure if I could move him or not, as he was so filled with hate and rage, but as I started the process, many other beings that work in death suddenly turned up to help.

This is a dynamic worth remembering: the magician is the *catalyst*, and if you start an action that will lead to a balanced resolution, then as soon as you start the work, any help that you would need will turn up. And it is only what you need: if you are capable of doing the work, however hard it is, you will not be helped. But if it is a bit too much for you, all hands will come on deck.

5.6 Composites

When we see scary haunting movies or possession movies, what is generally being depicted (often in silly, over-the-top scenes) is what is known as a *composite*, usually mislabelled as a demon.

A composite is where a long-dead person who is seriously out of balance and hostile becomes inhabited by intelligent parasites that move in, take over, and run the show. This creates a very nasty situation where you have a spirit that is seriously unbalanced, often aggressive and hostile, and a parasite that has intelligence, is manipulative, and uses the imbalance of the spirit to trigger destructive situations that feed the parasite.

These usually present as hauntings where fear is a major factor, as is physical violence, and the parasite uses the life experience of the spirit to target the other humans in the space.

So, for example, if the dead host was a rapist, the parasite would drive the spirit to continue that behaviour, which in turn gives the spirit an energy boost to help further their invasive behaviour, which in turn creates situations where the parasite can feed. That manifests as a haunting that targets women living in the house: they have nightmares of being raped, sometimes they get physically assaulted in their sleep, and they are kept in a constant state of fear. Don't forget: rape is rarely about sex, and more about power/control.

A composite can also get into the heads of the residents of the house, and the parasite uses the knowledge within the personality of the dead spirit to project specific behaviours into the minds of the people in the house. The ideas the composite gets from the mind of the dead person/host are impressed into the mind of a vulnerable living person in the house, and the composite attempts to drive the living person to behave in a way that will produce energy to feed from. This can all get very nasty and very destructive.

The knee-jerk reaction of most exorcists is to tear the composite out of the situation and cast it, complete, into the Abyss. The only problem with that method is that the dead spirit then has no chance at evolution or development, which in turn makes the magician responsible energetically for the stalled progress of that spirit. So the magician has to weigh up the consequences of such an action against the current danger of the situation.

Sometimes you just have to do it. But wherever possible the parasite should first be detached from the dead spirit and composted, and then spirit should be marched into death and handed over to the beings that work there. After that, the future of the spirit is not your responsibility: the magician's job will then be to deal with the house or invaded living person and get them cleaned, sealed, and balanced so that the situation cannot repeat.

And this brings me to another aspect of this situation that apprentices need to be aware of: once a vessel (a person, a house, a land area) has been breached and occupied, that vessel is vulnerable to further infestation if it is not cleaned, strengthened, and balanced. A pattern of behaviour becomes impressed upon the person or place that makes it easier for future parasites or composites to move in.

The media's depictions of exorcisms, where it is done and dusted and everyone moves on, is a fallacy: to truly rid a place or person of a composite and make sure it never happens again is a long, drawn-out job. The immediate act of getting rid of the composite is just the first step. The cleaning and balancing is the second step, and identifying how it happened in the first place is the third.

Often you will find that the building, the land, the person, or all three have an inherent weakness that enabled such a situation to occur in the first place. That weakness needs to be identified and strengthened, any natural portholes (wells, springs, burials etc.) need to be tuned and properly guarded (working with land beings or deities), and the pattern of behaviour or weakness in the human (feeding potential) that may have attracted the parasite in the first place needs to be addressed.

So you begin to see how complicated this can get, and knowing what type of haunting you are dealing with specifically dictates how it must be dealt with.

The first step towards being able to deal with these sorts of situations is knowing all the different types of beings, the different presentations of hauntings, and knowing how energy, land, and spirits operate.

And you will now see how a generic 'exorcism,' blessing, or clearing will for the most part be ineffectual. You will also now begin to understand just how dangerous these psychic 'reality shows' and 'quests' can potentially be. If the haunting is a composite or a standalone parasite, or a seriously disturbed dead person, then such playing about is only going to feed the situation and make it worse.

5.7 Warning—Please take note

I do not post this warning lightly, so please read it carefully, as it comes from years of direct experience as an exorcist. Simply reading about composites and parasites can draw you into a pattern where you become more visible to these types of beings. These are beings and situations that you will not have anything to do with magically until you are an adept, when you will know what you are doing and have the tools to deal with them.

Simply discussing specifics, or watching the films, or doing readings or visions around these situations can put you in a direct line of connection with them. I have seen this over and over again, and while it is not my job to dictate to you what you must or must not do, watch, or investigate, it *is* my job to outline for you the inherent dangers—after that, it is your own choice (and I will not clean you up from your mistakes if you do not follow advice).

My job is also to teach you basic skills but in a safe way, so while we will do practical work around 'recordings' and simple dead people hauntings, you will do no practical work around the more dangerous types of beings until you are an adept. So if you choose to look deeper into the murkier side of this subject matter before you are ready, then it is on your own head.

The deeper into magic you go, the more visible you become, and the more careful you have to be. Watching some of these films or going to some badly infested sites may or may not affect a curious ordinary person, and indeed some people develop a thick skin of natural immunity from exposure. But some do not and become infested.

For the magician, the training tunes you, which in turn can make you more visible. When you are working within the confines of balance and common sense, other beings step up to help you and keep an eye on you. But if you step away from that common sense and dip your toe into murky waters simply out of curiosity, knowing that it is a risk, then you are on your own: inner guardians will not help you.

Reading through parts of this lesson will be a minor risk to you, even though it is just words. But it is time for being grown up and not overprotected.

At the end of this lesson, do the ritual salt and water bath and also use the ritual salt and water cleanse for your work space.

After the cleansing and before you do anything else, any other lesson, meditation or exercise, do the hexagram ritual to tune yourself and the space, and when you come to stepping into the empty hexagram in the ritual, face south, be aware of your feet on the stone in the Underworld, of the Divine Breath above you, your sword in your left hand and your vessel in the right hand (the stance of the pentagram) and your flame in your centre. Anything that even remotely tried to connect with you will be swept away as the frequency of the ritual will make it hard for things to hook into you.

Anything that you watch, hear, or read, will, now that you are a magician, have an effect on you in some way or another. The key is not to get paranoid or avoid everything and get fearful; rather it is to be aware of how things can potentially affect you subtly, and if you feel that effect, to move away from whatever it is that is causing such a feeling.

Cleaning and retuning yourself is something you should learn to use whenever you get that energetic feeling of intrusion or imbalance. These beings work through your mind: thought is everything, and the imagination is the vehicle for everything: media affects and triggers your imagination, and this in turn creates a door that things can step through if you are not careful. The more you work with your imagination, the more you have to be careful what you expose that imagination to.

If you watch the movie I suggested earlier in the lesson, make sure you clean and rebalance yourself properly afterwards. Even if you are used to watching such films, as is commonplace these days, as a magician you are stepping into a whole different ballgame and you need to be aware of that and act accordingly.

5.8 The dead that cling

Before we move on to other Living Dead situations, there is something that is pertinent to the subject matter that an apprentice should be aware of, and that is a newly dead person clinging onto a living person.

Usually it is the person closest to them, like a parent, a partner, or a child. When someone dies in state of shock, or they were a person who was clingy, vulnerable, and fearful, they sometimes reach out for the closest person and *cling* to them. They will attach themselves to the inner spirit of the living person and will not let go. This creates an energetic drag on the spirit of the living person they cling to, and the living person not only processes their own emotions, but also the emotions of the dead person.

This most commonly presents as the living person having grief beyond what would normally be expected. Now I know everyone deals with death differently, but when you get a bereaved person who is not going through the different stages of processing grief, but is instead stuck in one expression of it in a major way, then the magician should suspect a *clinger*. This is easily identified in vision: you will see the dead person stuck to the living person.

This often presents from an outer perspective as someone displaying extreme grief, who is unable to function at all, who wants to die (sometimes the dead person wants to pull them into death with them, to keep them company), and has no resolution at all—the grieving person does not go through any stages of coping, and they get stuck in a very dark place emotionally. This can go on for years if it is not dealt with.

Gently detaching the clinger and accompanying them in vision on a daily basis to the plains of death slowly allows the dead to let go, and the improvement in the living person is often quite stunning: they start to go through a healthier period of grief and resolution, and can move on.

5.9 Staying in the land

I have already touched upon aspects of this phenomenon in other lessons, and have also written quite a bit about it in my books, so I don't wish to repeat myself here. But what would be useful is to outline for apprentices how these spirits present and under what conditions, so that should you come across this sort of situation you will recognise it. From there you can do further reading for yourself.

We have already looked at dead people who sleep in the land waiting for judgement, and also at working sleepers. There are also burials whose occupants have stepped into the sacred king or queen pattern and sleep in the land for the good of the people and the land, keeping balance simply by their presence.

Most of these types of spirits just get on with their job and are rarely connected accidentally with the living. But sometimes circumstances do occur where they are disturbed or have reached the end of their 'term of duty' and are ready to move deeper into death. It is useful to know which is which, as both situations often need the assistance of a magician.

Where a sleeper has been disturbed, either by building construction, digging such as happens in archaeology, or farm clearing of the land, they will start to appear to people in the vicinity. They often are tightly bound into a small, specific area, and will appear to the local people within that boundary.

Sometimes they simply project an image of themselves to those who can see: they expect you to know what to do. Often when these sleepers died, their spiritual society was vastly different to our societies today, and they are often not aware of such a shift and the modern lack of knowledge.

When the people to whom they appear do not do what is expected of them, the spirit can become frustrated and sometimes angry. The way to discern that it is indeed one of these disturbed sleepers that is causing the issue is that they will simply keep appearing, projecting an image, and trying to/asking the living to do a specific thing.

If something like this does occur, the first thing to do is to research the land and find out if any major building, excavation, demolition, or similar work has been done or is being done locally.

In such circumstances the solution is usually easy: open all the gates, light a fire outside as close to the disturbed burial as you can, and, working in vision, build a bridge for them through the fire to the gates (we will look at this in the next lesson).

They cannot go back to sleep, so they need someone to open the doors for them. This is not usually a job for an apprentice, but should you be directly presented with such a situation, then it is a job that you cannot do much harm to yourself with.

The thing to remember is that all you do is hold open gates—never ever try to force a sleeper into the death pattern. The same is true for a sleeper that has reached the end of their term of sleep: they will present asking for help, and all you need to do is light a fire and open the gates.

Sometimes, however, these spirits will present around a particular site, and it is not that they have awoken: what you can be seeing is a guardian projecting an image of the sleeper to basically tell you to go away. They can also present as black dogs, strange-looking cloaked/hooded men, or warriors.

If that happens, usually it is because a sleeper has been threatened in some way, or someone is trying to dig into the mound. If this happens, see if there is anything you can do practically to help. Are kids messing around a burial?

But most of the time there is nothing we can do, or it is that a house is on top of the burial. If that is the case, the issue can be resolved by incorporating the house into the role of guardian: the house becomes a part of the mound.

But in all circumstances of sleepers or guardians appearing, trying to banish or exorcise such a spirit is not only fruitless but hostile, and it will only aggravate any guardians connected to the site. Later in the course, you will learn skills to be able to deal with such issues; for now, knowing about them will not only lay a foundation for the future work, but it will also help you to spot these various situations in texts and histories, which in turn will give you a deeper understanding of those histories and texts.

As you go through your training and learn more skills, you will instantly recognise which skills can be applied in haunting situations. We will start that process in the next lesson, where you will learn some basic skills to deal with non-dangerous situations.

As an apprentice magician, you are very unlikely to be placed in a situation where you would have to deal with something dangerous, and of course, never go looking for it!

The other type of Living Dead that you can come across is what is known as an inner adept, inner priest, or inner contact. Because this type of spirit is very important for the work of a magician, they will be dealt with in their own lesson, Lesson 7.

5.10 About the practical Work

This practical work will be cautious because of the potential dangers in the subject matter for apprentices, so stay within the confines of the task boundaries and don't be tempted to peer into the murkier waters of this subject matter.

You are going to find, through research, certain haunting situations, and look at background information, presentation, and then do tarot readings around the situation to try and ascertain what in fact is/was going on.

This will teach you a basic process of investigation that any magician would do when presented with a potential haunting. It will help you to learn how to look, what to look for, and what to cast aside.

We will only look at the safer aspects of haunting, and we will not delve into demonic, parasitical, composite, or violent hauntings, as such investigation would open you up to the contact and place you in danger (even if it was a past event—it could potentially drag you back energetically into that pattern).

5.11 *Task:* Investigating sleeping warriors

The following is a folk tale from Wales that emerged during the 19th century Druid Revival movement, and was written by a Welshman called Edward Williams, A.K.A. Iolo Morganwg.

A lot of Williams' work is considered to be *total construct* ("made up") by scholars, but some anecdotal evidence of his stories in much earlier texts has been emerging recently. So we have an uncertain situation. What is most likely is that he found old folk legends, clothed them in an Arthurian dressing (which was fashionable at the time), and adapted them to fit his agenda.

Your job is to find out what is behind this story. This will teach you the basic steps of investigation as a magician, in a safe way. This story could be about faery beings, it could be about ancient sleepers, ancestral sleepers, or something else.

Different versions of this story, or similar versions of it, appear throughout northern Europe, which would point to either a faery type of contact or to a pattern of behaviour in ancient tribal people, or both. Also keep in mind as you read the story that there is more than one cave in Wales called Craig-y-Dinas.

Read the story, and then follow the tasks that come after the story.

This story is taken from Elijah Waring's *Recollections and Anecdotes of Edward Williams, Iolo Morganwg* (London, 1850), pp. 95-8, where it is headed *A popular Tale in Glamorgan, by Iolo Morganwg.*

A Welshman walking over London Bridge, with a neat hazel staff in his hand, was accosted by an Englishman, who asked him whence he came.

"I am from my own country," answered the Welshman, in a churlish tone.

"Do not take it amiss, my friend," said the Englishman; "if you will only answer my questions, and take my advice, it will be of greater benefit to you than you imagine. That stick in your hand grew on a spot under which are hid vast treasures of gold and silver; and if you remember the place, and can conduct me to it, I will put you in possession of those treasures."

The Welshman soon understood that the stranger was what he called a cunning man, or conjurer, and for some time hesitated, not willing to go with him among devils, from whom this magician must have derived his knowledge; but he was at length persuaded to accompany him into Wales; and going to Craig-y-Dinas,[1] the Welshman pointed out the spot whence he had cut the stick. It was from the stock or root of a large old hazel: this they dug up, and under it found a broad flat stone. This was found to close up the entrance into a very large cavern, down into which they both went. In the middle of the passage hung a bell, and the conjurer earnestly cautioned the Welshman not to touch it.

They reached the lower part of the cave, which was very wide, and there saw many thousands of warriors lying down fast asleep in a large circle, their heads outwards, every one clad in bright armour, with their swords, shields, and other weapons lying by them, ready to be laid hold on in an instant, whenever the bell should ring and awake them. All the arms were so highly polished and bright, that they illumined the cavern, as with the light of ten thousand flames of fire. They saw amongst the warriors one greatly distinguished from the rest by his arms, shield, battle-axe, and a crown of gold set with the most precious stones, lying by his side.

In the midst of this circle of warriors they saw two very large heaps, one of gold, the other of silver. The magician told the Welshman that he might take as much as he could carry away of either the one or the other, but that he was not to take from both the heaps. The Welshman loaded himself with gold: the conjurer took none, saying that he did not want it, that gold was of no use to those who wanted knowledge, and that his contempt of gold had enabled him to acquire that superior knowledge and wisdom which he possessed.

In their way out he cautioned the Welshman again not to touch the bell, but if unfortunately he should do so, it might be of the most fatal consequence to him, as one or more of the warriors would awake, lift up his head, and ask *if it was day*. "Should this happen," said the cunning man, "you must, without hesitation, answer *No, sleep thou on*; on hearing which he will again lay down his head and sleep."

In their way up, however, the Welshman, overloaded with gold, was not able to pass the bell without touching it—it rang.

One of the warriors raised up his head, and asked, "Is it day?"

"No," answered the Welshman promptly, "it is not, sleep thou on."

So they got out of the cave, laid down the stone over its entrance, and replaced the hazel tree. The cunning man, before he parted from his companion, advised him to be economical in the use of his

---

[1] "Rock of the Fortress"

treasure; observing that he had, with prudence, enough for life: but that if by unforeseen accidents he should be again reduced to poverty, he might repair to the cave for more; repeating the caution, not to touch the bell if possible, but if he should, to give the proper answer, that it was not day, as promptly as possible.

He also told him that the distinguished person they had seen was Arthur, and the others his warriors; and they lay there asleep with their arms ready at hand, for the dawn of that day when the *Black Eagle* and the *Golden Eagle* should go to war, the loud clamour of which would make the earth tremble so much, that the bell would ring loudly, and the warriors awake, take up their arms, and destroy all the enemies of the Cymry,[2] who afterwards should repossess the Island of Britain, re-establish their own king and government at Caerlleon, and be governed with justice, and blessed with peace so long as the world endures.

The time came when the Welshman's treasure was all spent: he went to the cave, and as before overloaded himself. In his way out he touched the bell: it rang: a warrior lifted up his head, asking if it was day, but the Welshman, who had covetously overloaded himself, being quite out of breath with labouring under his burden, and withal struck with terror, was not able to give the necessary answer; whereupon some of the warriors got up, took the gold away from him, and beat him dreadfully. They afterwards threw him out, and drew the stone after them over the mouth of the cave. The Welshman never recovered the effects of that beating, but remained almost a cripple as long as he lived, and very poor. He often returned with some of his friends to Craig-y-Dinas; but they could never afterwards find the spot, though they dug over, seemingly, every inch of the hill.

Tasks

Geography and history

Look on a map of Wales, or use a search engine online to look up places called Craig-y-Dinas. Look and research as to what natural features surround these places: springs, rivers that go underground, caves, ancient forest, or fault lines. Then research the ancient history of these places to see if any of them were the site of any battles between the Celts and the Romans (such as Anglesey).

Folklore

Do a search for local legends throughout Europe of caves or hills that have stories of sleeping kings and warriors, with stories that they will once again rise at some point in history. Compare the stories to the one you are working on. And for the ones that leap out at you, research further into the land features of those sites. Take computer notes of what you find.

Readings

Get your tarot deck and use the Tree of Life layout. The first skill you will practise is the skill of locking on to a partially or unknown element/place.

We do not know exactly which Craig-y-Dinas the writer was talking about, so you have to go by *what he was thinking of*.

Your first reading would be to ask:

"Does the place Craig-y-Dinas that Williams was specifically writing about actually exist?"

If the answer is no (either a card that denotes separation such as the Three of Swords, or the Fool, for example) then you know straight

---
[2]The Welsh.

away that this legend does not track back to a specific story of a burial in Craig-y-Dinas.

Then you need to ascertain if the story is about ancient tribes/a sleeper, or faery beings.

Ask first:

> "In this story, there are sleeping warriors and a sleeping king—are they, in this particular story, the spirits of long dead people?"

If the answer is no, ask the same question, but ask if they are faery beings. If the answer is yes, ask if they are still sleeping in the cave. If the answer is no, ask if they have gone deeper into death.

Write down your findings in a computer log. From the answers you get, think about what these stories are telling us. Are they telling us about ancient faery contacts? Or are they telling us about ancient burials?

These investigations will show you how stories repeat across different lands, sometimes because they are stories carried by travellers, and sometimes because they are patterns of behaviour found throughout tribal territories or faery territories.

If you want to, do further tarot readings around any other sleeper stories you came across in your investigations.

Interactions with humans

Choose one of the burial stories you have been researching, and ask, again using Tree of Life layout:

> "Are these burials (or faery areas) any problem to humans living on top of them or very nearby?"

From your answers, you will be able to see (or not) the potential issues with humans living closely to these places. If you get a yes answer, use the Desert layout and ask:

> "Show me why they are a problem for humans."

Read the results in context to a human community living on the site of one of these situations.

5.12 *Task:* Investigating the Treasurer's House in York

We looked at the incident of time recording in the Treasurer's House in York. The whole of York is one big ghost playground: there are so many layers of conquest, history, and successive waves of different inhabitants all *within a fully walled city* which contains it all, that it is a ghost hunters paradise.

But also, because of the strong influence of the Minster, it is relatively free of parasites, and the turnover of ghosts is pretty quick: few long-term hauntings tend to survive the influence of the Minster, so most hauntings there that are active are fairly recent.

York Minster is ancient indeed, and is kept very well tuned, which means the general muck of a city does not tend to accumulate: it is not a good feeding ground for parasites, so there is little if any issue with these beings in the walled city. So you can do readings around this place safely. You will look at some various 'haunting' situations to see what information you can get on the different various presentations that York tends to get.

Romans in the cellar

Using the Desert layout from this module, Lesson Two, we are going to look at the 'Romans in the cellar' haunting.

Your first question is:

> "With the apparitions of the Romans in the cellar of the York Treasurer's House, show me what is happening energetically when that apparition appears."

What you are looking for in the reading is specifics: what happened in the past to cause that apparition to become recorded in the first place (positions 4 and 5), what the trigger is (position 6), what is it that is actually appearing (position 8), what is still trying to resolve (position 7), how is it affecting the living world (position 9 and 11), what is falling away from the situation (position 10), and how long into the future is it going to keep appearing (short-term future 12 and long-term future 3).

Now you will start to understand how this layout gives you so much information and what a valuable tool it is.

Write down your findings and your conclusions in a computer log.

Anyone else there?

Your second question to do with the Treasurer's House is (and use the Tree of Life layout for a yes/no answer):

> "Was there another dead person haunting that building at some point in the past?"

There have been various hauntings over time in that house, but they were never able to stay for too long, as they were dispatched by the frequencies emitted from the Minster at various times in history when it was well maintained. However, it is possible to get a look at one of them.

The way to do that is to ask:

> "Show me the strongest haunting of a dead person who has haunted or stayed in the Treasurer's House in the past that I can look at."

It may show a male, female, a child, the lovers (more than one strong person). If it shows a trump personality (Hierophant, High Priestess, Emperor) than it is likely that you are getting a clergy member, or a Royal court dignitary, or a Roman in a position of authority.

This particular building has many layers to it, so you are likely to hit at least one of them.

If you totally draw a blank, it is not because is it was never haunted, but because you are being blocked for your own safety. If that happens, either you are about to get sick (get a cold) which would make you vulnerable, or you are too sensitive and would likely tap into some of the deeper layers of this place without realising it. Such a thing at this stage would be counterproductive for you.

The other reason you could get blocked is that you are not able, as yet, to reach the layers where these different 'hauntings' are. Simply write up your reading and take notes from the reading as to how you came to your conclusions.

If you get a yes answer, then use the Desert layout and ask:

> "What was the situation for that dead spirit that caused it to stay connected to that building?"

The Desert layout will show you how that person came to stay behind in death, and how the dead person came to be moved on.

5.13 *Optional task:* Your own investigation

If you know of a story of a non-violent, non-aggressive haunting or apparition in an area local to where you live or in a place that you know fairly well, go through the same process (research, land survey, and readings) to look at that haunting. Write down your findings and your conclusions in a computer file. It is really important that you do not dip into any sort of apparent haunting that is any way aggressive, parasitical in nature, or potentially dangerous. You do not have the skill as yet to get yourself out of a mess if you stick your energy into a badly unbalanced situation (and I will not rescue you... you're all grown up now!).

5.14 *Task:* Clean up

Now do the clean up outlined in the warning I gave you earlier in the lesson, and make sure you do it without delay. Do not put it off, and once you have cleaned up, do not go back to the subject matter until you are visiting it again in another future lesson. You will have learned what you need to know, gained the investigative skills you need, and you will be able to apply them to different things as you progress in your studies.

Lesson 6

The Thinning of the Veils

Within Autumn (Fall) there is a time where "the veils thin" throughout the northern hemisphere. Why this happens I have no idea, other than that it is a time where things are dying back for the winter. Nature has a series of tides that ebb and flow through the world, bringing in energy and taking out energy. It is a time where the various worlds seem to draw closer, and the thresholds between the living world and the Underworld become thin and permeable for a short time (one cycle of the moon).

Casting various traditions and their stories aside, over the years I have observed these tides and the effects they have on the inner worlds and on the outer world that we live in. As I looked through various traditions around the world, the one thing that stood out was times spanning October and November that were marked with light or fire festivals.

For the tides in my own land, Britain, I did notice from quite an early age that around this time there is an upswing in spirit activity and it becomes easier to connect to and with the newly dead: it was like a lot of people were hanging around, became more visible, and were badgering me to do things for them, to help them.

In my early thirties I still worked very much by instinct, and around that time of the year I would have the urge to light candles after dark and keep them burning all night. By the middle of November the urge would fade, and everything would settle back down. But one incident marked a turning point in my understanding, and gave me something more solid to work with.

It was the end of October, and I was living in a small town in Wiltshire. I lived with my family in a house that was very old—parts of it dated back to the fifteenth century. It was dug into an ancient, unexcavated burial mound, and in general was a very busy house in terms of spirits.

It was a few days before the full moon, and I got an irresistible urge to go and lay out on the mound one night (like you do). As I lay there, I looked up at the stars. It took me a moment to realise that I was lying on the mound directly under the constellation of Orion, which was lying across me in exactly the same position as me: head where my head was, feet where my feet were.

Suddenly I got a strong flash-vision of a man lying in the burial mound who was waking up. I was fascinated. It felt strange: the vision was strong, but I was still too young and dumb to realise what was happening. I went back into the house, and that night I dreamed of a man waking up and finding himself not only alone, but trapped.

Out of sheer curiosity, every night for three nights I went out and laid on the mound, with Orion over the top of me and the sense of the man awakening deep in the mound. I did not get the message—I can be a bit slow—until the fourth night, the night before the full moon (which was the thirtieth of October that year), that I was being asked to do something to help this awakening sleeper.

But I had no idea what to do. I laid and stared at Orion until a flash of fire dropped into my mind. Then I remembered the autumn fire festivals and the fact that although Bonfire Night (fifth of November) in Britain was supposed to be a tradition that only went back to the 1600s, there had been a bonfire at this time of the year on the town's common land for nearly a thousand years: a much earlier folk fire festival.

So I built a small bonfire and, as the full moon did its thing, I lit the fire and sat in front of it on top of the mound. Beyond lighting a fire I had nothing planned and had no idea what to do next. So I just sat there.

After an hour or so I was about to go back in the house when a huge pressure started to build up within me: something was happening. The pressure built and built, and I simply sat and watched the fire until the feeling became unbearable.

Without any warning, it felt like I was about to vomit into the fire when something passed through me and into the fire. At the same time I suddenly became aware of the gates: they were open, very present, and very strong. It was hard to stay sitting still, as my body was struggling with the sensation which I know now to have been a bridging action. I was hit with waves of nausea, sweating, and dizziness.

Suddenly the pressure released and something moved quickly through one of the gates: the spirit of the man in the mound had bridged through me and used the fire as a porthole to access the gates into death. I sat stunned for a short while, and as I sat I became aware of other spirits drawing near to the fire and then passing through it, heading west as they began their journey deeper into death. Many came, passed into the fire, and then vanished.

When I finally went back inside, I felt like I had been sitting on the mound for about an hour; but in fact, once I looked at the clock, I realised that I had been out there for six hours.

For days afterwards I felt like a piece of well-chewed toffee. But I had learned a lot. Also, the mound became very quiet after that night, which in turn brought peace and quiet to the house.

In subsequent years I worked with the idea of a fire as a gate for the dead at that time of the year, and I discovered that it was much easier on the body to work with a fire to do bridging if it was done over a three day period, or with a group of people all doing the same thing.

A few years later, when I lived in California, a small group of us decided to work with the same tide, and with a fire. We waited until the full moon that fell between the middle of October and the middle of November. On the days leading up to it, we visited the hill where we planned to do the work and we sat there each night, just keeping vigil with the intent of helping any lost souls wandering around the area.

On the full moon, we lit the fire and sat around it, at first chatting, until finally we fell silent and settled into our own thoughts. One woman, on instinct, starting singing a death song I knew from my childhood, the *Lyke Wake Dirge*.[1]

This old remnant of heathen folk tradition from Yorkshire was a song that was sung as the body was carried from the church for burial. It was often chanted without instrument but to the slow beat of a large drum, like a slow, deep heart beat.

As she chanted (it is more spoken than sung), we started to pick up on spirits drawing near, attracted by the singing. Over the span of about two hours, spirit after spirit drew near to the fire and then passed through it, vanishing through the fire and into the west: their deeper journey into death and separation from the living world had begun. They didn't pass through us this time; rather they gathered around us and then plunged into the fire.

We expected a handful. Two hours later they were still coming: it felt like hundreds of spirits

---

[1] See below.

had passed through the circle of women and plunged into the fire. None of us could move, speak, or break the pattern: we had to stay there, silent, until it was done.

We were all impacted for a few days afterwards, but we recovered quickly enough, and it gave us all a lot to think about. What we had intended, in a rather naive way, was to hold the gates open for a lost soul or two. We didn't expect half the dead population of the area to turn up; nor were we prepared for the amount of energy it would take.

The reason I tell you this story is because it is important to understand that while we as magicians think we have it all sussed out in our different traditions, with rituals for this and visions for that, to be honest, we do not have a clue—we are barely scratching the surface. We may have evolved technologically as a species, but when it comes to magic, inner worlds and power, we are still struggling to climb out of a dark age.

Because of that, while there is a lot of organised magical learning to do as an apprentice, there is also a lot for you to learn using your own intuition and instincts—and learn to listen to everything around you. Sure you will make some mistakes, and some of those may be major ones, but you will also have breakthroughs, make connections, and stumble across things that move you forward in your development. The key is to try and stay in one piece throughout the process, and that in turn comes from using your common sense.

In the decades since those events, I have observed more and more tides that flow across the land and that seem to do different things. I have learned not to try to overorganize them in my mind, but just to be aware of them, and to be acutely aware of how they make me act—am I suddenly needing to spring clean, or sleep a lot, or stay in after dark, or keep lights on?

The ancient wisdoms around these tides will not be found in books but in our ancestral knowledge that is buried deep in our blood; in our DNA. That knowledge can surface if you let it, and stillness is one of the keys, as is knowing what is your own imagination and what is something deeper. That comes from practice, common sense, and discernment.

When it comes to these tides of death, tides of scale-balancing, and tides of renewal, always observe and keep diaries of how they affect you. If you find yourself feeling out of character, or feel something strange happening to you, look around you. Is everyone else acting up, or is it just you? If everyone else seems to be going through the same thing, the chances are that a tide is flowing through to bring change or shake things up a bit. If you do observe something like this happening around you, simply take notes: write down the date, the moon cycle, the moods and actions of the people around you, and what is happening in the news (sudden increase in violent crimes or natural disasters?).

It is about learning how to observe for yourself rather than stick your head in a text: everything that is written in ancient texts comes from the direct experience of the people: it all started with someone taking note, someone observing and experimenting. Become a part of that process in magic by slowly becoming more and more aware of what is happening around you.

There are a lot of magical rituals, visions and so forth that can be used to work with a lost soul or a problematic spirit, but it is not yet a safe time in your training to dive into that. However, you can start that working process by tuning in to the next autumn death cycle, if you so wish. And this is something that you can do each year if you wish to, as a service to the land and to the people where you live. If you do work with this cycle, then work with your instincts and write everything down.

6.1 Working the death cycle

From what I have observed over the years in different countries, the tide seems to start with a new moon in October and finish with the new moon in November; and it peaks with the full moon in the middle. I find it interesting that at this time of year, lighting fires and lights in the window to guide the dead should come straight after a time of harvest, both of food and of the weighing of Scales/opening of the Book of Life in Jewish traditions. They dovetail together quite nicely.

What you can do as a magician is to start working with this autumn cycle on the new moon: start by keeping a candle burning at night, potentially where its cast of light can be seen from a window. Hang wind chimes outside near to the window where the light can be seen, and when you do your daily meditations, think about the many souls who get lost in the death process because they have no compass, no way of knowing what to do or where to go. Many figure it out for themselves, but some do not.

I would not use religious texts for reciting at this time; rather it would be better to learn to work with the tides of nature, to learn for yourself how to work and be with the dead.

A compromise could be to go out each night and talk to the dead—spend a few minutes each night standing in the darkness, and speak to the wind (the magical power of utterance): tell the dead who can hear you not to be afraid, that a fire will be lit at the full moon and the gates to death and renewal will be open for them. Tell them that in the meantime they are safe near you, and can rest a while around the outside of your house until it is time for the fire.

The fires for the dead, I have found, are most effective and have least impact on the worker if they are lit over three nights: the night before the full moon, the night of the full moon, and the night after. Either light a fire on the ground or in a fire bowl, and just sit with the fire each night, *with the intent of providing a gate for the dead*. As you light the fire, be aware of where the west is, and simply see in your mind the west gate. That is as much as you need to do magically.

This passive way of working can be a major lesson: often our rituals, visions, and actions can get in the way of a natural flow of power, and there are times when it is very powerful simply to turn up somewhere with intent, light a flame, and just be present. There is no need to behave as if you are in a church, with whispers and reverence. Just as it is with the dying, often simply being there, chatting, or singing is enough, if the sacred intent is held.

The major magical trigger is the lighting of the fire: treat the fire as if it was the central flame in your work space. Ground yourself with your feet upon the stone in the Underworld, the stars above you, the ancestors behind you, the Noble Ones before you, and with your intent of service and compassion. Then light the fire. That simple tuning will trigger a cascade of events that will culminate in the spirits drawing near and knowing it is safe to pass through the west gates via the fire. Some may bypass the fire and walk straight into the west.

You will know when you have done enough: the atmosphere will change and become more normal again, you will be sleepy, and you will feel that it is okay to leave.

While you sit around the fire, take note of everything that happens around you (and turn your phone off!): watch nature, watch the stars, listen to the sounds, and listen to how your body reacts.

Those of you who are sighted will have more than enough to keep you busy. For those who are not naturally sighted, learn to listen to the slightest whisper on the wind, the slightest change in how you feel, in what is happening around you. Don't, however, get jumpy and dramatic, nor think that everything around you is a sign: be grounded, be open, be aware, and use your common sense. None of this is paranormal; it is in fact perfectly normal.

If you are interested, do some research on old folk traditions about this time of the year. Don't fall into the trap of looking only for death-related traditions: cast your net wider and you may find some interesting things around the theme of fire, light, darkness, and a soul finding its way home.

6.2 Summary

As you will have noticed, this is not a heavy-duty lesson and there are no practical exercises or tasks for you to do. This is one of those lessons that is here for you to read, take note of, and then file away so that when this time of the year comes around you can revisit this lesson and decide if you wish to work with the idea of holding the fires of death.

I also thought, after the last heavy lesson, that you could do with some light relief! You have two more lessons in this module, which is a difficult module to study just because of its subject matter. Once you get to the end of this module, you will be back in full ritual mode for the next module, which will give your mind and spirit a much-earned rest from the heavy aspects that were covered in this module.

6.3 The Lyke Wake Dirge

(Written in old Yorkshire dialect.)

This ae nighte, this ae nighte,
Every nighte and alle,
Fire and fleet and candle-lighte,
And Christe receive thy saule.

When thou from hence away art past
To Whinney-muir thou com'st at last
If ever thou gavest hosen and shoon
Sit thee down and put them on;

If hosen and shoon thou ne'er gav'st nane
The whinnes sall prick thee to the bare bane.
From Whinny-muir when thou may'st pass,
To Brigh o' Dread thou com'st at last:

From Brig o' Dread when thou may'st pass,
To Purgatory fire thou com'st at last;
If ever thou gavest meat or drink,
The fire sall never make thee shrink;

If meat or drink thou ne'er gav'st nane,
The fire will burn thee to the bare bane;

This ae nighte, this ae nighte,
Every nighte and alle,
Fire and sleet and candle-lighte,
And Christe receive thy saule.

Note:

I have never found a recording that sounds anything like how it was back when I was a kid. Most recordings in the last few years all track back to a group from the 1960s called the *Young Tradition* and are very much styled in the 1960s folk revival. Traditionally it was more spoken to a drum than sung, with only the refrain sung ("And Christe receive they saule").

Lesson 7

Inner Contacts and Inner Adepts

We now get to, from a magical perspective, one of the most interesting aspects of death and the sort of variables that we see in death, and that is the subject of the inner adepts.

The phenomenon is as old as temple culture itself, and examples of people who once lived and who opted out of the usual cycles of birth and death in order to serve can be spotted in most ancient and not-so-ancient cultures. The one thing they all have in common is that they tend to come out of temple cultures of one sort or another.

More recent inner adepts are the product of mystical, spiritual, and magical traditions that keep a continued sense of service in their line. Like all things connected to humans, it sometimes goes wrong, but for the most part if you aim in the right direction in terms of contacts, these inner adepts can be very valuable.

However, in the last hundred years, and particularly in the last forty or fifty years, this aspect of human service has been co-opted by the commercial New Age and 'magick' community in order to sell product. It is not that the inner adepts themselves have been co-opted; rather that the concept has been misused. People channelling 'ascended masters' are more common these days than plumbers, and for the right price there are many 'teachers' who will connect you or initiate you into the 'Inner Order of Melchizadek'—something that does not exist.

Many esoteric orders have tried to pin these contacts down and organise them (giving them fancy names, imaginary lines of initiation, and made-up histories), something which never works and always ends up messy.

But the inner adepts themselves have throughout time interacted with various magical and mystical orders, working on the thresholds, and working in the inner realms with magicians who work in vision. So what are these inner adepts/masters/elder brothers?

7.1 The process of becoming an inner adept

We looked at the death process, the process of the Scales, and how some spirits who stand before the angel decide not to come back into life, but are not yet ready to go deeper in to the process, so they choose to serve in the inner worlds for a time. The spirit of the person steps into the inner worlds and operates through an inner structure that can be used as an interface with the living: inner temples, inner libraries, thresholds, and so forth.

Usually the personality that they last held in life is jettisoned before they step into the inner realms, so as not to cause a back-drag on the spirit or create a cult-type situation with the living humans with whom they will work.

This is one of the hallmarks of knowing when you have gotten a real inner adept contact: you will never know who they are. Any inner contact that appears as a known human or declares to be a certain person is most likely not, and is something else masquerading as them.

This can be for good reasons: an inner being trying to get a specific way of thinking across will pluck from your mind, or from the collective mind of the group, a person that they can dress up as who represents what they are trying to teach.

The bad reason would be a cross-dressing parasite. In such a case, anything transmitted from the contact to the living is usually banal or total drivel dressed up with light, aliens, crystals—you get the idea.

Sometimes fairly recently dead adepts will try to contact other magicians and work with them, but that is not the same thing. They are still going through the death process and have not yet moved deeper into the aspect of death that we looked at (the angel and the Vista). This is the most commonly mistaken type of contact: an adept in death who is waiting around, connecting with the lodge or other magicians, and who retains the personality/image from their life in clear terms is in fact, technically, a haunting.

Many of these types of magicians who hang around after death can become a bit of a problem as their ego and personality is still driven by a sense of control. We see this when lodge leaders die who cannot let go. They badger the living magicians, gatecrash into the temple, and generally become a nuisance. It is understandable: when a magician has spent their whole adult life trying to build something, to then feel in death that those left behind are not doing it properly must be frustrating.

But the dead magician has failed at the first post: upon death, everything that you held dear must be released and let go of: you cannot cling to a past life in death and still expect to be balanced. The net result of this type of behaviour tends to be the living magicians having to banish the dead magician from the temple or lodge. Very sad.

In such a situation (a magical leader/teacher dying), it is important for both the dead magician and the living ones left behind to realise that their old era is now over. Some living magicians, upon the death of a beloved teacher, will try to hold on to them, desperately trying to contact them and draw them back into the temple. Not only is that seriously unbalanced, it is also magically immature and a sign of bad or inadequate training.

A true inner adept will have shed their life identity, and what is left is the deeper knowledge, wisdom, skills, and intent to serve. Many will purposely not give a name, or if badgered by an inexperienced but psychic magician they will give a totally meaningless name. This is for good reason: this is not a personality show; it is deep reserves of service in action without ego attached.

The interactions I have had over the decades with this type of inner contact have usually involved me learning, or being shown something, or being asked to bridge something from the outer to the inner. I have never known who they were, where they lived in their life, or what they did. But they all bear the hallmark of the inner priesthood, the inner adepts; an inner frequency that becomes easily recognisable to the living magician.

And inner adepts do not always appear as humans, even though they once were. They can appear in different forms: the one I found the weirdest to get my head around for a long time was the inner adepts who were presenting as 'books' in the Inner Library.

Before we go any further, now would probably be the best time to start to look at the Inner Library in depth, as this inner construct is key to the understanding of inner adepts and how to work with them.

7.2 The Inner Library

The Inner Library is an ancient interface that has been known by various terms over the millennia, but what it is stays the same: an inner place where knowledge and the knowledgeable can be accessed. You are already familiar with the idea of the inner temples: inner structures that feed through and into an outer structure. The inner temples and the Inner Library are not naturally-occurring inner places (obviously), but are inner templates that were constructed using magical technique which were tied into or simultaneously created as their outer temples were built.

The main difference between inner temples and the Inner Library is that there are quite a few different inner temples (which are connected to outer world temples), whereas there is only one Inner Library and it is not connected to an outer library; rather it is *the root source of knowledge for all the inner and outer temples.*

All the acquired knowledge and wisdom that has passed through temples and through magical, mystical, and spiritual institutions is stored in the Inner Library, and it is also a major access point to virtually every inner temple that can still be reached.

All the temples connect to the Library in one way or another, and when a temple finally breaks up, all of the knowledge held in that temple remains in the library. As an inner temple falls into disuse from an inner point of view, it slowly breaks down and eventually sinks into the sands of the Inner Desert, or tips into the Abyss if the structure it maintains is to be composted permanently; only its knowledge remains as 'books' or 'scrolls' upon the shelf.

My earliest direct contact with an inner adept when I was a young magician was in the Inner Library, which is a safe and solid structure for a young, inexperienced magician to work in. I did not go into the Library with the specific intent to make a connection with an inner adept, it just sort of happened. The time that I spent going into the Inner Library and working with this inner adept was invaluable to me in terms of learning and experience.

A few years later I was to connect with inner adepts that were not in the Inner Library, but were in a very ancient temple that was preparing to tip into the Abyss. There was a sense of great urgency, almost desperation, in their contact with me. I wanted to know who they were, what temple culture they came from, and what I could learn on the spot from them (typical youngster attitude). In turn they wanted me to shut up and to simply take what they had to give so that I could bridge, process, mediate, and then externalise what it was they wanted to pass on. I was expecting a sudden download of instant knowledge (dork that I was), but what happened was something far more profound and which is still unfolding for me to this day.

In turn, each of them, men and women, stood in front of me in the ancient temple and literally shoved 'something' into me. Some of whatever they were placing within with me appeared to me as books, and some of it was...well, I could not even begin to describe it. And then they were gone.

At the time when this happened in my early thirties I felt special—a superior feeling that was very quickly slapped down by the inner adepts I worked with in the Inner Library. It was made very clear to me that I was an idiot, a novice in their eyes, and it was more a matter of me being the fool in the right place at the right time who was willing to take the burden on. Once I was quite rightly cut down to size, I slowly learned how to access what was in me and work with it. I was no more special than a library assistant helping to sort books.

Over the years I worked more and more with inner adepts, both in the temples and the Inner Library, until I came to a point where part of me is now always there as well as here: I don't have to *go* to these places any more, I carry them around with me always; you eventually become part of the 'hive.' And again that is not being special; it is just something that slowly develops over decades of work.

In the library, these inner adepts can appear in many different ways. Some appear as librarians or priests/priestesses within the Inner Library itself, and these are inner adepts who have stretched beyond the structure of the temple line they came from. They have become *generic* in that they no longer belong to any single stream of magic, spirituality, or structure: they are mediators of knowledge, plain and simple.

A deeper version of this generic knowledge contact appears in the Inner Library as a book or scroll. This is where the personality and the human dressing has fallen away and all that is left is the core energy and knowledge of that adept. This appears to us as a book (pure knowledge), but it is not *actually* a book and cannot be read as a book. This is a mistake that many magicians make: they go to the Inner Library, pick up a book, and expect to be able to 'read' the knowledge contained within it. But it doesn't work that way; this is not a movie with instant results.

The books in the Inner Library are energy patterns that hold knowledge and wisdom. To access that knowledge, the magician *takes the book into themselves* and gives that energy and knowledge a vessel that it can unfold within and bloom through. By taking the book into yourself, you literally absorb the knowledge of an inner adept, a knowledge that will unfold within you as time goes on. And boy does it unfold!

So you begin to see how the inner masters who are worked with in lodges, such as 'Plato' and 'Socrates,' are not *actually* Plato and Socrates: that grandiose claim is a dressing that tells you what sort of frequency that being is operating at, and what they are trying to convey to you. And when a true inner master dresses up, it is because they feel they have to 'talk slowly' to you; they have to dress up so that you will accept what they have to say.

But as always with 'personalities,' more often it is an intelligent parasite that is cross-dressing. That tends to happen most often if someone is using scrying methods, or brings the contact to them in their work space.

Working within the specific confines of the Inner Library or an inner temple gets rid of all of those and other issues—parasites just cannot get into these inner constructs. Occasionally you will come across a dead adept still holding on to their life persona in the Inner Library, but it is unusual and can often lead to issues as they want to connect to 'their magicians' through you. But such an occurrence is rare.

As an apprentice, the safest way for you to connect with and learn from an inner adept is to work with them in the Inner Library.

If you work as an apprentice in vision in the Inner Library and you perceive a grandly dressed adept who is talking at length to you giving you 'wisdoms,' it is most likely that it is your own mind that is talking to you.

For the most part, contact with inner adepts can be a bit weird, particularly if they are from a very distant past: it is difficult with such a contact to have a communal language as their concepts and ours are so vastly different. So a sort of pidgin sign language, symbolic displays, and lots of pointing at things tends to happen.

You can converse with some of them, but such conversation is usually quite simple, and yet profound. They will reach into your mind to look for a visual vocabulary, so be aware of that: they are looking for a common form of communication.

Teaching tends to come in the form of showing you things, pointing at things, shoving things into you, pulling things out of you, and/or taking you to different parts of the library and pushing you into side rooms to observe, or just simply to be there.

Eventually over time you gain a common language so that communication between you flows better and you learn to trust the contact.

The first inner adept from the library that I worked with communed fairly well with me, but would only give me lectures about food. We could have fairly clear basic conversation, but it was always lectures about what I should not eat. I became frustrated because I wanted magic, not dietary counselling.

And yet at that time, in my early thirties, it was exactly what I needed. I was being cleaned up, my body was being prepared to cope with high levels of power, and as someone with an autoimmune disease (at that time undiagnosed), the adjusted diet was spot on. My body coped well with the work thanks to the adept's advice. So don't dismiss seemingly non-magical conversation.

Working in the library should be a long-term, consistent discipline over decades, which in turn will change how the interface works for and with you: it gets to a point where a part of you is constantly in the Inner Library and the Inner Library is constantly in you. When you reach that point, it is made clear to you that you no longer need to work in vision in the library: you become a part of the interface at a deep level. When you die, as an adept, your stored wisdom, experience, and knowledge will be released into the library for future magicians to access.

The appearance of the Inner Library varies according to the lines of culture that the person comes from: its appearance to a magician is shaped by the collective consciousness of their culture. Someone accessing the Inner Library from a Hindu culture, for example, will see an Inner Library with the hallmark shape, but the dressing will look more like something from the ancient temples of the Indian subcontinent, whereas Western magicians will see something akin to the Great Library of Alexandria: it is the collective memory within your own culture and blood that often dictates how your brain will interpret the surface dressing.

One constant, though, is the shape of the Inner Library: it has a central circular area with four wings, like an equal-armed cross with a circle in the middle. Regardless of how it is dressed, it holds the same shape: the shape dictates how the power flows through it, how the temples connect into it, and also how all of those things come together (think back to your lessons on magical patterns and the four directions). The fine detail of the decor, dressing, etc. is what varies. But what it is and who is in it does not vary from person to person; it is itself, and the inner adepts, or whatever different traditions call them, are always the same.

It is also good to bear in mind that when you do make a contact with an inner adept, that the meeting is specifically relevant to you, to what time, culture, and mystical or magical system you are operating in. You are led to or introduced to an adept who is deeply connected to the line of magic/mysticism that you are studying. This ensures that the inner adept can pass their knowledge on to someone who can actually make use of it, and the magician receives something that they can actually do something with.

Saying that, I have had some very culturally different contacts in the library, and at times it was a bit of a struggle. But eventually it made sense as to why I was guided to such diverse contacts.

As an apprentice, it is time for you to start this connection process and learn how to first connect with an inner adept and then work with them. By now, after reading so far into this lesson, you should be aware that if any contact shows up in, say, Golden Dawn robes, or in white robes and tells you that they are Papus, then your mind is playing up and you need to clear your mind and focus. If you get an adept that looks very weird and unexpected, then chances are you have a very ancient contact.

The main thing to remember is that by staying within the confines of the Inner Library (and later the inner temples) most of the crud that is of any danger is filtered out: parasites cannot get in there, and the keep of the Library will connect you to the right first contact for you. If, over time, you have become used to working in the Library and you come across a known dead magician, the best advice I can give you is to quell your curiosity and steer around them—they are always trouble.

7.3 Making contact with the Inner Adepts

The way to initially make a contact with an inner adept that you can work with and learn from is to go in vision to the Inner Library. Before we get to that, here are the basic rules that will keep you safe, and help you to process what knowledge you are given.

And don't forget, if it is a grand presentation, it is likely fake or coming from your own head—really inner adepts are very simple, focussed, powerful, and unfussy.

Don't expect to open a book and be able to read it. You take the energy into yourself, absorb it, process it, and the knowledge contained within it springs to life when you start working on something that is relevant to that knowledge.

Don't be fooled by the apparent simplicity of the vision. Sometimes a powerful contact can seem easy while you are going through the process, but it will hit you like a wall afterwards. Everyone processes power in a different way, so when you come to do the visionary work, make sure you have some hours afterwards for downtime.

If you find it very difficult to form the images or make sense in vision of what is happening, don't overforce it: some people are strong visualisers, some magicians are not. You need to learn how *your* mind and body processes information and power. For some it is sensations, for others it is like a movie. Neither is better than the other; just do the work and see how it unfolds for you.

Now is also the time in your training to learn how to cope should you be suddenly disturbed in the depths of vision. If that should ever happen to you (the door bursts open and the dog leaps on you), learn to simply open your eyes while holding the energetic sense within you. Sort out the disturbance as simply as possible and return back to the vision: learn to put your mind on hold. It does not always work at first, but trying opens the pathways in your brain for doing that. Having kids is a good trainer: I learned early on to switch on and off according to which child was catapulting themselves at me.

Learn the access points of the vision by heart, really well, before you start to actually do the vision. Learn the paths, and then visualise each step in your head before you eventually sit down to the do the vision. The key steps are: knowing where you are going, how to get there, what the layout of the place is, how to make the contact, and then how to get out again.

7.4 *Task:* Meeting the Inner Adept—the vision

In your work space, light the directions including the central altar, see the gates open, see the Noble Ones in the south, and go around the directions at least once, seeing the gates open, seeing a contact standing on the thresholds, and then once you have finished in the north, stand with your back to the north in front of the central altar.

Spend a moment tuning in to the sense of your feet in the Underworld, the stars/Divine Breath above you, the sword to your left and the vessel to your right, and the path with the Noble Ones before you. Once you feel fully tuned and ready to work, walk a full circle around the directions and finish at the east. Sit down with your back to the central altar, with your body facing east, and close your eyes.

With your inner vision, build up an image of the east altar with the open gates behind it. Still yourself, be aware of your central flame, and when you are ready see yourself in vision standing up and going to the east altar. Bow before the altar and then walk through the altar.[1]

As you walk through the altar see the gates wide open and see that they lead to a long tunnel cut out in stone that leads off into the distance. As you step through the gates, a man steps forward: the guardian of the library.

He looks at you and you must simply stand and wait as he looks at the marks upon you and around you. He looks into your eyes and may ask you why you are here. Simply reply that you wish to access the Inner Library in order to learn. The man will look into your eyes again, and when he is satisfied that you are indeed an apprentice he will step aside and let you pass.

Walk down the long tunnel, and as you walk, think about the main thing that you think you

---
[1] See the note on walking through altars below.

need to learn from an inner adept. It will not be necessarily what you want to learn, but rather what you need to learn. You will not get that learning upon first contact, but it is important to have at least some idea formed in your mind as to areas of your magical or mystical life that needs focus: this creates something that the inner adept can work with. If you just flounder in without a clue, or with the wish for power, they will not waste their time with you. Think about what it is that you struggle the most with in your practice and study as a magician.

As you walk down the tunnel, you can feel all sorts of things happening around you, but there is nothing to see: it feels like the tunnel cuts through a vast building that has lots of things happening in it. That is exactly what the tunnel is. In the distance you see a light shining through a half-open door. Walk towards the door—and take your time.

Once you arrive at the door, carefully step through it, and you will find yourself in a wing of a vast library that seems to stretch in all directions. The shelves go up so far that the tops are veiled in mist. In one direction the wing vanishes into mist, but to the left of the door you emerged from, you see a vast circular foyer.

Walk to the foyer, and you find yourself in a large, circular library space. In the centre is a large ornate pedestal that holds a huge book, and in each of the four directions are entrances to wings of the library that stretch off so far into the distance that you cannot see the ends of those sections of the building. The building is very bright, light, and airy, and after the darkness of the tunnel it takes you a moment to readjust.

As your eyes adjust to the brightness, you notice that the library foyer is full of people milling around. Some are seated and reading, some are tending to books, some are chatting to each other, and some seem busily to be going somewhere. One of the people in conversation spots you, breaks away from their conversation, and comes over to greet you.

This is a Keeper of the Library. She asks you what you want, why you are here. Tell her that you wish to learn and you wish to meet an inner adept. Tell them that you are in magical training and wish to develop more.

She will indicate for you to follow her to the very centre of the library where all the directions come together. There in the centre is the very large and ornate pedestal with a vast book upon it. The woman stands up on the pedestal and asks your name. Tell her the name you were born with, your full name.

The woman sifts through the pages of the book, looking for your name. When she finds it, she reaches into that page and pulls out another much smaller book. She opens that book and then looks again at you to check that you are who you say you are. She is holding your Book of Life. She leafs through it, seeing everything you have done, good and bad, indifferent and odd, what you have studied, what your fate pattern looks like: all the things that make up your life so far. She checks to see if indeed you are working magically, how your work is going, and what you need next in terms of learning.

Instead of placing your book of life back in the vast book, she holds it up directly above her. A large hand comes down from the mists above that obscure the top of the library and takes the book from her before vanishing back into the high mist.

She nods at someone in the distance and then climbs down from the pedestal and walks away, leaving you standing at the pedestal. Stay where you are and just wait.

In time, someone walks up to you from behind, male or female, and places a hand upon your right shoulder. Turn around and greet them: this is an inner adept.

The opening of your Book of Life, and the handing up of your Book, signals a point in your life when your real learning begins in magic. That in turn *marks* you as a magician: you become visible to the inner adepts.

Let the person look at you, think at you, and interact with you. They may place books within you, they may talk with you, or show you things. Remember, this is a first meeting: it is about getting used to being in the presence of an inner adept and learning how they communicate. They may be able to converse well with you or they may not.

Spend as much time as you need to interact with them, and take note of everything that happens, however minor or strange it may seem.

When you feel it is time to go, or they indicate to you that it is time to leave, bow to the adept and thank them. They will walk away from you, and as you watch them go you will notice that the majority of the people in this place are now looking at you. Take a little while to look at them. You will slowly notice that they are from many different times, cultures, religions, and some of them will look very strange to you indeed.

You will also notice that they seem to group near each of the entrances to the four wings of the building that lead from the central podium. They do not seem to go down the wings of the building much; rather they stay in the central foyer, but browse the shelves close to a specific wing. Each wing corresponds to a direction, and the books that are held in that wing hold all the knowledge and wisdom that flows from the powers of those directions.

Now it is time for you to leave. You need to find which is the east wing, as it will lead to the tunnel that will take you back to the east altar in your work space.

Stand in the centre by the podium and look at each wing in turn. Look at the people, the magicians, priests and priestesses, the scholars, composers, writers, thinkers: you will notice that in one of the directions there is a debate going on, and people listening to the debate are writing down notes from what is being said. They are working with the power of the east.

Walk towards them, and as soon as you start to walk towards the east you will feel a slight wind on your face: you always get an elemental confirmation of the direction you are approaching in the Inner Library.

As you pass by the people gathered at the entrance to the east wing, stop and bow to acknowledge them: these are all inner adepts, magicians, or priests/priestesses. They acknowledge you with a smile, and some may bow back: these are teachers who are acknowledging your path as a magician. Pass by them and go down the east wing.

Part of the way down you will see a wall to your right that has many small doors in it. One of them holds a symbol you recognise: the X with a line through the middle of it. Go through that small door, and you will find yourself back in the tunnel.

Walk back through the tunnel until you pass over the threshold, through your east altar, and back into your work space.

Sit back down into yourself, and when you are ready, open your eyes. Immediately write down everything in your journal that you can remember. Then go around the directions starting in the east, bow, say thank you, see the gates partially close, and put the flame out, leaving the centre candle until last.

If anything pops into you memory later in the day, go back and write it in your journal, along with drawings of any symbols you see. Type up a summary for your computer log. Don't fixate on the presentation of the contact you made: it does not matter what they looked like, what their name is, or where they came from in life—what is important are the interactions between you in the library room.

7.5 *Task:* Routine

Do the Library vision once or twice a week for four weeks, and keep computer notes of the encounters. Also spend some time in each of those visions handling the books in the Library, feeling, them and interacting with them.

Once your month of working in the Library is up, set up a schedule to go into the library at least once a month for a year.

Working in the Library in vision is a major foundation feature of magical training. Throughout your training, you will work with the Library in various ways, learning more and more about its depths, its connections, and how it links into so many different things.

As you go back and forth into the Library, you begin to change at a deep level and wake up to dormant knowledge stores within you, as well as learning how to tap into the collective knowledge of humanity. It is a slow but steady evolution in how you learn, and it is not about learning facts or intellectual knowledge; rather it is a connection to very deep reserves of wisdom and knowledge that come from generations of experience. It will slowly unfold over your lifetime and will surface in every aspect of your life.

7.6 *Task:* Pondering

Remember at the podium, your Book of Life, that the Library Keeper handed it upwards into the mist? Think about what was happening to the book.

The Book of Life is not actually a book; we just see it that way in vision. The Book of Life is the same as the contents of your vessel, your Harvest so far: it is an energetic pattern that is constantly evolving according to what you do, how you do it, why you do it. It is woven tightly into your web of fate, and together they make a complex mix that is unique to you.

You will find throughout your magical work that this complex, ever-changing pattern that you create through your life actions and evolution appears in different magical realms in different forms. Learning the different ways it can appear will tell you a lot about the varied aspects of it and how it can be worked with in different ways.

Think about why it was handed upwards. There is a very specific reason for this, and it marks a turning point in your magical training. Think about what you have learned about the directions, what is up and what is down, and why the book would have been handed upwards. Note any thoughts in your computer log.

A note on walking through altars

By now you should be used to passing through an altar. There is a very specific reason for doing this in vision. When you pass in vision through an altar that physically exists and has been worked with repeatedly in ritual tuning, it becomes a guarded gateway: all the power that has built up over the time of your work is embedded within the altar, and also that direction in your work space. This in turn creates a membrane or filter that acts as a protection and a landing strip.

By walking through the east altar, not only are you protected by the power of the sword that you have been building up in that direction, but also by the nature of the contacts and the focused energy of the east that you have slowly been building. By walking through the east, you are guided to inner realms directly connected to the east: i.e. the Inner Library, inner temples, etc. It is a very safe, well guarded, and well trodden path that you can walk without having to worry about protecting yourself.

Study note

While you are doing the month of visions in this lesson, you can also move on to Lesson 8 which is a reading/study lesson and can be done concurrently with this lesson.

Lesson 8

The Bound Ones

There is an aspect of death that is not widely known about or generally discussed in magical circles, but which does appear in dogmatic terms in some religions, and that is the aspect of death that deals with the souls/spirits of the dead who are bound through a natural process or a ritual process.

We have looked at souls who stay close to the living, that is to say, a haunting; but there is also a deeper process whereby souls can become trapped in a cage of their own making, which prevents them from progressing through death or returning back into life. That process can also be exploited by skilled magicians, though it is uncommon in Western magic. We will look first at the sort of binding that is the direct result of the actions/inaction of the person who has stepped into death; then we will briefly look at the magical aspect.

8.1 A hell of your own making

There are some people that step into death and seem neither able to reach the living, nor willing to move forward into death properly, and end up trapped in a cage of their own making. Their inability to let go of the things that they clung to in life, and their inability to self-assess or to even be self-aware, slowly traps the spirit in a loop of obsessive frustration. It can also happen when the person has been very seriously out of balance to the point of total destruction.

In the last module we talked about the Grindstone and the Unraveller. These natural angelic forces that flow throughout creation can have a direct continuum effect in the dying and death process. We looked at how immersing oneself in the actions of the Unraveller can sometimes trigger an opposing action of the Grindstone in life.

If, however, the person dies in the midst of a serious immersion in the Unraveller, a much deeper opposing power can be triggered, and that is the *Binder*. When something has unravelled to the point of dissolution, or to the point of seriously destructive spirit unbalance, the power of the Binder is triggered and the spirit becomes trapped. They are not bound against their will; rather the deep unbalance within the spirit effects such binding for itself.

I confess that I do not deeply understand this process myself, but I have observed it enough times to know that it exists, it happens, and that there are many different variables around it. So rather than theorise around it, I will lay out what I have discovered and seen in vision, so that maybe that will provide a stepping stone for others to take it further. It is a mechanism that is reflected in Jewish Kabbalah, and is a major aspect of the creation/destruction process, so those of you who have studied Jewish Kabbalah (not

Hermetic Qabalah) will recognise the sefirot at work in this mechanism.

I think the best way to approach this, as it is a complex issue that I don't have a wide understanding of, is to explain it in terms of the sequence of discoveries I made over the decades. It is part of the death process, and as such is pertinent to apprentices should you come across it in your own work over time. I also feel that it would assist your understanding of the various dynamics involved in death, the evolution of the human spirit, and their relationship to themselves and the Divine.

8.2 Trapped in the sands

Decades ago, when I first started working within the various death visions, I noticed an area away from the river, deep in the sands on our side of it, where many souls were trapped in the sands. Some were trapped up to their waists, and some were trapped up to their necks. Some were asleep, some were talking, and some were really angry. Some were cocooned and looked like larvae, and they had angelic beings that seemed to be tending and watching over them. I was fascinated.

After watching this process for a while when I was working in vision, I approached one of the angelic beings who was tending a cocoon and asked them what it was and what they were doing. The angle placed a hand over my eyes so that I could see through their filter, and I saw into the cocoon. Inside was a human who was full of destructive rage, imbalance, and fear. Every emotion of the person inside was heightened to a destructive level and they were completely engrossed in their turmoil: they were not aware of anything or anyone around them.

I asked if they were all like that and the angel said "no," and showed me another one. Inside was a person who exuded so much suffering that it caught my breath. The suffering of the person in the cocoon was so great that it hit me in the chest like a punch and I started physically crying.

As I watched, my body and mind felt assaulted and I quickly pulled back out of vision. I realised that whatever I was observing, it was seriously energetically imbalanced, and if I wanted to learn more I would have to do this in short bursts of visionary work and not stay too long in any of the visions. So over a period of months, I went in and out of this part of the death vision and simply watched.

I slowly began to notice that those who were up to their necks in the sand were totally wrapped up in themselves: they talked and talked to themselves, shouted, gossiped, spat, struggled, and were generally very unpleasant. Some were shouting threats and some just raged, full of hate and spite.

Over time as I went in and out, some of them slowly quietened and began to look around them. As they did this, the sands seemed to withdraw a little bit and more of their 'bodies' became exposed.

The ones who were buried up to their waists were still very negative, but they were looking around more, and were trying to communicate with the angelic beings.

I noticed something that struck me quite strongly: as some of them tried to communicate with the angelic beings and the beings communicated back, some of the trapped people immediately rejected whatever was said to them and went back to ranting to themselves. As they did this, the sand seemed to tighten around them.

In the vision, I got a sudden flash of people I knew in life who were like that—very negative, very dismissive and insular, and very self-destructive with it. These are qualities that we all have to a greater or lesser degree, but in these people they were so intense that they were the overriding qualities that ruled them.

At this point, I started to try and make sense of it in terms of the living, and why/how this binding happens to some people and not to others, and I just ended up tying myself in knots. So I gave up trying to rationalise it, and just went back to observing—which as an aside is a good way to operate as a magician if you want to learn about something: don't theorise, just observe.

As the months went by, some of the souls slowly released themselves out of the sands and began to walk towards the river; others seemed to dig themselves deeper or stayed in exactly the same state.

But the most curious group of all was the souls in the cocoons: some of them stayed there unchanged, some slowly became unbound, but some vanished in increments down into the sands. I asked the angelic being where the cocoons were going, and the angel just pointed downwards. I asked if they were going to hell (I know…I was still young at that time) and the angel had no idea what I was talking about (and I am sure the Catholic visuals in my head did nothing to help its confusion).

After a few months of looking into this, I seemed to get no further other than understanding that some souls got released, some stayed put, and some went 'down.' I became frustrated because I didn't fully understand why some people where there and others were not, nor could I figure out what (if any) role a magician would have in the process. I was too young really to grasp it, and did not at that time have any deeper experience in the death, creation, and destruction cycle. So I left it and moved on.

A year later I had started working in the Inner Desert in vision in a limited way. During one particular visionary session in the Desert I was walking with the Sandalphon when I noticed, off to one side in the Desert, people and other types of beings trapped in the sand and seemingly asleep.

I asked if I could look closer, and the angel nodded. So I wandered over to these trapped souls and walked around them. Some were obviously people, buried up to their shoulders deep in the sand (just like in the death vision), and they looked to be deeply asleep.

Some were not human. I saw what looked or presented to me like angelic beings sleeping standing up, buried in the sand up to their waists or necks, and other strange, powerful-looking beings were in a similar bound state. Some had what appeared to me to be 'mummy bindings' on them, some had layers of sacred script around them like bandages, and all of them were deeply asleep.

They reminded me of the people in the death vision, and I had not at that point connected up the dots—that the sands of the death vision and the Inner Desert were different areas of the same inner realm.

I asked the angel why they were there, and the reply that I got was that these beings of different types had no place in the living, manifest world at this time. I asked if they would ever be released, and the angel said that some would eventually, and some would not. The some who would not would slowly descend 'down,' and again the angel pointed 'down.'

I was getting a bit fed up with this 'going down' malarkey, as I did not understand it and was therefore dressing it in my mind in the dogmatic dressing of 'Catholic hell,' which I knew instinctively was not true.

I asked about the angels that were bound. And I was told that they would be released from the sands when it was their time to be active: they were very destructive and would be released when the time for that massive destructive period arrived. I was then unceremoniously booted out of vision. After that, I gave that area of the Desert a wide berth for a while.

Moving on a few years, I was back working in the death vision when I saw some activity around one of the cocoons.

A few angelic beings were waiting around a cocoon that was slowly cracking open. I asked if I could watch, and when it seemed that it was okay, I moved closer to watch.

Inside the cocoon was a human that exuded the energy of a psychotic mass-murderer. I took a few steps back, but an angelic being came up behind me and pushed me forward again to watch. As I looked closer, I saw something inside the human, as though the human's energy was a cocoon in itself.

Fascinated, I watched as first the outer cocoon and then the human structure cracked open, and a bright, beautiful spirit stepped out and began a walk towards the river of death. I followed. The spirit went to the river and drank deeply before climbing on to the bridge. Fascinating.

I went back to the shell of the cocoon. The angelic beings were busy breaking it apart and composting it into the soil. I asked what that was all about. I was shown the physical shell of the human and told to look closer.

Its structure, besides giving off the energy of a mass killer, was badly put together: the bits did not seem to fit. I was confused. I asked the angelic being for clarification and it immediately grabbed me by the hair and 'transported' me to a living scene.

In the scene was a psychotic killer pacing around a room fighting an urge to kill. I immediately thought of a parasite driving it. I was shown that although there were parasites around this person, a parasite was not what was *driving* them. I was pushed to look closer.

I then spotted the spirit of the person within the body. It was a good energy, intelligent and bright, but it did not fit in the body properly, and the body looked strange, mismatched, as though it was not a good fit. The angelic being once more put its hand over my eyes so I could see better. The body was inherently flawed: the brain, the gut, and the whole of the structure was so badly damaged that it was like a feral car plummeting over a cliff with the driver unable to stop it.

I was then immediately back in the death vision, and I got it. The damage to the body, whatever had caused it, created a situation where the spirit or soul of the person was not in control of the impulses of their body. Their brain was so badly damaged or unbalanced that the soul could not operate properly through the body, and the body's impulses were so strong that it was driving itself. The spirit in the body watched helplessly as the outer person wreaked more and more destruction.

That in turn damaged the spirit, plunging the spirit into deep trauma. The spirit had to slowly, carefully detach from the outer personality driven by the body, and that took time. Once the spirit was able to disentangle itself from the outer personality, it could begin the process of breaking out of the cocoon.

This radically changed how I thought about 'good' and 'bad' spirits/people, and made me realise that sometimes the issue was far more complex than I had understood it to be. It was also the time when I realised that being judgemental about a person and a spirit was limiting my understanding, and was also at times just plain wrong.

I then swung the other way for a while, and assumed that every cocooned spirit was simply a victim of their body. This was also a wrong assumption, as some were indeed just deeply imbalanced and destructive spirits. So I eventually learned to take a 'wait and see' approach.

8.3 Sinking into the Abyss

I spent quite some time observing these souls and cocoons held in the sands, and after seeing some of them sink beyond trace, I wanted to know where they went and what happened to them.

Eventually I managed to figure out how to track them, and I watched as they sank into the Underworld and became trapped in the substance of the rock. Slowly the rock would absorb them and they would become unreachable even in the Underworld.

For a few years I was unable to ascertain what happened then. Did they stay in the rock? Did they dissolve? If so, what happened to the idea of an 'eternal spirit'?

I got no answers for the longest time, but years later, I was working down in the Abyss and had to go down one of the tunnels for the work I was doing. At the end of the tunnel was a small cavern, and in that cavern was what looked like a stone cocoon. I asked the being I was working with what this was, and the being told me it was a spirit that was suspended in stone, and that while ever the planet existed, it would be held in that stone, taken out of circulation until living physical beings no longer existed. Hell indeed.

This was a turning point for me in a lot

of ways. As a young teen I had rejected the religious dogmas I was raised in, but I also knew there was a grain of truth within them; I just could not find that grain or understand it. After total rejection and then spending my late teens and early twenties searching, the shift into deeper magic took me down this road of discovery that I still walk to this day.

I learned that some of the dogma in all religions is just made up for the sake of various agendas. Some dogmas have their roots in folk myths that in turn developed from direct communion with the vast array of spirits within nature, and some of the dogmas were the tiny fragments of a much more profound understanding. Those tiny fragments had survived in the human consciousness and had been dressed in layer after layer of dogma, agenda, and just plain silliness.

What was once ancient magical knowledge that emerged out of the Mediterranean areas, North Africa, and the Near/Middle East has over millennia been reduced down, through generations of ignorance, to dogmas designed to control.

What I have observed, for example, with the Bound Ones, is I think the root of the Christian concept of hell. A lot of Christian structure is cobbled together from Egyptian, Greek, and Babylonian streams (as well as many other influences), and if we look deeper into those ancient structures, we see the seeds of magical wisdoms that were converted into shock horror tactics.

So we go from an understanding of natural tides and forces, of the dynamics of cause and effect, until, through the dogmatic development of religion, we end up with stories which tell us that if we do not adhere to that religion's particular laws, we will "burn in hell" or be "trapped in hell."

Yes, a spirit can be trapped in the Underworld, but not from punishment; rather because that is the safest place for it to be for all concerned.

I have to say that after decades of exploration around these subjects, the older I get, the less I know, and the less I understand. And I think that is a good thing. This magical universe is far beyond our understanding: we do what we can to understand what is relevant to us and to interact with it, but the more you dig, the bigger it gets.

The best advice I can give at this point in my life—and I do hope I progress more so that my understanding changes over time—is that when you come across something in magic that you do not understand, don't try to theorise and fit it into something. Just watch it, observe, follow it around, and let whatever understanding you can grasp rise up to you through exploration.

8.4 Ritually Bound Ones

This is something else for you to begin learning about, but which you should not be working with as an apprentice for obvious reasons. All magical technique is a structured application that has its roots in a natural process: the magician uses a mechanism that is already inherent within nature and then applies it in a ritualised, visionary way.

One of those ritualised mechanisms that has been used in magic is the process of the Bound Ones. Where nature cocoons, locks in, and binds something that is a potential threat (and the human body does the same), so too the magician follows that same mechanism in order to bind something out of the life cycle. This is pretty nasty magic for the most part, and when it is necessary to ritually bind something using magic, the magician forestalls what would otherwise be a natural process.

There is a middle ground in this, and that middle ground comes into play when magic is the catalyst which caused the problem that subsequently needs to be bound up. If a spirit needs binding, nature responds and deals with it—though often not in the time frame humans would like. But if a magician releases a destructive and powerful being that would not naturally have been released, then the natural process does not always seem to respond properly.

To fix this magically by using ritual binding opens the door for lots of things to go into disarray: as humans, we do not always get the right picture, or our intentions are not always what they should be, and many times it becomes an ego issue for the magician. Nevertheless it is possible to ritually bind something that should not be out in the world, and to do it without upsetting the balance even more. The Egyptians were pretty good at this.

But the middle ground is where something has already been triggered and released by magic: the magician can work within the natural process along with the beings who would normally work with this issue, and as a combined team, it is possible put the being back and seal it back up. Under such circumstances, the human magician does only what is needed in proportion to the original magical act, and the rest is dealt with by the beings who take over nature's side of things.

This is something that is really important to grasp as apprentice magicians: ninety percent of your magical work as an adept is collaborative, and is often work where you only play a limited part: the angelic and other beings do their bit, and you do yours. This means you often do not get to see the finished results, or at times even get to see what it is you are doing: you become a bit-part actor in a massive blockbuster movie (alternatively, you can stay in control and be a leading actor in an amateur production at the local village hall). It's all about ego and control.

When you get to work as an adept, if you cannot get past yourself and your own need to control, your work will be limited. If you can learn to do your job and let others do theirs, you become part of a major team. This lesson about the Bound Ones is a very good example of a natural and powerful process that can potentially be reduced down to petty magical acts of revenge or control, and the common denominator in those petty acts is the limited thinking and ego of the magician.

The ritual binding of a soul/spirit is something that has been used in various religions, particularly ones that have reincarnation as a mainstay of their system. And of course, wherever you get magicians of great skill, corruption can so easily creep in, and those skills end up being used to bind souls into their bodies and into the land in order to make sure that an agenda is followed.

There is no practical magical work that an apprentice can do around this theme, as it is a mechanism that is energetically dangerous to be around in its natural inner form, and fraught with serious difficulties in its ritual presentation. But as apprentices it is wise to know about these dynamics early on in your training, as spotting them in different texts around the world will tell you about the depths of understanding in the roots of that religion/culture, so that you can then understand what it is that the religion stands upon as a foundation. In turn, it tells you about the magical skills of the early priests/priestesses who operated within that religion.

It is also handy to know about ritual binding early on in your training so that you can spot inherently imbalanced and flawed magical systems that incorporate such methods. In the early days of magical training it can be a bit of a minefield when you read and research, and often an apprentice magician has no reference point to be able to measure the balance, knowledge, or degeneration of a system.

By casting your net of understanding to the peripheries of magical texts, myths, legends, and systems, you will slowly learn to spot where a system's problems are, where its weaknesses are, and where there are gems hidden within the dogmatic bullcrap. So your task for this lesson will be to hunt down these ancient wisdoms hidden in ancient texts so that you can see the fragments of knowledge and magical wisdom buried among the dogmas and agendas.

The best way to approach this is to be able to read texts without getting drawn into their dogmas and manipulations: look for the magical keys, the fleeting mentions of deeper, more ancient magical powers at work, and learn to extract from the dogmas the roots and foundations of older wisdoms however fragmented they may be: and by "older" I mean going back up to five thousand years or more. By 2000BC the rot had already set in, and by the time the Greeks had come along after their dark age, it was well and truly over. But fragments of knowledge and wisdom from those very ancient times have continued down to us in a variety of texts.

8.5 Practical Work

What follows are clips from various religious texts. Read through them, wade through the dogma, and see the dynamic you have been reading about in action. You have a choice once you have read through them:

Either choose one of the texts/authors and read/research further into those writings to spot the various creation and death dynamics that you have been learning about.

Or, once you have read the texts, use key words to do a search for similar presentations in other cultural myths, legends, and religious texts. They will of course present in many different ways but the foundation mechanism will be the same.

If you are interested in tracking the dissolution of understanding of the Mysteries and the rise in dogma with Christianity, first read further into the texts that I have outlined, and then read the various gospels and epistles in the New Testament around the same subject matter. You will immediately spot the loss of the ancient fragments of knowledge and the rise of hellfire agenda-driven dogmas designed to frighten and subdue the masses.

Some of the New Testament writers still carried through the more ancient wisdom fragments in their writings, while others display a sad degeneration into fearmongering and flashy visuals, probably co-opted from the Greeks (hellfires). This also marks the rise of the idea of hell as a place of punishment as opposed to a deep Underworld place where things are taken out of circulation: similar, and yet very different.

As you read, take computer notes about anything that leaps out at you and any connections you make. It is up to you how much or how little you explore, but it is an important skill to acquire—learning how to learn about magic by reading non-magical texts.

Don't forget that the separation between magic and religion is not that old; many ancient texts are stuffed with magic hidden away in the corners. The skill of the magician is to be able to spot those hidden gems and to read around them to see what else can be discovered. This method of reading old texts is also a very useful habit to get into when you work as a visionary magician. Often what you see in vision appears strange and can make no sense. But once you then visit ancient texts that talk around that topic, you find your weird contact, and it is often written in a context that helps you understand it a bit more.

Many young magicians fill their shelves with tons of magical books. But in fact the best magical library is stuffed with ancient and religious texts, myths, and folk legends: that is where a lot of the real magic hides. But often these days people expect everything in bullet points and laid out in obvious paths for them. The real Mysteries are found by working in ritual vision, and then reading ancient texts which then give you a clue as to the next step. This module has been the beginning of that process for you.

8.6 *Reading tasks:* clips from classical and older religious texts

The Book of Enoch, Chapter 10

> And again the Lord said to Raphael: "Bind Azâzêl hand and foot, and cast him into the darkness: and make an opening in the desert, which is in Dûdâêl, and cast him therein. And place upon him rough and jagged rocks, and cover him with darkness, and let him abide there for ever, and cover his face that he may not see light. And on the day of the great judgement he shall be cast into the fire…

…And when their sons have slain one another, and they have seen the destruction of their beloved ones, bind them fast for seventy generations in the valleys of the earth, till the day of their judgement and of their consummation, till the judgement that is for ever and ever is consummated. In those days they shall be led off to the Abyss of fire: and to the torment and the prison in which they shall be confined for ever. And whosoever shall be condemned and destroyed will from thenceforth be bound together with them to the end of all generations."

The Book of Jubilees, chapter five

And it came to pass when the children of men began to multiply on the face of the earth and daughters were born unto them, that the angels of God saw them on a certain year of this jubilee, that they were beautiful to look upon; and they took themselves wives of all whom they chose, and they bare unto them sons and they were giants.

And lawlessness increased on the earth and all flesh corrupted its way, alike men and cattle and beasts and birds and everything that walks on the earth—all of them corrupted their ways and their orders, and they began to devour each other, and lawlessness increased on the earth and every imagination of the thoughts of all men (was) thus evil continually.

And God looked upon the earth, and behold it was corrupt, and all flesh had corrupted its orders, and all that were upon the earth had wrought all manner of evil before His eyes.

And He said that He would destroy man and all flesh upon the face of the earth which He had created. But Noah found grace before the eyes of the Lord.

And against the angels whom He had sent upon the earth, He was exceedingly wroth, and He gave commandment to root them out of all their dominion, and He bade us to bind them in the depths of the earth, and behold they are bound in the midst of them, and are (kept) separate.

And against their sons went forth a command from before His face that they should be smitten with the sword, and be removed from under heaven. And He said "My spirit shall not always abide on man; for they also are flesh and their days shall be one hundred and twenty years."

And He sent His sword into their midst that each should slay his neighbour, and they began to slay each other till they all fell by the sword and were destroyed from the earth. And their fathers were witnesses (of their destruction), and after this they were bound in the depths of the earth for ever, until the day of the great condemnation, when judgement is executed on all those who have corrupted their ways and their works before the Lord.

Epistle of Jude

These people are blemishes at your love feasts, eating with you without the slightest qualm—shepherds who feed only themselves. They are clouds without rain, blown along by the wind; autumn trees, without fruit and uprooted—twice dead. They are wild waves of the sea, foaming up their shame; wandering stars, for whom blackest darkness has been reserved forever.

2 Peter 2:4

For God did not forgive the angels that sinned, but cast them down into the deepest Abyss (Gr. Tartarus) and delivered them into chains of darkness, to be reserved unto judgement.

The Theogony of Hesiod II

And amongst the foremost Cottus and Briareos and Gyes insatiate for war raised fierce fighting: three hundred rocks, one upon another, they launched from their strong hands and overshadowed the Titans with their missiles, and buried them beneath the wide-pathed earth, and bound them in bitter chains when they had conquered them by their strength for all their great spirit, as far beneath the earth to Tartarus. For a brazen anvil falling down from heaven nine nights and days would reach the earth upon the tenth: and again, a brazen anvil falling from earth nine nights and days would reach Tartarus upon the tenth.

Round it runs a fence of bronze, and night spreads in triple line all about it like a neck-circlet, while above grow the roots of the earth and unfruitful sea. There by the counsel of Zeus who drives the clouds the Titan gods are hidden under misty gloom, in a dank place where are the ends of the huge earth. And they may not go out; for Poseidon fixed gates of bronze upon it, and a wall runs all round it on every side. There Gyes and Cottus and great-souled Obriareus live, trusty warders of Zeus who holds the aegis.

And there, all in their order, are the sources and ends of gloomy earth and misty Tartarus and the unfruitful sea and starry heaven, loathsome and dank, which even the gods abhor. It is a great gulf, and if once a man were within the gates, he would not reach the floor until a whole year had reached its end, but cruel blast upon blast would carry him this way and that. And this marvel is awful even to the deathless gods.

There stands the awful home of murky Night wrapped in dark clouds. In front of it the son of Iapetus stands immovably upholding the wide heaven upon his head and unwearying hands, where Night and Day draw near and greet one another as they pass the great threshold of bronze: and while the one is about to go down into the house, the other comes out at the door.

And the house never holds them both within; but always one is without the house passing over the earth, while the other stays at home and waits until the time for her journeying come; and the one holds all-seeing light for them on earth, but the other holds in her arms Sleep the brother of Death, even evil Night, wrapped in a vaporous cloud.

And there the children of dark Night have their dwellings, Sleep and Death, awful gods. The glowing Sun never looks upon them with his beams, neither as he goes up into heaven, nor as he comes down from heaven. And the former of them roams peacefully over the earth and the sea's broad back and is kindly to men; but the other has a heart of iron, and his spirit within him is pitiless as bronze: whomsoever of men he has once seized he holds fast: and he is hateful even to the deathless gods.

There, in front, stand the echoing halls of the god of the lower-world, strong Hades, and of awful Persephone. A fearful hound guards the house in front, pitiless, and he has a cruel trick. On those who go in he fawns with his tail and both his ears, but suffers them not to go out back again, but keeps watch and devours whomsoever he catches going out of the gates of strong Hades and awful Persephone.

And there dwells the goddess loathed by the deathless gods, terrible Styx, eldest daughter of back-flowing Ocean. She lives apart from the gods in her glorious house vaulted over with great rocks and propped up to heaven all round with silver pillars. Rarely does the daughter of Thaumas, swift- footed Iris, come to her with a message over the sea's wide back.

(Sigh…they are all such happy souls…—Josephine)

8.7 Task

Research in ancient Egyptian funeral texts the concept of a human soul (depicted as a heart) bound and trapped forever in Duat.

8.8 Task

Watch the following clip from the film *What Dreams May Come*: the hell scene (if the link I give below stops working, search for the hell scene). It is a good fictional depiction of the various things you have been learning about in the module.

Some of this film has been analyzed by film academics/psychologists, who postulated that the imagery in the film comes from eastern influences (Buddhism) as (they state) none of this imagery appears in Western culture (head hits desk in despair).

In fact, the majority of the Underworld imagery in this film comes directly from the Western Mystery Tradition (and that academic is a badly-read idiot).

www.youtube.com/watch?v=HwrmILnrzbk

8.9 Module Summary

This has been a tough, though interesting module for apprentices, as it has been less about ritual and magical learning, and more about visionary and textual exploration. Setting down this foundation before you move on to work with ritual tools is important, and it will help you to understand the deeper powers at work as you begin to learn about ritual tools, what they are, and how to work with them.

Now you are at this stage in your training, you have worked with a variety of different magical skills, and I am sure you find some easier than others. Some will struggle with meditation, some will struggle with tarot, and others will struggle with visionary work. What is crucial is that you do not give less attention to one skill and more to another: learn them all equally, practise them, and do not give up or let one slip to one side if you find it difficult. Magic is not easy, and all the skills in this course are necessities.

Keep up with your regular meditations, keep working with your tarot deck, and keep your working space tuned. Keep up with your journals and computer notes.

The idea I suggested in an early lesson that you have a journal for each module (use thin exercise books) is so that you can go back to that journal later on in the course, and add notes around the subject matter. Your learning will expand, your understanding will deepen, and as you revisit a topic, the new layer of learning can be compared to your old notes, and then added on. At the end of your training, these journals will be like unique textbooks that you can then use in so many different ways as an adept.

The next module is far more practical, and will be a bit of a view-change for you. The rhythm of ritual/practical and then visionary/reading through the modules allows things to settle within you as you switch from one format of learning to another. The last two modules have been about intense powers, and that learning needs to bubble away now under the surface as your attention changes gear. You will very likely find that by the end of the next module your understanding of death and creation will have deepened quite a lot, not because of what is in the next module, but because it has had time to percolate away in the background: your subconscious mind needs to sit and sift through it while your conscious mind gets on with other things.